# New Zealand

–

## My Adopted Home

A cross-cultural trainer's personal portrayal
of New Zealand and Germany

–

and what it's like to live between two worlds.

For Verena

He who returns from a journey is not the same as he who left.

*Chinese Proverb*

New Zealand

–

My Adopted Home

A cross-cultural trainer's personal portrayal of New
Zealand and Germany – and what it's like to live
between two worlds.

**A catalogue record for this book is available from the National Library of New Zealand**

First published: December, 2019

ISBN: 978-0-473-50714-5
Editor: Marja Stack
Illustrations: Edgar Noll
Photos: Silke Noll, Ineke Chapman (217), Janet Nikora (219)
Cover & Design: Claudia Troßmann

# Endorsements

For my work as a cross-cultural trainer and consultant, I read many books and articles on the subject. They are very often dry and scholarly, with few interesting examples to illustrate some complex concepts. It's strange when you consider that cross-cultural studies are actually based on the observation of human activity. This book was an enjoyable read because of the colourful anecdotes the experienced traveller and recent immigrant to New Zealand references.

The young author seasons her experience with some intercultural theory, and blends these with observations made on her travels around the world into a fascinating and entertaining memoir about life in New Zealand and Germany, garnished with bits and pieces of trips to other places. Cultural facts in conjunction with introspection is a good recipe for cross-cultural competence. *New Zealand – My Adopted Home* demonstrates how to do it. I award full points!

– Susan Hoppe, Intercultural trainer, Hawaii

Anyone who has ever been to New Zealand says, 'It's a wonderful country and its people are so great and relaxed...!' I worked for a year in New Zealand and shared a flat with three Kiwi girls. I could never say why exactly it was so hard for me to leave New Zealand. As I read *New Zealand – My Adopted Home*, there were numerous 'Aha' moments. I got a lot of answers to why I love the country and the inhabitants. As you read what the author shares about her personal experiences, you will learn a lot about your compatriots and other countries.

– Petra Lenz, Returnee from New Zealand, lives in Hamburg

It was a pleasure to be one of the first people to read *New Zealand – My Adopted Home*. The author vividly captures the Kiwi soul through her personal experiences, flavouring it with deep intercultural knowledge. I am a born-and -bred New Zealander, and reading the book got me excited and emotional about my own country! I even gave some pages to my Mum to try to translate, as she took German for fun in her fifties. My mother is 94 and still sprightly.

One example of my mother's adaptability – one of the things described in the book – is when I picked her up at the airport the other day, she had no hesitation in coming to our bach where there was no power on. So she coped with no

electricity, no running water, no flush in the toilet, no oven to cook or quick way to make a cup of tea! She took it all in her stride and enjoyed the simplicity of it. She brought out her knitting as she said she could still do that no matter what! I put it all down to the pioneering spirit.

My father, aside from his chosen profession as a medical doctor and engineer, had many skills up his sleeve. Carpenter skills – he added a new room to our house each time a new member of the family came along – there are six of us(!) and electrical skills. He sorted these problems out in our house and built retaining walls and garden sheds. He could also upholster and deep button furniture, lay out vege gardens and make compost. He built us kids a 15-metre concrete swimming pool with solar heating! He even cut his own hair – you would never have guessed! He was also a reasonable artist, violinist and could whip up a decent dinner.

Of course, some of these skills were passed down from his father and mother but at that time the DIY was even more strongly evident than today. He said sometimes you could easily do a job properly and better yourself! Do a good job. Be independent. Be resourceful. Instead of relying too much upon others. The pioneering spirit is still alive! The early settlers (1840s and onwards) needed to be resourceful, self-reliant, adaptable to survive a new life in a strange land inhabited for that time only by strange people. These traits are clearly seen in my parents. And in theirs before them.

The book stirred up so many memories! It is a must read for people who love New Zealand and like to live in this beautiful country. Long live the Kiwi pioneering spirit!!

– Susan Sellers, a genuine New Zealander with a pioneer spirit

*New Zealand – My Adopted Home* not only gets you in the mood for New Zealand, but it examines unique characteristics and cultural differences with lots of humour and introspection. The result is a comprehensive, world-embracing account that depicts not only the author's childhood country, but her new home in the South Pacific. You can experience the interaction, lifestyles and quirks of New Zealanders through the eyes of the author, as well as their problems and worries, all delivered with a smile. It's an absorbing read, a diverse compendium of information about New Zealand and a wonderful comparison with Germany and Europe and how people there master their lives. The author's love for the country she grew up in shines

throughout, even as it throbs for her island home. It is an accomplished work of storytelling and interwoven cross-cultural insights about a rather unusual life on the other side of the globe.

– Marika Mochi, Editor

I have been living in New Zealand for nine years and have read several books about life here from the German perspective. *New Zealand – My Adopted Home* is different, because the author has successfully managed to reflect daily life in New Zealand and its people with authentic examples and a lot of humour and charm. The most important cultural differences have been cleverly highlighted by enlisting the help of her companion, the tui, Kaitiaki. The author clearly identifies and analyses background information to the many hurdles we immigrants must conquer. The New Zealander's view is also present; the book actually looks at two cultures in tandem with tangible descriptions by the author. Her knowledge as an intercultural trainer is built into the story without being too dry. Adventure, humour and deep inter-cultural insights are guaranteed.

– Manuela Mühlbauer, German immigrant to New Zealand

# About the author

For a long time she was there, never here, until she discovered New Zealand. Of course, seafaring discoverers found it first. Nevertheless, author Silke Noll eventually discovered the far ends of the Earth for herself.

A certified cross-cultural trainer, author and New Zealand expert, Silke has always been keenly interested in other cultures and peoples. As an Agile Coach and Scrum Master, she has worked on projects all over the world. Recently, she mutated from world traveller to New Zealand immigrant, and lives (most of the time) in her beach house in Wellington. A New Zealand Christmas tree, a pōhutukawa, grows in her front yard and blooms in the Antipodean summer.

In this book, Silke shares her very personal experiences of the multicultural world of New Zealand. She interweaves many other stories from visits to other countries into this comprehensive look at New Zealand from a cross-cultural perspective. Her trainer expertise and her background in the Palatinate region of Germany provides an additional dimension. (That is, as a Palatinate, not as a German – she would probably be the first to admit to actually being typically German, something Germans don't typically do!) Silke's love of both countries shines through every hurdle and stumbling block to successful immigration. With Middle-earth now at the centre of her life, only a closer look unmasks what at first appear to be similarities with other Western cultures. Yet, there are so many unexpected challenges – even one that made her lowly wall clock go crazy. Germans are not usually known for their humour. Trying the impossible, Silke luckily had lots of support for the writing of this book from her multilingual companion and mentor, the cheeky New Zealand tui, a native bird – named Kaitiaki. Without his help, the attempt to keep a light-hearted tone throughout might have failed.

More information:  www.wahlheimat-neuseeland.de.
Instagram: https://www.instagram.com/wahlheimat_neuseeland/
Faceboook: https://www.facebook.com/wahlheimatneuseeland/

Linkedin: https://www.linkedin.com/in/silke-noll-79a609/
Kanban University: https://edu.leankanban.com/users/silke-noll

Beach House overlooking three seas. https://bo3seas.co.nz
Facebook: https://www.facebook.com/bo3seas/

# Stages of a journey

## He kupu whakataki – Introduction

Who hasn't experienced that wonderful feeling of being back home? Throughout my life, I have returned home to Germany from holidays, from my studies abroad, or from a great job in another country. Each time, a little less of me went back. Each time, a little more of me remained out there in the big wide world. And once I discovered New Zealand, my wanderlust only grew. After every visit to that far-off land, more of me stayed behind, until I finally decided to move to the 'most beautiful end of the Earth'.

On my most recent return to the country of my birth – the first time since permanently moving away – I decided to look closely at Germany from the outside in, and explore, through writing, the differences and commonalities between New Zealand and Europe; what it feels like to reintegrate. I wanted to take a good look, in a light-hearted way, at my perception of myself as a German, and of Germany as well as Europe, New Zealand and the rest of the world. This trip begins and ends in New Zealand, and transits through Cuba and Nicaragua. In Europe it takes us through Germany, Barcelona, Tuscany, England and France. Accounts of adventures with my Italian friends are a feature, and a trip to Brazil, which played a crucial role in paving my way to New Zealand.

All of these places have helped me to understand my own culture – and many others – better.

No matter where we are in the world, whether a traveller or an immigrant, we cannot avoid comparisons. Usually, we view our own culture uncritically as *normal*. Deviations might capture our attention. But our own way of life is the yardstick against which we measure ourselves and other cultures.[1]

Such comparisons have become daily a feature of our increasingly global and international lives. Therefore, I can't reflect on New Zealand only from a German/European point of view. Asian cultures and many other influences have shaped the originally bicultural and nowadays multicultural society of New Zealand. Aspects of British culture, and certain facets of the indigenous Māori people, build the historical base for my observations. My experiences in Cuba, Nicaragua and Europe impacted on my perspective from a Western

angle, while other observations result from my perceptions as an immigrant to the other end of the world.

In particular, I was interested in figuring out how New Zealand has influenced me, culturally speaking. As a facilitator and trainer for intercultural communication, I advise and coach people who are relocating to a foreign country (integration) or people who are returning to their home country after spending time overseas (reintegration).

Countless publications document the characteristics of specific countries and what to look out for when immigrating to a foreign land. There are far fewer books and articles about returning home, though it is often a far more dramatic experience. In a foreign country you expect to encounter strangeness. When you return, you don't realise how much you have changed and how much your home might have changed in your absence – or not. Both can turn out to be a surprise. I was interested in what would happen to me when I returned to Germany and Europe. Would I experience the usual reverse culture shock? Shouldn't someone like me be well prepared? We shall see.

While travelling, cultural mannerisms and differences manifest themselves on many levels. In intercultural theory, these are often explained using the analogy of an iceberg. Language, clothing, literature, symbols, etc., are visible above the water line in the model. Values and expectations are located deeper, below the water line. The tip of the iceberg is only the smallest part of a given culture. The essential qualities are hidden, and are often only subtly discernible. The structure of this book will emulate the iceberg model, though I would like to base it on a special *berg*: White Island, one of New Zealand's many volcanoes. The craters on this active volcanic island, located off the north-eastern coast of the North Island, are mostly submerged. Under the sea it is superhot and eruptions occur unexpectedly.

A native bird, called a tui, and which I have named Kaitiaki, will accompany me on my journey. He is able to analyse and explain what is happening below the surface.

The Māori use the word *kaitiaki* to denote a protector, guide or

anchor. Kaitiaki reflect the ancient Māori custom of assigning a mentor to a stranger. The mentor will instruct the newcomer on the internalised rules of Māori culture and society. My personal kaitiaki is the tui, which chirps around my house in Lyall Bay, Wellington, as I drink coffee or splash water on my face to wake up in the mornings. The tui is a typical New Zealand bird, both dashing and serious, with its neck feathers arranged like a white bow tie. Tui are known for their ability to imitate other birds. Kaitiaki can also empathise with others. He speaks several languages, so please don't be surprised if he interrupts with a chirp or whistle. He insisted on coming along on my trip to Europe, because he has never been there. Above all, he loves to be the cross-cultural smart-aleck.

In addition to the index and bibliography, starting on page 232, you will find a small *Kiwi Wiki* – or mini glossary – to aid you on your reading journey.

By the way, the cross-cultural content structured around White Island is the heart of the book – you can start reading the book from wherever your attention draws you. You can read it from beginning to end, or any way forwards or backwards as you prefer.

## Intercultural (Cross-cultural) content

Designed to help you navigate the cultural differences between Germany and New Zealand, the following six pages highlight the intercultural/cross-cultural content of this book, modelled on New Zealand's volcanic White Island.

Above the water line in the picture you will find topics listed that you might already be aware of. These generally cause fewer problems in the understanding and communication between cultures.

Below the water line in the picture are the issues that often remain hidden and unconsciously tend to cause miscommunication and misunderstanding.

The page numbers refer to the corresponding intercultural/cross-cultural commentary in the book. The fonts are used to make these paragraphs easily distinguishable from the rest of the text, just as they do here.

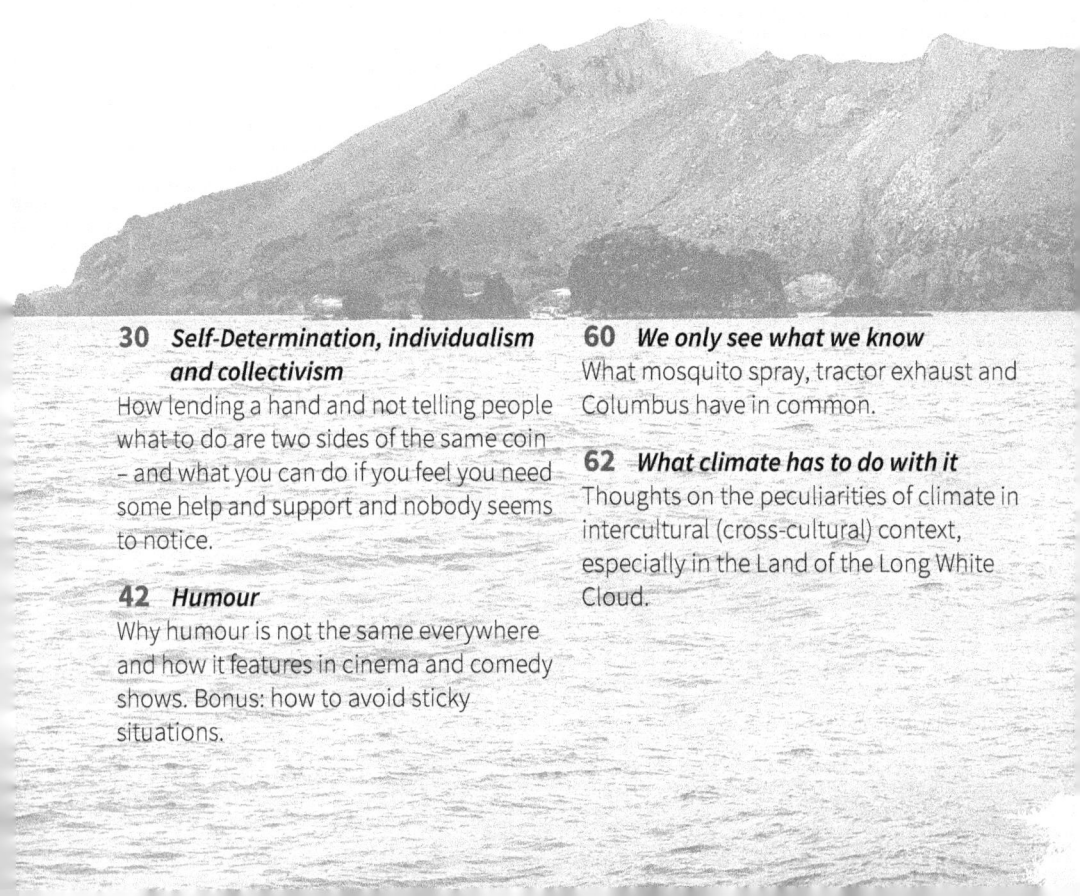

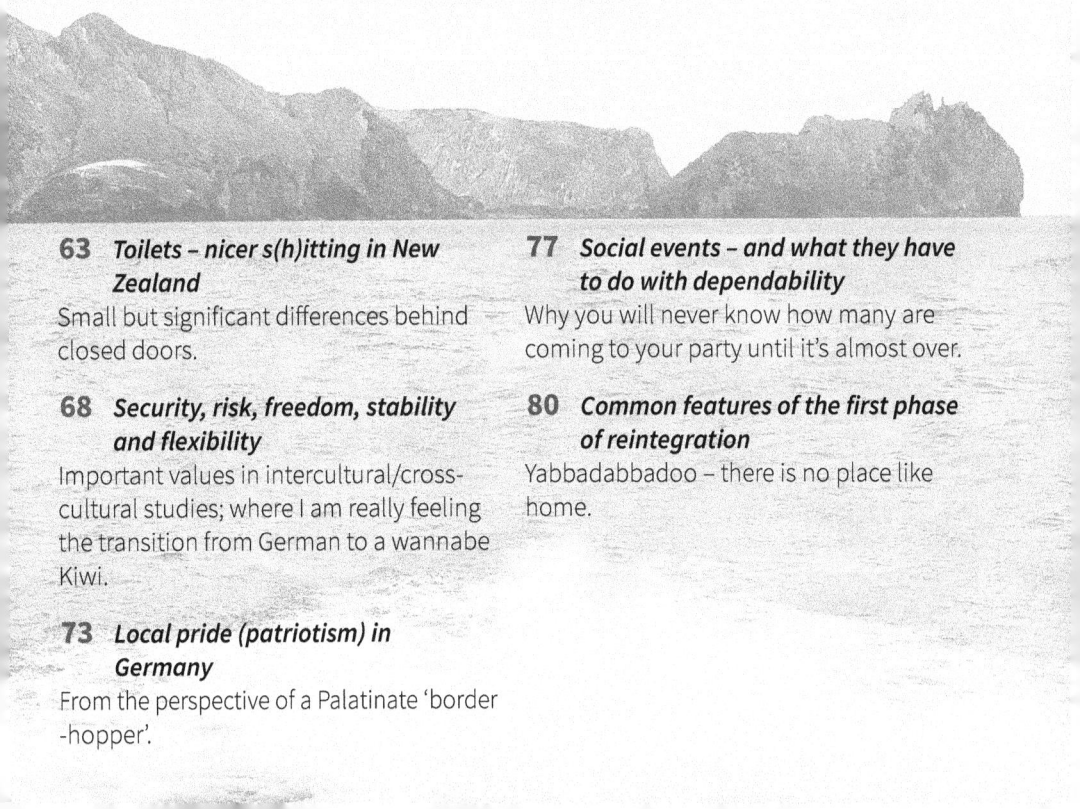

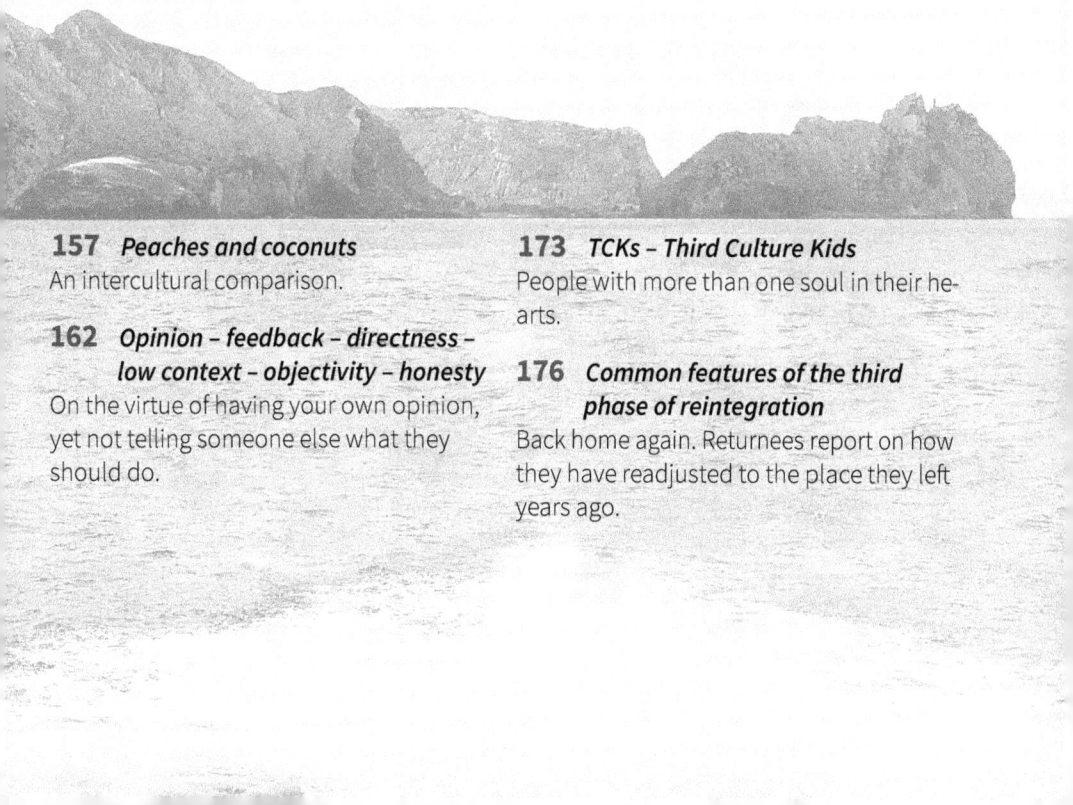

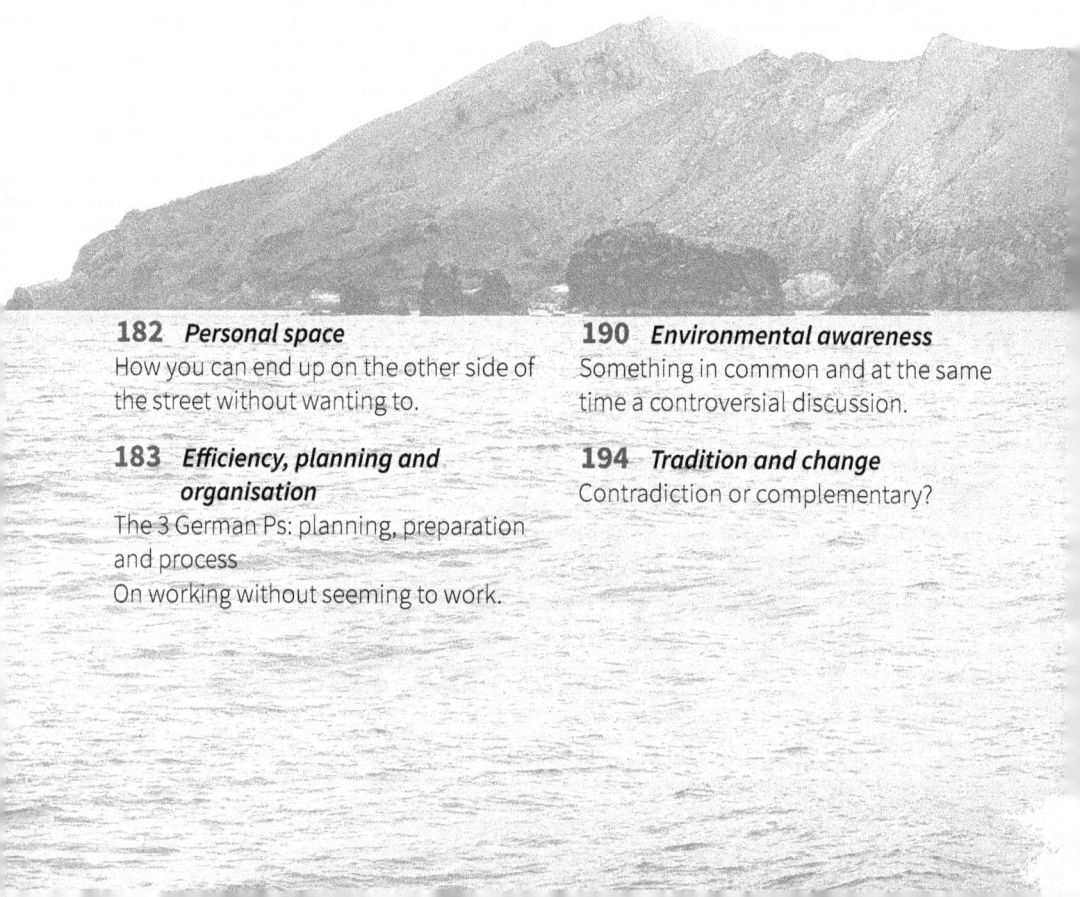

## How did I come to New Zealand – or, how did a world traveller become an immigrant?

I have always been fascinated by other cultures. My love of travel was sparked by a primary school exchange programme to Nancy in France. I was homesick – it was my first time away from home – and on my first night I called my parents. My world was going under! After that, though, never again.

After graduation, I completed a two-year training course in banking in my hometown of Kaiserslautern, Germany. The highlight was an internship in London for a month, after which nothing would ever hold me back. This experience changed my life forever. Ready to go, I rolled my suitcase towards the car. Come to think of it, I don't think there was any wheeled luggage back then. I lugged my suitcase towards the car. That was when I noticed my mother was crying. I looked at her, and said, 'Mama, it's only a short time in London. I'll be back in a month.' She answered, 'No, you won't ever be back.' How right she was.

At the end of my internship in London, I came home for three days. Then I left for a job in Tuscany, Italy. After that I started university in Passau, Bavaria. I was like a kid in a playground. I tried out as many jobs through internships in as many countries as I could, so that I could learn as many languages and cultural conventions as possible. I was an intern at a TV station in London, England, an intern at a newspaper in Munich (yeah, yeah, not technically abroad, but foreign nonetheless), an intern at a bank in Barcelona. And so forth.

For my year of study abroad in Toulouse, France, I packed everything in my room into my Fiat Panda and took off. The overloaded Panda's tyres needed pumping up every few hundred kilometres.

What a time I had! Sometimes I wish I could go back to the days when the only responsibility I had was a car full of stuff and the freedom to roam the world. I had no plan, not even for a place to stay in Toulouse. I assumed I would find what I needed when I needed it. The plan to have no plan worked, and I arrived safely.

I first became acquainted with *small talk* in Toulouse. This is a

concept Germans find suspicious. Why should we talk about things that are not really important? I felt I'd rather not talk at all than go on about trivialities. After a year, though, I started enjoying chatting about the weather and other everyday happenings with the lady in the bakery. Why not be friendly and talk about this, that and the other? It was much nicer to pick up my croissants in the morning that way rather than being what everybody always thinks of as a 'grumpy' German.

*Small talk, making contact and keeping a distance*
Kaitiaki found the ritual of small talk absolutely understandable.
'Small talk is how people in many nations of the world make contact and start conversations with each other,' he said.
'Except in Germany,' I replied. 'Unless we are used to it from our travels somewhere, we tend to find it completely unnecessary to talk about unimportant things.'
Kaitiaki countered with: 'Don't be so hard on your fellow Germans. Look at it more positively. A German has a different idea about small talk: complaining. You whine a little and get into a conversation that way! Why else would you complain about a late train, the slow cashier, or the weather – which can't be helped anyway?'
*Alors!* Viewed that way, the Teutonic penchant for grumbling sounds a lot better.

In Germany, people will expect to shake hands if they are being newly introduced or are only slightly acquainted. The importance of any such encounter is emphasised with the appropriate facial expression. Kaitiaki learned how to do this very quickly, perfectly serious with his fancy bow tie. At this stage, people are still very formal with each other, unless the introduction is among friends or they are still kids or teens. If you are being introduced to a colleague who is older or has been with the organisation for a long time, it is very important that you behave formally and use the *Sie* form of address as a sign of respect.

In other countries, you might be greeted with a little air-kiss to the left and right or even a hug. We Germans only hug when we know each other well. Then, there is nothing better than a good, strong handshake and a solid German hug. Kaitiaki thought hugging – after being formally distant for a long time – was strange. But once the hug comes, it means a casual friendship is budding and you can transition to the more informal *Du* form of address.

Generally, we Germans can be fairly distant for a very long time; decades even. It has only recently begun to change, and younger people might jump right into using the informal *Du* and being more chummy right from the start. Even in business relationships, it used to be inconceivable that you could be so casual with a salesperson or cashier in a store, yet it is becoming quite common in Germany. An article in the *Süddeutsche Zeitung* daily newspaper tells about how venerable German companies are espousing the convivial style of start-ups, even at top management levels. What is often overlooked is that – for Germans – the *Du* insinuates a kind of intimacy that is not really applicable to the relationship of CEO to employee. In English-speaking cultures, addressing someone of higher rank with you doesn't mean you are friends – there is still a respectful distance. Unfortunately, this can fall away too easily in a German business context if the informal *Du* is used.[2]

In intercultural theory, *interpersonal distancing* is one of the German cultural standards – a concept coined by Alexander Thomas, Emeritus Professor of Intercultural Psychology. Standards describe the mentality of a given culture.[3]

Germans tend to take their time getting to know someone. If you are called *friend* then you are already a really good one. A German friend is a

friend for life. You can read more about this bond in the chapter on *Friendship* on page 111.

My bird friend began telling me about his country. 'In New Zealand, the Māori people have the hongi, where they press their noses together, although it is something really only reserved for cultural situations or between Māori people. I revere this custom and would hate for our culture to lose it. Then we have small talk, raising our eyebrows, the handshake and the hug. How each of these comes into play is different from your country,' Kaitiaki said. 'Small talk is always appropriate. Raising both one's eyebrows is a common greeting, often from a distance and even between strangers. It signals that you acknowledge eye contact in a positive sense. Your head tips back slightly, your eyebrows go up and you smile. This is not to be confused with how Germans might tilt their head back suddenly with a wary look, as if to say, "What are you staring at?"' Kaitiaki chirped. 'But it is something that usually only men, especially young men, and Māori people would do among themselves, and also maybe as a joke between friends. It would be considered impolite in more formal circumstances. We exchange hugs among friends and, if we know each other well, also among colleagues. Handshaking occurs almost exclusively in business, mostly in international settings. New Zealand women don't generally offer their hand to people. Instead, they say "Hi, good to meet you".[4] We also don't have the problem of *Sie* and *Du*. Everybody is addressed with *you* and their first name in both business and in private life.'

True enough, I thought. Kaitiaki had no problems chatting away with me while I hung out the laundry or sipped on a glass of wine on the balcony. 'By the way,' he continued, 'in emails here, we always address people by their first names, even in business emails and even in cover letters for job applications. Writing "Frau Schmidt", or "Mr Smith", as in Germany or Britain, would be very odd indeed.'

When Germans attempt to engage in small talk, we generally try to turn the conversation to something we consider more meaningful. Discussing work, career moves, education and training are important topics. These are things we can measure ourselves against and see how we are doing. Kaitiaki continued his little lecture. 'This is different in many other countries. Favoured topics are family, what you did last weekend and

generally anything you would do in your free time. It's what we do in New Zealand, too. The question "What do you do for a living?" comes up much later in the conversation, if at all. There are regional differences: In Wellington, a conversation could start with "What do you do for living?", in Christchurch with "What school did you go to?". In Dunedin you might be asked "What are you studying?", in Auckland the question could be "In which suburb do you live?", and on the West Coast, "Where are you from?". Māori people will present themselves in the context of their tribal group.' For more information, please refer to the chapter *Self-determination, individualism and collectivism* on page 30.

Germans often don't understand why an English-language conversation has to start with 'How are you?', or the New Zealander's 'How yah doin'?' or 'How's it going?'. They prefer open, yet specific, questions, like, 'What's the weather like there today?', 'How was your holiday?', or 'How was your weekend?'[5]

In business, many topics in Germany are taboo, such as discussing salary. You might voluntarily tell a good friend what you earn, but you would never ask. It is also very hurtful to ask a German why they are not married, has no children or to inquire about similar things considered to be extremely personal.

You can learn a lot about a country just by looking at how people greet one another.

One thing for sure is that not many Germans immigrate to New Zealand for career or financial reasons.

After graduating from university, I ended up in the hamster wheel for a while in investment banking. Others call it a shark tank. For me, it was like being spun around in a washing machine and coming out dripping wet, asking myself what I was doing there. The only good thing was that I could afford to take a few months off between new jobs. And that was like winning the lottery, allowing me to do once-in-a-lifetime things. I ran my first half-marathon in Berlin, took my first kite surfing lessons in Venezuela and went on a backpacking tour through Australia.

Backpackers are those tourists with the big pack on their backs. At first you think you are being less touristy, blending in, getting to

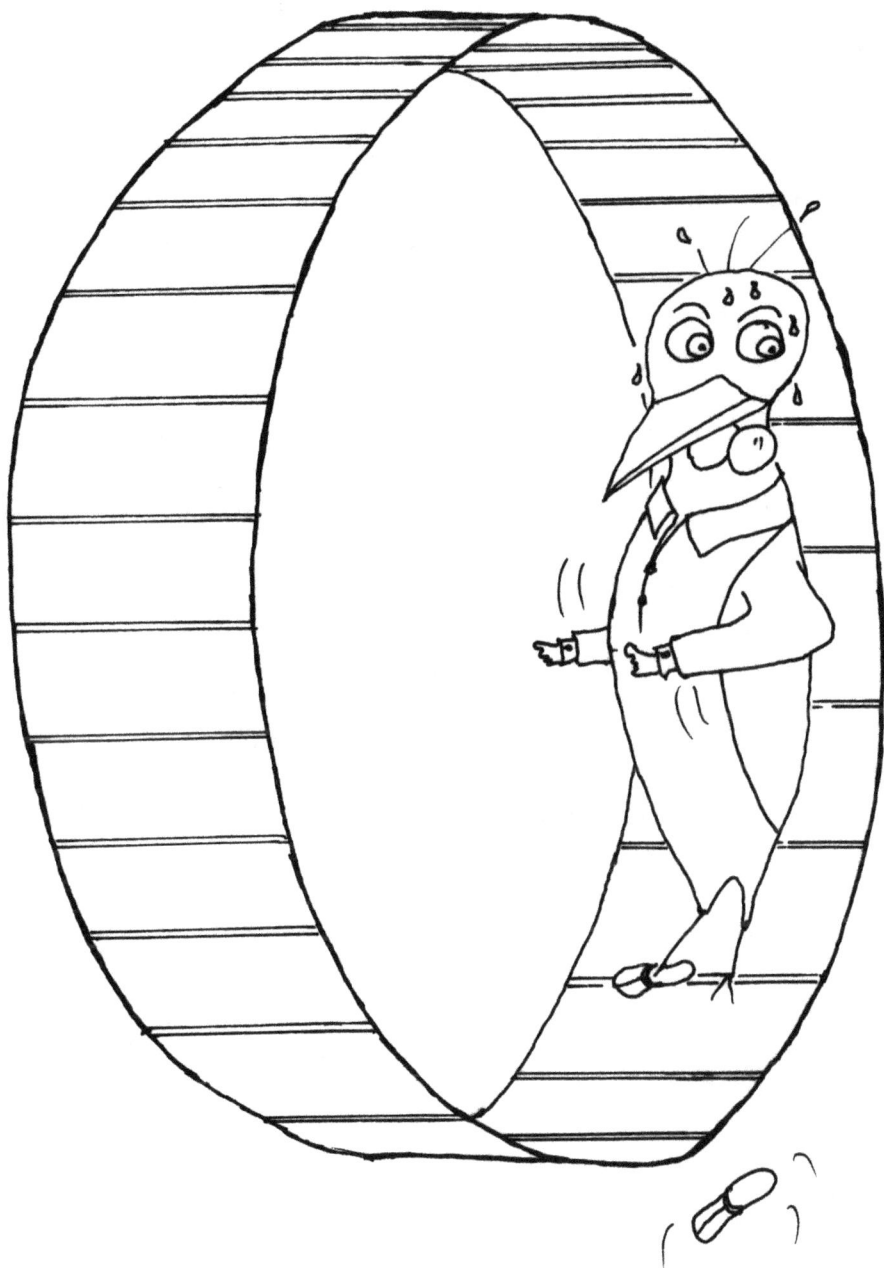

know both the land and its people. In retrospect, I find that backpacking really only means paying a little less and not using a suitcase. The only way to get to know the land and the people is to live there a while.

So, Australia. Back then, I thought I would never travel so far away from Germany again. Huh. A further trip to Australia and four more to New Zealand – the rest is history. And now I have a tui companion.

Travel changes you. Living somewhere even for as short as a month changes you even more. Seeing things in a different way becomes normal. You start questioning your previous interpretations and are glad to have a chance to try new things. The German pop band Rosenstolz sings, 'I love the moment when I fall.' That's me, evolving with every tricky situation that takes me out of my comfort zone.

Eventually, I switched careers and became an IT consultant. IT is used a lot in the world of finance. There are lots of computers and systems to be dealt with. Not much is done manually or on paper anymore. Living out of a suitcase followed: new projects in new towns, flights every weekend. On Fridays, I could choose whether to fly home to Hamburg or to visit one of my friends who live all over Europe. I loved it. I felt like I had homes everywhere! The downside was spending less and less time in Hamburg. And if I happened to be in Hamburg, housework and other mundane things kept me busy until I had to pack my bags again.

I travelled so much each weekend, I found it difficult to decide where to spend my holiday break. I know, it sounds like a terribly self-indulgent problem. But I had accrued a lot of vacation days.

In the end, I decided to go to Brazil. I hadn't kite surfed beyond a few tries, but I really wanted to become good at it. Brazil guarantees a lot of ocean coastline and lots of wind. So off I went – and this trip really changed my life.

The wind in Brazil comes up mostly in the afternoons, so you can have a leisurely start to your day before heading to the beach to kite surf. One day, I was dozing with a mug of coffee in a hammock in the garden of the Cumbuco Guesthouse. Other kite surfers were

staying there too, some of whom became such good friends that we have visited each other on several occasions since. Suddenly the gate opened, a Jeep drove through and everybody started running around excitedly. The arrivals were Louis and Trevor, well known for their mischievous humour. I was just too chilled in my hammock and watched the goings on with a breeze on my face, and soon went off to kite surf.

As a beginner, you must learn how to stay upwind. I wasn't quite there yet. I spent the afternoon kiting downwind so that I could walk upwind along the beach afterwards. The kite seemed to have a mind of its own, especially as I got tired. It jerked me out to sea and back again. Boy, was I glad no one saw me struggle!

In the evening, Louis, one of the kiters from the Jeep, suggested some things I could do to make it easier. Oh no! There had been someone watching after all! We got to know each other and eventually I found out he was from New Zealand. He was in Brazil, training to attempt to set a world record – kite surfing over 2,000 kilometres along the Brazilian coast.

A few months later, I paid Louis a visit in New Zealand. This was not one of the travel destinations I had envisioned at the age of 35. I had been considering it more in terms of retirement travel. However, rather than ticking off places, I prefer to visit people and getting to know the real deal. So, I booked a flight, glad that Louis had time to spend with me. For a few weeks, we travelled around, camping, kite surfing, kayaking and standup paddleboarding (SUPing), which was unknown in Europe at the time.

New Zealanders have an activity for every kind of weather. My father once tried to persuade me to move back to Germany, saying that I could do all of that there, too. Not so. In New Zealand, everyone does all of it, all the time. Life happens outdoors. Their values and priorities are very different, and I really liked this kind of life. I got to know some New Zealanders on this first trip and was able to experience daily life first hand. One of Louis' friends often accompanied us. Travelling with them was relaxed. That's just how New Zealanders are; sometimes even too mellow.

## Self-determination, individualism and collectivism

Kaitiaki fluttered about restlessly when this topic came up. He looked at me with disdain. 'You're nuts. How can someone be too laid back? Isn't that one of the reasons people want to come to New Zealand in the first place?' I was curious, so he continued.

'We New Zealanders are basically no different from Germans when it comes to self-determination and individualism. This is a perfect example of a cultural dimension from the theory by Geert Hofstede, Professor Emeritus for Organizational Anthropology and International Management at the University of Maastricht in the Netherlands. His research shows that individualism is a cultural dimension which New Zealand and Germany share. Compared to collectivist regions of the world like Asia or Latin America, Germans are individualistic. New Zealanders are even more so.[6]

'We are used to taking things into our own hands. We call it the "Number 8 wire mentality", "Kiwi ingenuity" or just plain "DIY". It's no wonder that there are so many old cars in New Zealand. We don't mind repairing old vehicles and our other toys like kayaks, surfboards, buggies, mountain bikes and so on. Our garages are full of them! Our toys, I mean! We park our cars outside. None of it is a problem: *Shbireitmeit* (which means, "She'll be right mate". We like to mumble it). It means everything is fine.

'We wake up every morning with the expectation that we can handle anything. "It's a piece of cake".[7] It's not such a surprise if you consider that we are historically a rural country with a small, widely spread out population, mostly surrounded by sheep and cattle instead of humans.

'Take kite surfing for example. Anyone can get the kite up into the air and land it again safely. In most countries you have a mate to hold down the kite to park it or to hold it up to get it into position for flight. Many people in New Zealand can launch and land the kite without help from others. Here, the "I can do this alone" mentality comes to the fore.'

Kaitiaki explained further that he could never count on finding another tui to help him. He was poking fun at himself, of course. 'Calling on sheep for help wouldn't be a problem, though, as I have yet to learn to imitate sheep bleating.'

Geert Hofstede confirms Kaitiaki's statement on his website.

'New Zealand, with a score of 79 on this dimension, is an Individualist culture. This translates into a loosely-knit society in which the expectation is that people look after themselves and their immediate families. In the business world, employees are expected to be self-reliant and display initiative. Also, within the exchange-based world of work, hiring and promotion decisions are based on merit or evidence of what one has done or can do.[8] The German society is a truly individualist one (67). Small families with a focus on the parent-children relationship rather than aunts and uncles are most common. There is a strong belief in the ideal of self-actualization. Loyalty is based on personal preferences for people as well as a sense of duty and responsibility. This is defined by the contract between the employer and the employee. Communication is among the most direct in the world following the ideal to be "honest, even if it hurts" – and by this giving the counterpart a fair chance to learn from mistakes.'[9]

German culture is also characterised by a standard called *objectivity*.[10] An example: if we factually and objectively have no time, a person in need must wait.

Interestingly, the collectivist Māori culture in New Zealand is at odds with the individualist German, *Pākeha* (European New Zealanders) and other similar cultures. This includes a different understanding of time, as I will describe later in this book. The term *Kiwi*, however, is used much more in daily life than the term *Pākehā*. A Māori saying goes like this: *'Kāhore taku toa i te toa takitahi, he toa takitini'* and means that we cannot succeed without the support of those around us.

**Māori people define themselves through their relative position in the social network. At introductions among Māori people, they name the tribe and subtribe (*iwi* and *hapū*) they belong to. The following interview with Harata Ria Te Uira Parata reflects how identity and self-perception is established.**

**'I do not see myself as an individual, rather a part of a group. This is the difference between our and Western culture. In Western culture the**

individual comes first. Amongst Māori, my given name "Harata" is the last word someone would use in greeting me. He would first say the name of my tribe "Ngāti Toa" or "Ngāti Raukawa".'

Social ties are eminently important for Māori people. Standing out or embracing the ideal of independence is considered unhealthy, since Māori people value interdependence. This does not mean that they cannot act on their own; only that actions are traditionally carried out in a harmonious manner with the group. This is the very definition of collectivism.

Pākehā, all the way back to the first British settlers, are quite the opposite. They are individualistic and independent in thought and actions. This Western concept represents autonomy, liberty, self-determination, entitlement and achievement, while collectivism stands for values such as relationship-orientation, reciprocity and solidarity.[11] Note also that including past generations in decision making is a feature of the Māori people's contrasting perception of time. Please refer to the corresponding information on *perception of time* on page 82.

Kaitiaki relaxed again. 'It's normal that we can help ourselves. We assume this in others as well. Pragmatism and independent behaviour are expected[12], not that someone will come to the rescue. In Germany you might assume you can help by showing a new colleague the ropes, for example. Fresh off the plane in New Zealand, however, you might feel abandoned and think we don't care. That's not true. We just assume you will figure things out on your own. To clarify: anybody will gladly help you. You only need to ask for it.'

On my first trip to New Zealand, I found everything to be okay, and a lot like what I was used to at home. Western. My great love for the country came later. It was a slow process. Six months after my return to Germany, I realised that the country had me captured. I emailed Manu, a friend from Germany living in Christchurch, and asked if I could come to visit.

What luck! I was able to stay with Manu and Tim! At first I looked around for jobs. Not earnestly though, so nothing turned up,

either. Most of the people who interviewed me assumed I was only country-hopping. A year later I returned, and when I contacted the same companies, they realised I might actually be serious. That time around I stayed with a friend in Dunedin for a few days and then spent the rest of the time driving cars and campervans back to home base for rental companies. Most tourist guidebooks recommend driving from north to south, so that's what tourists do, with one-way rentals. The rental companies pay part of the petrol for the return and the ferry. So I had a roof over my head on the way north. I would fly back south on stand-by, pick up another rental and return via another route.

On my next trip to New Zealand, I worked in a hostel in Raglan, learning how to surf while I applied to openings in the IT sector through which I hoped to secure a visa. In between interviews, I kite surfed if there was enough wind. On the day before I had to leave, I got the news that I had been offered a job!

I had to return to Germany for work I had signed on for before this trip, not anticipating that I would land a contract in New Zealand. For the next three months I worked weekdays and packed up all of my belongings on the weekends. I brought my boxes to the container terminal and terminated the lease on my flat. When I handed in my resignation at work, my boss wasn't all that surprised; he just hadn't expected me to quit so soon. I am grateful that he understood. Two weeks later I was gone for good.

Even the best salary and perks couldn't have kept me in Germany. I cancelled everything: insurance, bank accounts, mail delivery, etc. 'Don't you want to wait to see what it's like?' people asked. 'No,' I replied. 'I'm not coming back. Unless it's for holidays or short-term projects.'

That is how my life in New Zealand started. I am asked so often, 'Why here?' Several years on, I can say that every trip formed me. I am a German, and that will never change. But my ambitions have changed and I feel that I can realise my potential in this country better than elsewhere.

All of my travels were a search to discover my place in the world. I have found it in New Zealand. I have not regretted the move, not

even for a second. Sometimes you just know what is right. Eventually other people start to accept it, too. Many people I know in Germany think I'm not normal. Courageous, maybe. For some of them it's an inspiration to make more of their own lives.

In New Zealand and on my travels, I meet people like me all the time. We speak the same language – and I don't mean German – and we often feel like others don't understand us. I guess it applies in the other direction, too. That's okay. It would be so boring if we all were the same and wanted to move to Aotearoa (the Māori name for New Zealand, meaning *Long White Cloud*).

Sometimes it feels like immigrants have their own culture somewhere between the old and that of their new home.

Alexander Thomas describes culture as an orientation system which influences our emotions, thoughts, actions and judgements. Fons Trompenaars, a Dutch-French researcher in intercultural communication, wrote: 'For us, culture is like water for fish. A fish only realises it needs the water once it is no longer in it. We live and breathe through it.'[13]

So, I think if one culture is a river and the other a sea, then perhaps immigrants feel most comfortable in the deltas.

Cross-cultural understanding refers to the priorities and values of different cultures. If we belong to a certain country, region, town and family, we subconsciously acquire certain values. These values can change over a lifetime, through the course of a career or by living abroad. From time to time, we may question our values and consciously adopt some new ones, or acquire some without noticing. Some, we might purposely let go. Values determine most of our thought processes and actions. Throughout this book, you will learn about German values, how they differ from New Zealand values and how many similarities there actually are between them. Kaitiaki sat on my shoulder and nodded briskly first, then cocked his head as if to say, 'You, dear reader, can decide for yourself.'

## DIY, or 'Don't you miss anything from Germany?'

The questions I hear most often at the beginning of conversations are about why I emigrated. Of course, I miss a lot of things from Germany and Europe! I haven't heard of a deficiency syndrome in New Zealand because of a lack of beer coasters, though.

Some of the things don't exist, like fancy ice cream sundaes (with fruit and sauces and whipped cream on top) or Germany's famous 'spaghetti' ice cream, which is vanilla ice cream put through a press to look like a small plate of spaghetti, garnished with strawberry sauce and grated white chocolate. Vanilla ice cream with hot strawberries, raspberries or other fruit is typically German; however, New Zealanders would call it Grandmother's Secret Recipe.

I have searched high and low for things like Leibniz-Butterkekse, Kinder-Schoko-Bons, German Händlmaier mustard or the extra-large tins of Nivea cream. I've had to learn how to make pan-fried potatoes and other specialties served in German restaurants at home and go without the many varieties of lovely mushrooms.

White asparagus is hard to find in New Zealand. The national craziness around white asparagus is a German phenomenon. From other countries' point of view, the German calendar tends to revolve around white asparagus season. It almost seems like the asparagus season is competing with what the Germans call the "fifth season" around carnival/mardi gras. By the way: the fools in the carnival capitals of Duesseldorf, Cologne or Mayence don't need to waive their fifth season when in New Zealand.

New Zealanders adore going to **themed parties** and wearing costumes year-round, even on their surfboards, downhill skiing or running a marathon. A favourite is, wearing a Santa outfit at water sports.

Thinking of Christmas and New Year: Surprisingly it is a British comedy sketch, *Dinner for One*, or *The 90th Birthday*, that the Germans watch

every year at Christmas. It has become a tradition in Germany, albeit unknown in Britain, and is the most frequently repeated television programme ever.

One thing Germans need not miss are big hearty breakfasts. Just put out everything your fridge contains and sit for hours talking, nibbling and drinking coffee with your friends. Until the great outdoors

Dubbeglasses

calls with some sporty activity or other. Germans also prefer mixing juices or white wines with sparkling spring water. We love anything with bubbles. Where else in the world is a wine spritzer served in half-litre *Dubbeglasses*? *Dubbe* means that they feature concave bumps, so that the glass perfectly fits into your hands, with the fingers right in the bumps. A glass of wine in the Palatinate is an honest quarter-litre, not a percentage of it.

I can always improvise, of course. Still, there are things that are sorely missed. That's why I had a container bring my things from the other side of the world. I realised very soon that many supplies are limited in New Zealand. And whatever is available is not quite the quality I am used to in Europe, besides being terribly expensive. An Apple store, IKEA or dm-drogerie markt (a health and beauty retailer) – those would be a dream come true. In New Zealand, there are always specials and sales going on. The steep discounts partly make up for what is lacking in quality and supply.

Were I packing for this move again, I would stock a supply of German washing powder, because so far I have found nothing in New Zealand that smells nice to me. You can get front loading **washing machines** here, but more common are top loaders, whose washing qualities are most vehemently defended by New Zealanders and hotly contested by Germans, making it a standard discussion topic at get-togethers.

Kaitiaki twittered, 'I don't know why you want to wash everything in hot water. That ruins the material and the colours. Cold-water washing saves us a lot of money!' I just had to disagree. 'We would never wash

things in cold water! They can't possibly get clean and sanitary. And how is washing a towel after a single use being thrifty? I know that at least 20% of New Zealanders do that.'

Life in New Zealand means having nothing in abundance, besides nature and Number 8 wire. Some love this life and make do; others give up and move back to what they can't do without. For me, it's the former and I hope things don't change too quickly. It makes you creative and handy. Many people enjoy upcycling second-hand furniture or even build their own and we bake our own German-style bread (until you find a bakery with terrific bread which is willing to ship it all over the country). DIY is luxury, New Zealand-style, for people from countries that live in abundance of everything. We do it ourselves. Proudly.

## Kiwi ingenuity, pioneering spirit and the German engineer and handyman

Kaitiaki fluttered around excitedly, landing on my shoulder after a while with his breast proudly swollen. He pointed his beak up towards the top of the tree, showing me where his nest was.

'Kiwi ingenuity is an attribute or even value we New Zealanders are very proud of,' he lectured. 'It's part of our national consciousness. It is the ability to get things done or fixed with minimal resources. Being handy with tools and solutions is typical for a archetypal Kiwi outdoorsman, who is just as often celebrated as joked about. The pioneering spirit simply means "giving it a go" and is best described by a well-known joke: a hostess asks a guest if he or she can play the piano. "No, but I'll give it a go."[14]

'We are so far away from the rest of the world,' Kaitiaki continued, 'that we had to invent things we didn't have at hand. That's where the expression "Number 8 wire mentality" comes in. It's a standard thickness of wire. We use it to make and repair all sorts of things. There's always been plenty of Number 8 wire in New Zealand. It's become the symbol of our inventiveness and how we can adapt to anything.'

Māori people were adept at weaving, carving, canoe building, making stone tools and building a walled pā. A pā is a Māori village or

defensive settlement. It is the centre of social life, home and hearth. The first Europeans in New Zealand were pretty astonished when they saw how skilled the Māori people were.

New Zealand is a record holder for superlatives. One of them is the highest number of patent recordings per capita. This was in the year 1900. In 2006, New Zealand ranked fourth worldwide for Gross Domestic Product (GDP) and fifth in population density.[15]

Famously, New Zealand also invented bungy jumping. The world's first bungy jumping operation was opened in 1988 in Queenstown. The stamp vending machine, the disposable syringe, the wire whisk, the whistle and the jet boat are only a few more notable examples of New Zealand inventiveness.

Quality handiwork and tradecraft is an attribute Germans share with New Zealanders. The major difference is that Germany has more

variety and high quality (and yet affordable) products. What would a German homeowner do without a DIY home store like Baumarkt, or a New Zealander without Bunnings or Mitre 10?

Once Germans live in New Zealand, they love to be able to deal with even less – just like the New Zealanders – and use Number 8 wire, too. In any case, it's a paradise for do-it-yourselfers and talented craftspeople.

If we look at the Number 8 wire phenomenon in an intercultural context, applying Schulz von Thun's Values Quadrant Model, which I explain more fully later in the book, Germans may think that using Number 8 wire for everything is an unsatisfactory solution. They could think that: obviously New Zealanders are happy with cheap compromises, they don't think things through, they go in for quick fixes and are not generally very accurate. Under such criticism, New Zealanders will feel that Germans are pedantic perfectionists, everything takes too long and everything costs too much. Why do more than is necessary? What show-offs.

Without their ingenuity, Germans could not have come up with genius technical inventions like the Otto automobile engine, rockets, SLR cameras and pharmaceuticals such as the contraceptive pill, to name only a handful. Nor could New Zealanders be as proud of their genius at fixing things. Thus, the cultural value of *ingenuity* carries exactly the same significance for both, although how they express it differs greatly.

German engineers are sought after the world over, including for our recent expertise with insulation and green buildings. It's no secret that **New Zealand's houses** are more like wooden sheds in regard to insulation.

A popular weekend abode is called a bach. The downside to this kind of construction is that they are often damp and musty. Mould grows fast and copiously. However, since the huge earthquake in Christchurch in 2011, we know why New Zealand builds with wood. It was for the most part the brick and cement buildings that collapsed. Kaitiaki proved his point by taking a nice branch up to his nest. 'Time will tell if German-style construction in terms of insulation and heating standards has a future,' he squawked. 'An entertaining video on this

Palatinate Wine Princesses and Silke Noll (centre) in vineyard

subject is the *Kiwi–German Life Swap, Episode 3: The Winter Deniers* by the Goethe Institute in New Zealand.[16] If you are interested in more information about the intensity and frequency of earthquakes in the region, please refer to geonet.org.'[17]

Besides things that one might miss in New Zealand, there are many available that are simply different. For example, **wine**. It is to be expected that wine produced in Aotearoa from the same grape species will turn out differently than it does in France or Italy. So, I do miss European wines. No big surprise there, since I grew up in the German wine country. Yes, we Germans produce beautiful wines, not just beer. The climate and soils of New Zealand are very different, resulting in distinctive taste experiences. For instance, I would never drink a pinot noir in Europe because it has too little body for my taste. In New Zealand, a pinot is refreshingly tingly. Here, my favourite wine is a Bordeaux-style merlot cabernet sauvignon blend. If you like lighter wines, you will find quite a good variety in New Zealand. Make sure you order it New Zealand-style: 'Can I have a sav, please?', otherwise you might not get what you are asking for.

My favourite reds come from Waiheke Island and the Hawke's Bay. Good reds are also produced in Northland (Kerikeri) and in the Waikato (Bay of Plenty). The only red exception is pinot noir, which is also grown, along with white grapes, on the South Island in the Otago region around Queenstown, and in Nelson (merlot also grows here), Canterbury and Marlborough, as well as in Martinborough (Wairarapa) in the southern part of the North Island. White grapes grow around Gisborne on the North Island.

Life here can be fun and creative. A well-known joke is the one about the pilot who had just landed in New Zealand and tells the passengers over the PA system: 'Welcome to New Zealand. Please set your watches back 20 years.'

On Facebook, there are a few active groups discussing 'where to' or 'how to'. Some are for people wanting to immigrate to New Zealand; others are for immigrants to New Zealand or Kiwi immigrants to Germany. You can find all manner of advice on international bank transfers, where to find special ingredients like quark (a kind of smooth cottage cheese), if someone has had success baking pretzels, where to find fluffy bread (for the Kiwis in Germany) or what to pack into your overseas container for the move because you probably won't find it in New Zealand or Germany. You might not have to bring your wardrobes, kitchen furniture or lamp fixtures, as they are mostly installed in New Zealand homes.

I enjoy the fact that you can't take anything for granted in New Zealand. It's back to the roots. Away from German consumerist glut, where people complain all the time that everything they have is not good enough. Not that New Zealanders never complain. But there seems to be more of a humorous, self-deprecating slant to their griping, spiced with a pinch of 'shbireitmeit'. Since you can't change things right away anyway, why not laugh about it?

## Humour

'Why are *you* talking about humour?' Kaitiaki pecked at me cheekily. 'You have no idea about it.'

It happens regularly that people laugh heartily when someone brings up German humour, since the two words seem to be mutually exclusive. Kaitiaki almost fell off my shoulder, chuckling, once, as I tried to convince him that we Germans are funny. But our brand of humour does take some getting used to.

So, I smiled as I replied, 'Yes, I am a German. I have no sense of humour.' It's the only way to demonstrate that we aren't serious all the time. We have a dry kind of humour that other cultures can rarely follow. Even within Germany, people of the different regions of the country like Bavaria, Hesse, Hamburg, The Palatinate, etc., claim the others are completely humourless. It should come as no surprise that British and Kiwi humour are divergent too.

Kaitiaki had to explain. 'Down Under, we like to poke fun at ourselves. You get points for self-mockery. All the same, you can blunder badly. New Zealand humour is short and to the point; unassuming and dry. A joke or an ironic remark should appear to come easily. You should never try too hard.[18] Humour is the opposite of the painful reality that we try to soften this way. A good example is a 2010 film called *Boy* by Taika Waititi. Waititi says, 'It is "colonial outsider" humour, the kind that people develop when they have ended up on the other side of the Earth. You just have to laugh at all of the misadventures that happen to you. Māori humour is rather self-deprecating. It is close to life and its tragedies – laughing and weeping at once – so as to see both sides of the coin."[19] Kaitiaki thought for a moment, and then continued. 'There are rules you have to follow when poking fun at each other. I've listed some further on in this book under the heading *Hierarchy and egalitarianism* on page 137. The basis for equality (egalitarianism) was historically founded as a kind of social contract. On this level it is absolutely essential that you take your opposite seriously, even as you joke with each other. It is an implicit rather than explicit understanding. Things do not escalate; they stay on a light-hearted plane. We can mock each other without overshooting the mark and losing respect.'

At times, German and English humour crosses the invisible line which

New Zealanders have drawn. *Schadenfreude* is a word that has no apt translation, which is why the British have adopted it into their vocabulary. British jokers often get into trouble in New Zealand.

Kaitiaki nodded. 'This kind of English or German humour is not compatible with our sense of equality. The words are subtly twisted and the meaning is diametrically the opposite of what you'd think. New Zealanders generally make fun of themselves and deride others less than Germans can do, unless it's respectful joshing.'

Watching comedians from both countries is insightful. The musical comedy duo *Flight of the Conchords* is known internationally. On the About Us page of their website, there is this: 'Bret and Jemaine first met in 1996 at Victoria University Wellington. Jemaine vividly remembers the first time he met Bret; "he was wearing a hat". Bret doesn't remember meeting Jemaine, but says it was unforgettable.'[20]

German comedians and cabaret artists like Detlev Schönauer, Kaya Yanar, Stefan 'Das Eich' Eichner, Hella von Sinnen, Mathias Richling, Hape Kerkeling, Urban Priol, Anke Engelke, Bodo Bach, Gerd Dudenhöffer, Lars Reichov, Cindy aus Marzahn, Vince Ebert, Bülent Ceylan, Badesalz and Dieter Nuhr represent the German *zeitgeist*, or spirit of the times (another word adopted into English, by the way). German and ethnic Turkish jokes have become commonplace in Germany next to banter on the regional and national issues of the day. Some comedians really punch hard below the belt at the target's expense. Sometimes it's political humour that would be totally unacceptable in other countries.

Much of Polynesia engages in comedy that New Zealanders can appreciate. Recently, I was howling with laughter at a comedy show called *The Laughing Samoans*[21] while – interestingly – my English friend did not find it funny at all.

I am comfortable in New Zealand because of how people deal with scarcity. Somehow it all works out, one way or another. Shbireit. Nothing is set in stone; anything goes.

On Facebook, there are a few active groups discussing 'where to' or 'how to'. One of them is for people wanting to immigrate to New Zealand; others are for immigrant Germans (German Expats living in New Zealand, German–Kiwi Network, Germans in Wellington

(and other cities), Deutsche in Neuseeland, and the Goethe Society Wellington). You can find all manner of advice on international bank transfers, where to find special ingredients like quark (a kind of smooth cottage cheese), if someone has had success baking pretzels or what to pack into your overseas container for the move because you probably won't find it in New Zealand.

You might not have to bring your wardrobes, kitchen furniture or lamp fixtures, as they are mostly installed in New Zealand homes

## Departure from New Zealand

The idea was overdue: visit my family and friends in Europe and travel a bit on the way there and on the way back home to New Zealand, where I'd just received my residence visa after two years. Once I had made the decision, everything went quickly. I booked flights, and I even had a tenant for my beautiful home in Wellington. I was a little ambivalent too, though – maybe you know the feeling. I didn't want to leave, but I was ready to go.

So much had happened in the last two years. New Zealand had become my new home – by choice. I had had some nice and some not-so-nice experiences.

After being a flatmate for a year, I decided to buy my 'beach house overlooking three seas', as I like to call it. I really can see Lyall Bay and Evans Bay, along with Wellington Harbour and the Tasman Sea from my deck!

I had hesitated to buy a home in Germany because I always felt that I would live abroad someday. Buying the house in Wellington felt right and was proof that I had arrived. It is a dream house with its beautiful views – to me the best in New Zealand. A view that mesmerises, an urban location in the capital, yet close to nature and the ocean.

Over the course of those two years, I also worked on building a new private and professional life. It's not as easy if you're a little older. New friends and work relationships, and a life not at all like the one I was used to in Germany.

I planned four months for my trip to Europe, so getting some work there would make sense. It didn't really matter where, since I was planning to travel around to see friends all over the continent during the weekends.

As I began applying for work, I realised I would be visiting good old Germany where the hiring process is very rigid. Years ago, an application in English was quite sufficient. This time, an email popped up in my inbox which made me smile. "So! Ms Noll. First of all I need your curriculum vitae (CV) in German. Then also in Word format. Otherwise I cannot proceed with your application." Okay, okay, got it. So Germany was still Germany.

There were countless goodbyes and last get-togethers in Wellington. Many of my new friends couldn't understand why I didn't want to leave for even a few months. Me, a Travel Queen in my 'former life', who was on the go every weekend, always feeling like I should be *over there* when I was still *over here*. In this new life, I was taking leisurely weekend trips with my campervan, with tui and sheep as my companions, totally happy with everything. The heartfelt goodbyes only confirmed that I had found a home at the other end of the Earth. And though it was hard to say 'bye for now', I felt that it was the right time and the right thing to do.

My intuition told me that seeing things from another perspective would bind me closer to New Zealand. Some distance would do me good, as always; looking in from outside the box, as I had done in my life so many times before. It was time to step out for a clear view. So, I left for six months. Four in Europe and two in South America. I used to travel to get away, and was always sad as a journey neared its end. This was the first time I was actually looking forward to coming home. I mean that, even before I had even left,

I was looking forward to my return to New Zealand! I had finally found my place. Still, I was curious to know what would happen in the next few months. Life is full of surprises, and I have always embraced them. Would I want to return to Germany after all? My parents would be thrilled. I was curious to know how my Germanness would feel now, outside of New Zealand for the first time in two years. Had I become a New Zealander, even a little bit? No, I think I will always be a German, in spite of all the years I have spent abroad.

'I'm not really that German' is a common statement made by my fellow nationals. I said it all the time too, until one of the participants in my intercultural training course told me that it's a typical thing for a German to say. Part of it is because of our history. None of us want to be regarded as a Nazi.

I think Germany is one of the few countries in the world whose citizens have real trouble saying 'I am proud to be German'. It's difficult for me to say that with my German soul. I'm afraid people will secretly imagine me saluting and clicking my heels. Others might refrain from showing German national pride because of what they think their neighbours might say, and I have heard of Germans telling other Germans that it is totally inappropriate to be proud of being German. The only exception to the rule of 'no patriotism' is German soccer. The flags come out when an international soccer tournament is on and Germany is on a winning streak. And that has only been happening since the World Cup was held in Germany in 2006. It was so magical that people are still talking about it.

Kaitiaki snorted. 'What nonsense! You Germans are admired for so many things. And lampooned for others. But I know that each of you are proud of the region you hail from, your hometown and your local traditions. That is **typically German**!'

He was right again. Whenever I spoke to my friends abroad about these things, they are just as confused by our discomfort as Kaitiaki.

I am often asked about our history and how it was handled in school. This is pure and honest curiosity. People are thrilled when they find a German who they can talk to about it. Our history is just that – history,

they say. We don't have to be ashamed, they say. Unfortunately, it is not that easy for us Germans.

There are things we can be proud of: our efficiency, planning and organisational capabilities, for example. I can also state, all bias aside, that we Germans are good travellers. We're open and curious, flexible, uncomplicated, willing to try new things, and are mostly grateful for the opportunity, even if you have seen a Helga and a Herbert wearing white socks with their Birkies, a Hawaiian shirt and their bum bags.

My first client in New Zealand asked me if I was a typical German like the ones he had already met. I asked him what he thought was typical. He told me there are Germans who scream and shout around at work. I replied that I was familiar with that kind of behaviour, though I wasn't planning to do it myself. I was hired.

In one of our later feedback rounds, I wistfully said that I would like to become a little bit more like a New Zealander. Kaitiaki had to laugh at that. 'In New Zealand you will always be a German slash European. This upcoming trip will show you, however, that there is a tiny New Zealander in you after all.'

## Food – or what a New Zealandert misses while abroad?

I'll never forget the time my friend dragged me through a super-market on my first trip to New Zealand. Grabbing packages left and right, he tossed everything into the cart saying, 'You must try this!' It turns out that most of the things were what he loved best in his childhood. Our friends were there when we arrived home. What an oohing and aahing there was as the shopping bags were unpacked.

It is always surprising to me how many visitors to these islands, even to my own B&B, never really discover New Zealand's true specialties, though they are of course aware of Kiwiana. I don't just mean the fruit, the locals (Kiwis) or the funny-looking national bird of the same name. Kiwiana is everything rolled into one: culture, history, language, traditional symbols, etc. The list continues with gumboots (called rubber Wellington boots elsewhere), the Haka (a war dance), a buzzy bee wooden toy, sheep, Kiwi ingenuity, Weet-Bix, as well as the iconic tributes to a local specialty that adorn the entrance to many towns in New Zealand, for example you can behold an enormous Kiwi fruit in Te

Puke, a giant carrot (really!) in Ohakune, gumboots size XXXXXL in Taihape, a huge bottle of Lemon and Paeroa (L&P for short) in Paeroa, a large trout in Taupo and a very large dog and sheep fashioned from corrugated iron in Tirau.

Two more unique birds in New Zealand besides the tui are the pukeko and the kea. The national plant is commonly called the ponga, or silver fern, and is featured in the names of dozens of sports teams and on unofficial flags. A Māori legend says the fern helped hunters and warriors find the way through dark forests with the reflection of the moon on its leaves.

To understand New Zealanders better, you need to know the local lingo: Choice bro, sweet, sweet as, good as gold, beaut (for excellent). Then there is 'Bob's your uncle' (meaning Gotcha!), Bro (brother), Mate, 'Good on ya, mate' and 'Give that man a chocolate fish!' (both mean well done!). A good one to know is 'Yeah, nah' (which means no), while the ubiquitous 'Shbireimeit' (for German ears)/'She'll be right, mate' basically means 'Okay, no problem'. There are many more: Tiki tour (take a drive), 'You can handle the jandal' (you can do it), koha (a Māori word for contribution or donation), and kai (Māori for food). If something rips your nightie, then you are angry about something. There are some sly ones: yonks (a very long time), smidgen (a tiny amount), ankle-biters (little kids, toddlers), home and hosed (very successful), wet blanket (party-pooper), wicked (clever, tops), squizz (to take a quick look) and tu meke (Māori for literally too much). You can be Kiwi as (very Kiwi) or German as (very German).

Sports teams have their own nicknames, of course. New Zealand's top men's rugby team is called the All Blacks while the women are the Black Ferns. The national wheelchair rugby team are the Wheel Blacks, the softball team are the Black Socks, netball are the Silver Ferns, cricket the Black Caps, hockey the Black Sticks, the men's national basketball teams calls itself the Tall Blacks, the women the Tall Ferns and, in a twist, the national soccer team styles itself as the All Whites.

All of these are very strong national symbols indeed. But what did my friends think they would yearn for in terms of food if they ever had to leave New Zealand?

– Fush 'n chups (fish 'n chips) – (note the Kiwi pronunciation) is a favourite family dinner on the beach on Friday nights. Or even better: because it's too windy, in the car watching the 'bitch' (Kiwi pronunciation of beach).
– Feijoa – also called a Brazilian guava – is a fruit you can learn to love after a few tries. It suddenly appears in markets in autumn, is available everywhere for a while and then disappears just as suddenly again. There are also a number of products with feijoa flavouring, including teas and chocolates. It is available in Russia and some other countries, but it is a barely known tropical fruit in Europe.
– Manuka honey – my favourite. It also has medicinal properties and is used on external injuries and for sore throats. It can be exported legally.
– Fritter or patty – New Zealanders eat a lot of these with a huge variation of fillings.
– Whitebait – these look like mini herrings and are often served in fritters.
– (Marinated) green-lipped mussels – which look just like common, black North Atlantic mussels, only with green edges, or 'lips'. They are wonderful as an appetiser or snack. The marinade has a delicious taste that I can't even begin to describe.
– Pāua (abalone) – the interior of its single shell glows like a pearl and is often used for jewellery. The meat itself is black outside and white within. It looks like a tongue, and if you hold a fresh one just out of the sea, it will try to 'lick' your hand. Pāua are very strong and will attach themselves to a rock if they feel danger. You need a special pāua knife to carefully pry them away without damaging them. Freshly caught from the sea, they taste best fried up in olive oil and garlic or in fritters. Please make sure they are cooked by a New Zealander who knows how. Avoid getting them from a fast food stall. You can only legally harvest pāua of a certain size and the limit is 10 per person per day for personal use. Also, the use of scuba diving equipment to catch pāua is illegal.
– So many species of fish that we don't have in Europe, such as hoki, moki, kingfish, tarakihi, warehou and more. New Zealanders often catch their own.

- Also Kina are very popular in New Zealand.
- Tuatua and pipi – two other kinds of shellfish. Pipi are usually found in the mouths of rivers flowing into the sea and on the beach when the tide is far out. You stomp around on the sand to bring them up to the surface – if they aren't already lying there for you to gather. Tuatua live in colonies. A good place to dig for them is Ninety Mile Beach in Northland. If you find a colony, you might think it resembles a Chinese town, with so many of the mussels stuck together. Just grab some sand and you will have a good handful of them. They should be kept in water for at least five hours before cooking so that they spit out all of the sand inside them.
- Whittaker's chocolate – good old New Zealand chocolate that also doesn't contain palm oil, etc., and therefore is known as being more ethical than other brands. Even I miss it when I am abroad.
- Hokey pokey – is a kid's favourite, delicious vanilla ice cream with lumps of honeycomb toffee. There are also many other types of hokey pokey-flavoured food in New Zealand, such as Whittaker's hokey pokey chocolate.
- Chocolate fish and pineapple lumps – the former are fish-shaped, chocolate-covered, pink marshmallows. Here is my secret recipe: toast the chocolate fish on a stick instead of regular marshmallows at your next campfire or barbecue. Yummy! Pineapple lumps are small rectangles of a soft, pineapple-flavoured middle covered with chocolate, and are similarly beloved by Kiwis.
- Twisties and Rashuns – a corn snack with a cheesy, floury coating.
- Dilmah tea
- Pavlova – named for the famous Russian ballerina, this is a dessert dream made of meringue, fruit and cream and the subject of a never-ending argument over whether it was invented in Australia or New Zealand. The Kiwis jokingly like to declare many things their own invention or at least the best in the world or in the southern hemisphere, etc. (refer to the chapter on *Kiwi ingenuity, pioneering spirit and the German engineer and handyman* page 37). Often this is even true. Something could be the tallest tree, the cleanest water, the furthest jump.

- Marmite – looks like automotive oil and to Germans tastes like their strange yeasty soy sauce Maggi, which some people use as a condiment for everything. There is also a popular Australian competitor brand called Vegemite, which tastes very different. I actually prefer the Kiwi marmite compared to the English and Australian version! You should have a New Zealander serve it up for you on toast with just the right amount of butter.
- Crumpets – a kind of pancake made with yeast. They're originally from England and one of the things New Zealanders remember from childhood.
- Afghans – my favourite biscuits. My mother's too. She's always happy when I send her a parcel of them.
- Lamingtons – little cakes which are terribly sweet and somehow artificial-looking. Sometimes you get some that aren't as sickly sweet; then they can be quite delicious with their chocolate and coconut coating.
- ANZAC biscuits – these are a tie with Afghans as New Zealand's favourite biscuit and are made of oats and optionally with coconut flakes. There is a delicious soft type, and also a caramel-flavoured hard-baked type. As with pavlovas and lamingtons, Australia and New Zealand are still quarrelling over who came up with the idea for these particular biscuits.
- Barbie – nothing to do with the skinny, blonde doll. New Zealanders love to shorten words, so it's a barbie instead of barbecue. There is nothing cute about the Kiwi method, though. They place the meat on the grill, start what looks like a bonfire, wait a few minutes in a safe place and then the food is done in no time. In my German hometown of Hamburg, the start of the barbecue season is a highly anticipated great tradition and ritual. German men love their barbecues.
- Raw milk – meaning the creamy, untreated milk straight from the cow. Also freshly churned butter. Unlike in most countries nowadays, both are available from certain farmers with a license to sell them.
- Tamarillos – also known as tree tomatoes. Though they're originally from South America, their more exotic-sounding name

was coined in New Zealand.

- Boysenberries – a fruit which is a cross between the European raspberry, the European blackberry, the American dewberry and a loganberry.
- Gingernuts – a type of hard, ginger-flavoured biscuit.
- Sally Lunn Buns – a sweet, large bun or teacake, usually served warm in slices with butter.
- Scones – a sweet bakery product, usually served warm with butter and jam.
- Relish – a cooked and pickled product made of chopped vegetables, fruits or herbs, typically used as a condiment, in particular to enhance a staple.
- Gregg's Mixed Spice – blend of spices made up of coriander seed, cassia, cinnamon, nutmeg, allspice, ginger and cloves.
- Primo – a flavoured milk.
- Kumara, potatoes and carrots – In New Zealand the latter can still be found in their original colour (purplish-black) and are available on farmers' markets. The Dutch started breeding orange carrots as we know them, and it's thought to be in honour of William of Orange.
- Sunday roast.
- New Zealand apples, like Pacific Rose.
- Fresh spring water – in Petone (a suburb of Lower Hutt, Wellington), you can see queues of people waiting to fill their containers from the spring fountain there. In general, most town water is from water reservoirs which are filled from rain water. There is also still spring water on most farms. On the Canterbury plains on the South Island, for example, the tap water is often artesian well water – straight from the mountains and filtered through the gravel water table.
- Vogel's toast bread – especially the gluten-free bread.
- Hāngi – a traditional Māori method of preparing a meal by baking it in an earth oven. Meat and vegetables are wrapped in ferns and laid on hot stones in a pit. With another layer of wet ferns and packed earth on top, it is left to bake for several hours.
- Steak 'n' cheese pie – honestly, I've never tried it, but it was one of the first things that came to a friend's mind when I asked him what he would miss if he had to leave New Zealand. Especially that re-

heated pie you pick from the transparent, heated cabinet at your local dairy at 3 am.
- Pic's peanut butter.
- Wattie's tinned spaghetti (on toast or as a pizza topping) – kids (and a certain ex-prime minister) adore it. And it's palatable only to Antipodeans and the British.
- Cheerios – a pink sausage, also called a 'cocktail sausage' or a 'little boy', which is traditionally eaten with Wattie's tomato sauce.
- Tip Top ice cream – found on every street corner and on many banners on the outside of dairies. I can't imagine New Zealand without it.
- Sparkling duet – soft drink flavoured with real orange juice and lemon juice.
- L&P – short for Lemon & Paeroa, a soft drink traditionally made by combining lemon juice with carbonated mineral water from the town of Paeroa.

There are New Zealand specialty cookbooks available for anyone who is into Kiwi cuisine.[22]

And when it's not about food? I've heard Kiwis in Germany say:
- Kathmandu.
- Mini tongs.
- The wind.
- The beach.
- Ibuprofen and paracetamol from the supermarket.
- The smell of salty sea water.
- Sunsets, and the night sky with the Milky Way and all the stars.
- New Zealand nature.
- Fly spray that actually kills flies.
- Soft toilet paper. Germans find it hard to find *good* toilet paper in New Zealand that doesn't dissolve.
- Pounamu/greenstone.
- Good and cheap merino clothing.
- Kmart toaster and generally cheap appliances.
- Making plans, changing them halfway through, and nobody cares.
- Coming up with an idea, and everybody joins in.

- Apparently, a mop is not a mop. Many Germans like the ones you wring out with your hands because they think it is the only way floors get properly clean. New Zealanders find this absolutely unhygienic. Therefore, they prefer self-wringing mops, which in German perception only spreads the dirt.
- Being late to parties.
- Jandals out of season and walking barefoot in general.
- Friendly, open, less perfectionist people, and friendly people at the counter without being stared at.
- Not sending kids to school if you don't feel like it.
- Allbirds shoes.
- Repco, Mitre10, The warehouse.
- Building a house in Germany – a disaster!
- New Zealand pillows.
- Rugby shorts.
- Flixonase.
- New Zealand roll-on deodorant smells the best.

## The New Zealander – Hunter, spearfisher, angler

This subject made Kaitiaki nervous. 'Easy to get into trouble with. How can you explain it without treading on someone's toes?'

Besides nectar, pollen, fruits and seeds, Kaitiaki also enjoys eating insects as a particular delicacy.

New Zealanders like to hunt, spearfish, fish and catch their own food, whether it be pāua (abalone), lobster, scallops or butterfish. Spearfishing is very popular, as is fishing, diving and snorkelling.

One of Kaitiaki's human friends achieved a number of New Zealand and world records. He crowed proudly, 'This tiny person shoots game as big as she is. She and her boyfriend are the epitome of the Kiwi way of life. They are in their mid-thirties and completely self-sufficient. They have made their hobby their life and live off what the land and sea offers. In spite of their sporting records, they are at harmony with nature (see Chapter Kiwi ingenuity, pioneering spirit and the German engineer and handyman for more on records page 37). This is not a contradiction. New Zealanders find hunting to be perfectly natural and see nothing wrong with it.'

Kaitiaki was in his element again, so I just listened as he continued. 'New Zealanders seem to be born with a hunting gene, so fishing and hunting are normal activities. Those I know are very conscious of which species they're allowed to hunt, and they are very clear on the seasonal limits. This is one reason why there are still pāua in the waters here, but none left in South Africa. If the pāua is too small, according to the rules it is thrown back into the water without further discussion.

'Spearfishing is particularly resource-friendly. You don't catch what you don't want or need and there is no net or line to harm any other creature. If you have the chance, have a spearfisher tell you some stories about how they wait in the deep, hidden behind a rock with only a snorkel (no diving equipment, no mask) and a harpoon at the ready. How a camouflage wetsuit makes them virtually undistinguishable from the sea floor. And how a tug-of-war begins when they spear a big one. The stories get really dramatic if a shark shows up and tries to steal the catch.'

This book's reference list features an article about a record-breaking catch if you're interested in more about the world of spearfishing.[23]

My tui continued his commentary about game hunting on land. 'Since there were originally no mammals in New Zealand, except for seals on the shores, and also birds, reptiles and insects, and since the only poisonous creatures were spiders, the katipo and the redback spider, the indigenous fauna was not endangered. Over time, small deer, rats and possums as well as other mammals were introduced to the islands. Hunting certain species is officially allowed to help preserve endemic wildlife.[24]

'If you ask a New Zealander for advice and they about "doc", they don't mean to send you to a doctor and don't think you are nuts. DOC, or the Department of Conservation, has a website and information posted all over the islands, at campgrounds, on hiking trails and in cabins to make sure everyone knows how to protect New Zealand's unique natural environment.[25] The Ministry for Primary Industries is responsible for determining fishing and angling limits.'[26]

# En route to Europe – San Francisco

I had decided to book my flights to Germany via the USA and Cuba, so I had a two-day stopover in San Francisco. I met up with Bastian, who was coincidentally on his way to Wellington, where he was going to take care of my house in my absence. He had lived in San Francisco some years ago, so he shared some highlights of his time back then with me.

He told me that he found Wellington more attractive. After two days I was beginning to understand what he meant as I scratched on the veneer of local attitudes a little bit. One thing I observed was that while Germans are always full of praise for American service standards, arriving now from New Zealand I didn't feel it was that great anymore. To me it seemed that service had become something you have to pay for with tipping in the US, whereas in New Zealand it is still a gratuity in the original sense. I found it interesting how a shift in my cultural perspective from Europe to New Zealand had changed how I saw things.

On the one hand, San Francisco is very multicultural; on the other hand, there is a huge homeless population, and lots of noise. No matter where you go for dinner or just to hang out, you hear sirens, traffic and loud music. Sensory overload. I wasn't used to it anymore; only to the sound of the ocean. It was not surprising that Bastian was looking forward to staying in my house for a few months.

As far as culinary things go, San Francisco is like a mini Europe. I was really impressed with the fine food I ate. Gourmet food shops were all over the place, as well as authentic Italian pizza and ethnic restaurants. These are the things I really miss in New Zealand, even though I live in Wellington, which is proud of the variety and quality of its culinary offerings.

There's an international food scene and locals are always keen to hear appreciative words about it. Auckland has a good selection, too. There are some gourmet shops where you can find most of the ingredients you need to make your favourite specialties at home. Improvising is a lot of fun. French and German immigrant forums on the internet might

have some information on the ethnic restaurants or markets that carry specialties from 'home'. Either you content yourself with that, or you adapt to local tastes, which is not the worst route to take if you immigrate.

Back to San Francisco. I wanted to tour the city unmotorised, so, the second morning, I jogged to a bike rental station. Then I biked all through town, over the Golden Gate Bridge (ok, I took the ferry back) and then jogged back to my accommodation after returning the bike. I picked up my bags and took the rapid transit train to the airport.

For most of the exercise through town, I had been gasping for breath because of the urban air pollution. Wow, I really have become a nature lover. Does that mean I've developed a simpler mindset, or do I just have higher expectations on air quality than before?

## Enroute to Europe – Cuba

Havana. Great! Colours! New Zealanders generally use fewer colours. Nature is colourful. So is my beach house. Often when I ask for colours in New Zealand, I am offered grey or beige. No, I mean c-o-l-o-u-r-s. Like the Cadillacs parked in front of even more colourful buildings. What a feast for the eyes!

The air was, however, just as bad as in San Francisco – the downside of all of the old Cadillacs. Lots of people. Lots of history – and lots of historical buildings. You don't see those things too often in New Zealand. The air in New Zealand has fewer exhaust fumes too.

Cuba is a country where you need to be good at haggling so you don't get ripped off. In my earlier travelling days, I didn't mind it so much. Now it just made me wonder why I had to pay for every little kindness.

I thought of New Zealand and how people help each other – whether you're local or a tourist – with no strings attached.

So, automobile fumes, people everywhere, the constant haggling... I was glad to escape the city for the seaside.

Varadero. Much better. A few days' stay turned into more than a week. I liked it very much here, but I was on a trip of discovery, after all, so I decided to take a day trip to Matanzas, an old, typically Cuban town inland from Varadero.

I caught a local bus. I had been told at the beginning of my trip to Cuba that tourists are asked to leave this cheap mode of transport to the locals, especially for long trips – one of the obvious signs of a parallel tourist world where it is very difficult to connect with Cubans and get to know their culture. I politely asked the driver if there would be enough space for me, and I was invited on board.

I was so glad I was allowed to experience a Cuban bus ride, even for the short distance to Matanzas. There were no specific bus stops, as is often the case in Hispanic countries. The locals merrily

flag down a bus and squeeze in. No embarrassment with touching body parts. One happy fellowship. I was the only stranger, and my rear end was not thrilled with the hard, wooden seating. The Cuban seniors obviously had no problem with it. Well, if I wanted a deluxe experience, I shouldn't have got on that bus. Eventually the bus arrived in Matanzas, where my derriere and I had a nice short stroll through town. I escaped from the crush of people back to Varadero as soon as I could.

New Zealand, what have you done to me? I couldn't function without the sea and sand and especially not in an inland city.

Back in Varedero, I felt much better. I relished the wide, open sea and the fabulous Caribbean beach.

If only there wasn't that noisy tractor polluting the air with unbelievable amounts of white smoke. Unbelievable, too, that that rattling socialist relic was still running. As for the air, a German acquaintance who was married to a Cuban explained to me that the smoke wasn't gasoline exhaust but that the tractor was actually spraying an insecticide to kill dengue fever-carrying mosquitoes. Well, if that's true then let me find a cloud of it to stand in!

**We only see what we know**, right? Insecticide from what I thought was the tractor exhaust pipe was unknown to me, but I was familiar with plain, stinky exhaust fumes. I had come to a premature verdict, for me logical yet faulty, about air pollutants in Cuba. Another example of seeing only what you know is this legend which is often cited in intercultural literature: when Christopher Columbus discovered America (technically the island of Hispaniola), the indigenous Arawak Indians overlooked the ships nearing on the horizon. Why? They had never seen such large vessels before, nor could they have even imagined them. So, when they 'suddenly' appeared in the waters close to shore, they were stunned by their 'magical' arrival. The point of this story is that it is important to ask 'what and why is that?' When dealing with other cultures, so many things have a different meaning or logic to them than what you may have actually experienced yourself. In other words, you simply can't see it if you don't know it.

For the rest of my time in Varadero, I kite surfed when the wind was good. There were nice people to talk to and a beautiful sea to look at. When the wind died down too much for kite surfing, I decided to feed my curiosity and have a look at other parts of Cuba. I haggled a great price for a rental that needed returning to Havana, or rather the airport, so I wouldn't have to re-enter the crowded metropolis. It was a win-win situation. I was autonomous, needed no guide, no tour groups, no buses or taxis, and I ended up paying less than I normally would have done.

I jumped in the car and drove off, flicking my indicator on for a right turn... and the **windshield wipers** turned on. Yes, a beginner's mistake. It should have been the 'other' right indicator. I don't think I can ever be reprogrammed. Whether I am driving on the left in New Zealand or on the right in Cuba or Germany, like most other immigrants, I will forever be turning on the wipers instead of the indicator.

I took the six-lane highway. Three lanes in each direction – completely empty. Well, not quite. There were the garlic vendors who tried to sell me some while barrelling down the highway at 120 km/hr (in an 80–100 km/hr zone). Suddenly three horse-drawn carts appeared and I had to step on the brakes. The horses were trying to pass each other, causing a horse jam on the highway.

Another thing I noticed as I was driving, was my **German lead foot**, as we call it. It was impossible for me to stick to the speed limit when I had this totally empty, straight road ahead of me. It rarely happened in New Zealand, but there are no empty six-lane highways there either. Even after more than two years at much slower speeds, I had the worst time trying to keep myself in check. It was as if driving fast is hereditary.

When I turned off the highway into a little town, I came upon a roundabout. How do these work in Cuba? Easy. You go with the flow, easing into traffic, much as I had experienced in Asia or Italy. You yield to whoever is in front of you. Just drive. The others will take care of themselves. There seems to be no rule; only a mutual understanding of trying not to hurt each other.

## Roundabouts in New Zealand and Germany

There is a different rule for using signals governing these. In Germany, you enter the roundabout without your indicator on and signal when you want to turn out. In New Zealand, you enter the roundabout with your signal to the left if you are leaving on the first exit. If you intend to exit half way around, you must signal right as you come up around the roundabout and indicate left as you pass the exit before the one you wish to take. If you are going straight through, don't signal as you come up, signal left as in the previous case.[27]

In Cuba, I drove through countryside I would never have seen had I taken a bus. The people have most likely lived there, in the middle of nowhere, for generations. Those first ones, why did they stay exactly there and not move on? Far away from population, surrounded only by red sand. Why not on the beach or by the sea, for example? Of course, everybody has a different taste. Some like the mountains, some like the sea. Did the first human being there just get tired of walking or searching? It's in these moments I realise how lucky I am to mostly be able to choose where to live.

Many cultural characteristics have developed over time because of geography. The slower pace of life in Spain, including the traditional siesta in the heat of the afternoon, is due to the **climate**.

Officially, New Zealand has two climate zones: subtropical in the north, temperate in the south. Actually, the northern end of the North Island is tropical, turning subtropical and temperate, dry or alpine or as you travel further south to end up at the colder southern tip of the South Island. A trip through New Zealand will feature different vegetation and fauna at every turn. New Zealanders love to be outdoors, spending as much time there as possible. Some of their habits stem from their attachment to nature and the pleasant climate. Generally speaking, many career choices, industries, local cuisine and countless natural remedies can be explained by climate and nature.

On my Cuban road trip, I met two German couples at a rest stop who were visibly upset. Their experiences so far had been of

Cubans jumping in front of the car, terrible signage, potholes and horse carts travelling in the wrong direction on the highway. They were totally aghast when they heard that I had no GPS, only an old road map, some broken Spanish and an innate sense of direction. I did admit to stopping to ask for directions often because there were so few signs, especially ones listing distant destinations, the way they are in New Zealand or Germany. The next town, the next step is enough, or not? Must we Germans always know what to expect in the tenth leg of a journey? Take a look around, regroup and move on to the next stop. You will still arrive where you want to go.

Trinidad and Cienfuegos. Somehow I found these towns even without proper signage. I was interested in seeing these two old towns and also the mountains beyond, do some tramping (hiking) and jump into the natural pools up there. In German, *tramping* can be translated as *Extremwandern* or *Wandern*, and *hitchhiking* as *Trampen*.

Of course, I was also going to visit the beaches on this side of Cuba. Welcome to the parallel universe of tourists: 1 Euro for parking, 10 Euros for 'admission' to walk through the forest; a 'donation' is required even for a piece of toilet paper. I know they are poor. Still, this was my perception in that moment: What was I doing there? I already lived in a place of true natural beauty where it can be enjoyed free of charge. Let's hope it stays that way for a long time. Tourists and locals are unfortunately doing a 'good' job of destroying some of that nature. Here was another opportunity to be grateful for what my favourite country has to offer.

## Toilets – nicer s(h)itting in New Zealand

Kaitiaki blushed and hid his head under his wing, peeking at me through his feathers. You read right. A national toilet comparison is worth our time.

In Germany, there is a kind of toilet that has an internal ceramic ledge , something that foreigners never fail to wonder about. The reason for this construction is that we like to examine our elimination with respect to colour, consistency or foreign objects, and to determine

how things stand with our health. These toilets are on their way out, but still found in many older buildings.

Women's bathrooms. Every time I return to Germany, I am annoyed by how dirty the toilet seats are in public toilets. German women believe that sitting on it is terribly unhygienic, so they crouch over it and often don't hit the target underneath. The result is truly dirty toilets. Even the ones in London with a higher volume of traffic are cleaner. I find myself always having to clean the seat myself in Germany.

Kaitiaki could not opine on German women's rooms, but he did like the ones in his country. 'New Zealand generally has clean public toilets,' he declared. 'Toilet paper is usually on hand, and where there isn't and when you are in nature, you can fall back on traditional rangiora leaves, also called 'bushman's toilet paper'. Even the famous Hundertwasser public toilets in Kawakawa are free of charge. The Austrian artist/architect Friedensreich Hundertwasser became a citizen and lived in New Zealand in the Bay of Islands for many years.'

I had to agree when I read how German newspaper *Die Zeit* described the experience of New Zealand's public toilets as 'comfortable crapping' ('Schöner Scheißen').[28]

Playa Larga – the next stop on my trip through Cuba. What a wonderful surprise! On my way, I rented snorkelling gear for five dollars in Punta Perdiz. The rental shop's owner spontaneously decided to swim out with me and showed me a shipwreck featuring Chinese vases. With bits of bread, he lured brightly coloured fish closer for a while, and then we swam out to where the reef ends and the ocean floor falls away into vast darkness. The ocean never fails to impress me with it's awesome power of the natural world.

I met two Germans who have travelled to Cuba every year for two decades. They advised me to go back to stay in Playa Girón, a place I had already been through. Really? The only thing going for it, as far as I'd been able to see, was a pizza place. I almost did go back, but curiosity for the next place won me over and so I continued on to Playa Larga, just to see what there was to see there. The place was so much nicer. I really liked the cute restaurants and range of

ocean-side accommodation. And best of all, I saw kites! I grabbed my gear and within 15 minutes I was kite surfing with the locals. In the evening they invited me to stay and drink a beer.

Sports are such a great way to get into contact with people and feel less like a tourist. It's a lot like the way Germans make friends through membership of a club, called a *Verein*, where people meet regularly for sports, singing, craft and dozens of other hobbies. I was so glad I had followed my own star and given in to curiosity.

Viñales. The next day I had a long drive ahead of me. By now I was pretty good at driving in Cuba. It was easy to see who had just picked up their rental and who had already been on the road a while. Europeans, especially German newcomers, stubbornly stuck to their accustomed rules: pass on the left and otherwise stay to the right. In Cuba there is no such rule, really. Rule number one is to avoid potholes. If that means pass on the right and then keep left, that's perfectly okay. Rule number two: avoid horse-drawn carts on the wrong side of the road at all cost.

So, I made good time and arrived in Viñales in about the same time it would have taken on a German autobahn, and without the flat tyres that featured so prominently in other German travellers' stories of driving around Cuba.

The landscape around Viñales is very beautiful – lots of caves. Of course, you have to pay admission to visit one and parking has an obligatory 'watchman's fee'. Same thing at the beaches. I lost interest in all of it. What was one more cave or beach to my life? After three weeks in Cuba, I was ready to go. Now that is something I had never experienced on my previous travels.

On this trip I often found myself wondering 'Why am I here?' until I realised it must have to do with the great change in my life over the past few years. I would never have thought that I would become travel weary. Was it the place, or just me?

Due to the parallel worlds of tourists and locals, I felt like my usual way of travelling wasn't possible in Cuba. I found it difficult to connect with the locals and to get to know the culture. But speaking the language definitely helped and I did find something in common

to talk about with my *casa particular* (bed and breakfast/Airbnb) hosts, thanks to being one myself. I know I was a guest in all the countries I travelled to. In Cuba more than in other countries, I felt like a tourist guided along well-defined routes.

Of course, it was mostly me. For years I had roamed the world to get away from home and find my perfect paradise. Now that I had found it, I wasn't that interested in travel anymore. Yet without all of those experiences on my trips, I certainly would not be the person I am today. Just think – I wouldn't even have found New Zealand! Kaitiaki grumbled. 'You cannot simply lose interest in the rest of the world just because you like my country so much. Get off your high horse! Cuba is a new experience worthy of our continued attention and understanding as long as we are here.'

It was time to leave for Germany. I still hadn't secured a job, but I was completely calm, and thought, 'shbireit'. It was great to be on an extended holiday. In New Zealand, people get around four weeks' paid leave a year and five to ten paid sick days a year. So, people take unpaid leave without hesitation. Quite different from Germany, where sick days are not deducted and entry-level employment starts with about 21 days paid holiday days.

Kaitiaki and I arrived at Havana airport four hours before departure. I was hoping to check in early so that I could do some writing before boarding. How could I have forgotten that I was booked on Condor, a German discount carrier, to Frankfurt? Fellow Germans were already queued up outside the terminal, waiting to be let in so that they could queue again at check-in. I sauntered up to the security guard at the barrier. Of course, someone gave me the evil eye, and snarled, 'The queue ends back there.' Ashamed, I looked at Kaitiaki. Welcome to Germans – we are bad at queuing, unlike New Zealanders. As if I hadn't learned how to queue properly there. Who was being more German anyway? Them or me? In Germany's supermarkets people charge ahead if a cashier opens up, regardless of where they were in the original queue. The brazen are always first and no one says

anything. Kaitiaki was confused. 'Why queue in front of the airport anyway?' he wondered. 'It doesn't make sense. Why do you have to be first at check-in just so you can sit around longer until boarding?'

## Airports, baggage belts, lifts and the German evil eye

I remember an episode from when I was a consultant. I was in Frankfurt Airport waiting for the luggage to arrive. Perhaps you have already seen the impatient, reproachful glare Germans give to every bag that is spit out on to the belt if it's not theirs. Especially people who travel for business and really don't have time. Poor suitcases really have to put up with a lot! I swear, only Germans can do the evil eye. It cannot be learnt. It's very difficult to untrain because it's completely unconscious. You will experience it if you try to push your shopping cart against the 'natural' flow in the supermarket, or if you try to get in a bus through the 'wrong' door. Don't ever think about leaning on someone else's car or putting something on the boot lid even for a moment! You will suffer for it immediately, skewered by the evil eye and lashed by the loud accusing voice of the owner.

That's not all. There is also the unmalicious German stare. I experience this all the time if I am speaking at a seminar or to any kind of German audience. The stare is completely empty of expression or emotion. In elevators you might see the same inscrutable stare, but aimed at the floor or the changing numerals until the doors slide open again. There appears to be a secret understanding that you never look at someone in a lift in Germany. Laughing is forbidden.

I've tried bouncing into a lift with a merry New Zealand smile and a 'good morning!' It only perplexes people, making them genuinely uncomfortable and stare even harder at the floor.

At some point, I managed to check in and pass security at Havana airport. Near my gate, I sat down at a table where a middle-aged gentleman struck up a conversation. He told me that he was thinking of immigrating to Cuba. I told him I had immigrated to New Zealand.

On my trips, I have met a number of people who were considering

leaving Germany for good. The reasons why weren't ever very clear to me. Why that particular country? Did they know what they were getting into? What were they planning to do in the country they were going to live in? Strange to know of so many Germans, normally so mindful of their security, who would throw all caution to the winds. Yes, they really do. They even have a TV show about the boldest German emigrants into the world. One needs to understand that the German word for security is so portentous for their culture that it means many things, such as comfort, security, safety, guarantee, quality, financial security and *Geborgenheit* (a feeling of being homely, safe and warm). It may have as many implicit meanings as the Inuit have words for snow.

During my flight on Condor, I was pleasantly surprised and a bit confused. Their safety video actually tried to be entertaining. Do you know Air New Zealand's hilarious **safety videos**, some of them straight from the Land of the Hobbits?[29] Funny as!

I can't imagine something like that being shown on an early morning business shuttle from Munich to Hamburg. The passengers would probably short the circuits with their evil eyes. Having said that, the video on Condor was a nice attempt at showing that Germans have a sense of humour, too. It finished with the words: 'a small step for you; a large step for airline safety', which, besides echoing Neil Armstrong's famous quotation, tapped into a very important German cultural value.

## Security, risk, freedom, stability and flexibility

Kaitiaki was very quick to explain that by security he didn't mean personal safety in New Zealand. 'People will run after you if you forget something and search for the owner of a lost item. We trust each other for the most part and help each other willingly. I hope it stays this way for a long time. New Zealand regularly has trouble with tourists, often backpackers, stealing things from supermarkets. Isn't that sad? If visitors abuse our famous hospitality, someday there won't be any left. They should take our good vibe home with them and share it there.'

This section is about the cultural value of *security*. People like to feel secure – some more urgently, some less so. For historical reasons, Germans are

a very anxious people, even if you only consider the ruin of the two world wars and the hyperinflation in between. There were many other vicious wars, like the Hundred Years' War, the Schmalkaldic Wars, the Thirty Years' War, the War of the League of Augsburg and the Napoleonic Wars, fought in earlier centuries and carried out on German soil. They weren't Germans' fault; Germans just happened to live where the larger powers' armies crossed paths. They rebuilt their country numerous times from the ashes. Anxiety is deeply rooted in the German soul and so they value security very highly.

In intercultural studies, this is a cultural standard and dimension called *uncertainty avoidance*.[30] In German culture it manifests as the need to be extremely organised and efficient, highly ethical, dutiful, perfectionist and thrifty, and with very high regard for regulations and relying on government agencies. It is uncertainty avoidance that makes us stop at a red light even if nothing is coming. Regulations, traffic lights and an innate sense of order have, however, reduced our concept of responsibility and accountability. Why are we not allowed to look out for ourselves? If you have ever tried to cross a street in India on foot, you will know what I mean. In New Zealand it makes me dizzy to think of how few retaining walls and fences have been built to protect its climbers and hikers, for example at the Paritutu Rock in New Plymouth or the Escarpment Track between Paekakariki and Pukerua Bay. Not even a warning sign. This is unthinkable in Germany. No wonder my father felt it necessary to yank me back onto the sidewalk one day while I was in Germany, admonishing me to remember I was not in New Zealand.

Uncertainty avoidance makes us plan and save for old age. It can also get in the way of living life. To a German it might be frightening to think you can just try something out without knowing if you will succeed, or do something without overthinking it. However, people from many other cultures don't interpret this as being irresponsible. They just do it.

There are two significant exceptions: one is the stretches on the German autobahn with no speed limit, and the other are the private fireworks on New Year's Eve everywhere in the streets. While flying along at 180 kms/hr or blowing things up at least on that one night a year, it appears our need for security is suspended for a brief time.

On my first New Year's Eve during my time at the university in Toulouse, I

automatically stepped outside at midnight to watch everybody let off fireworks. I was hugely disappointed. There were none. Boring darkness. In New Zealand there is always Guy Fawkes, a tradition adopted from the British, though they don't go as crazy as the Germans do with their firecrackers.

New Zealand has taught me about liberty. Life has taught me that there is no real security. It makes more sense to stay flexible and grasp every opportunity. You will always land on your feet. So what if I don't land a new freelance contract when I return to New Zealand? I'll find some other job. And what if my immigration plans hadn't worked out? I would have returned to Germany.

'Be careful with generalisations,' Kaitiaki said as he wobbled his little head from left to right. 'Not all Germans are such-and-such, and neither are all New Zealanders. Do not think in black and white. In comparing cultures, we find there are tendencies that grow from a deeper value and stay with us our entire life. Generalisations about countries and cultures are basically a national average, a mid-point on a scale. Individuals will slide this way or that based on how they were raised, their education, friends, travel experiences, other countries they have lived in and their environment as a whole.'

If you imagine the scale of a value like security, I tend to personally be more comfortable with uncertainty than many Germans because of my many experiences abroad and my life in New Zealand. Though compared to people from other countries, I am probably still more of a worrywart.

If I look at uncertainty avoidance of New Zealanders as a whole, or of Germans, there is an average with variations. A bank employee or insurance employee might be more risk averse than others, and civil servants might have the greatest sense of security, especially compared to the self-employed.

Freelancers in Germany might be slightly more risk averse than their counterparts in New Zealand. The city or region they come from in their respective country might affect things, not to mention their individual life experience.

New Zealanders tend to react flexibly to situations that are not going well. 'Shbireitmeit.' If one way doesn't work, you can improvise. New Zealanders' expectations are generally lower because they believe you

can't know the future. Very often the outcome is totally different anyway. They almost expect things to turn out differently than originally thought. 'If you want to just let things happen, let life happen, then New Zealand is a good place to try it out.' Kaitiaki flew past me. He had a piece of Number 8 wire in his beak, intending to add it to the nest he was building.

A German psychologist and communications researcher, Friedemann Schulz von Thun, introduced an expanded version of an older model called the Value Square. It helps us to explore the relationship between pairs of values such as security and risk taking, liberty and obligation, and stability and flexibility, for example. On the website of von Thun's Institut für Kommunikation, he describes the Value and Development Square as the premise that every positive value is effective only if viewed in context of its complementary nature, and that without that tension between the two, values become useless exaggerations of themselves.[31]

On the bus from the plane to the terminal after landing in Frankfurt, I overheard this exchange: 'Helga, we should have got on the first bus.' 'You are right, Herbert. Then we'd be at the baggage belt sooner,' expressing the German-style desire to optimise everything – even to save a few seconds.

The first step was passport control, however. Would the immigration officer let me in after more than two years away, I wondered? Yes, he did, as if I had never been gone. Little did he know...

# Europe – German winelands – the Palatinate

From German friends in New Zealand I had recently heard that Germany felt less secure nowadays. There were many more police at German airports, they told me. I was pleasantly surprised that things seemed to be the way they always had been. Things bounce back to normal so quickly, even after a terrorist attack or a stock market crash. The human brain is very good at repressing or recovering from things.

I originally come from a rural area in Rhineland-Palatinate, a German state that borders France, Luxembourg and Belgium. I hadn't felt very content being here in a long time. The trip through blooming, yellow fields of rapeseed was beautiful.

Everything smelled different somehow. The bird sounds were exotically familiar to my ears. Kaitiaki was thrilled with everything and warbled his first notes in German, a language he hadn't known until now. As I messaged excitedly to a friend back in New Zealand about how I felt, she replied with different memories of springtime in Germany. She has hay fever. In Wellington, she suffers less from her allergies.

In a way, if you look at our local history, it's surprising that the people in the Palatinate corner of Germany are German at all. Of course, this could be true of any group of people who have lived on a country's borders in Europe. My own family is a good example: my great-great-grandfather was an Italian named Casagrande (pronounced as it would be in Italian). He married my great-great-grandmother, who hailed from the border region between Germany and France. Together they had a theatre troupe and travelled extensively, making music and entertaining the villagers throughout the region. During World War II, they lost everything they owned, and when the war was over, the border was redrawn to where it still is today. Not 100 kilometres to the north or south, but exactly there. As a result, the Casagrandes became French and the pronunciation of their name was drawn out, as the French do, to 'Casagrawnd'. My side of the extended family ended up on the German side of the border. Alsace, as this region is known, has been a bone of contention between Germany and France for centuries. The borders were redrawn several times

throughout its complex history. The Alsatian people laugh easily about it, saying that they always ended up on the 'losing side', whether they suddenly turned French or German. Had the border been drawn a bit more to the north, I would have been born French; or a bit more to the south, they would be German nowadays. The history of the region is preserved in the local dialect, which is very similar on both sides of the border. When I was a little girl visiting the French Alsace area, I

Rye burger with stuffed pig's stomach, onions and sauerkraut

marvelled at the lady in the bakery who seemed to be speaking German to one of her customers. Actually, she was speaking her local French dialect, which sounds very similar to the German dialect in my hometown. In culinary things, the Palatinate has as much to offer as the French. Now that I had returned to my childhood home, I was in foodie heaven. **Local pride** is no coincidence, as Germans tend to identify with the region they grew up in. I have lived in Munich, Lower Bavaria and the Palatinate (which are the southern regions of Germany), in Düsseldorf (the Rhineland in the western part of the country), and up north in Hamburg. I can attest to the fact that Germany could be two separate countries, so disparate are the cultures: the Prussians in the north and the Hohenzollern in the south. That's not even taking into account the enormous differences between former East Germany and West Germany, based on their more recent histories.

In comparison, New Zealanders' local pride is rather modest, though they do love to distinguish in a rather derogatory fashion between Dorklanders, or Aucklanders (also know as Jafas – Just Another F\*\*king Aucklander, not to be confused with the popular orangey-chocolate biscuit called Jaffa), Cantabs from Canterbury, Coasties from the coasts, Tronners from Hamilton, Naki Lads from Taranaki, Welly Wooders and Dunedinnites from Dunna Vegas.

I really enjoyed being in my childhood home again. On Sunday, the entire village of Weilerbach came out to the farmer's market, where I ran into people I hadn't seen in over a decade. Most of them still aren't on Facebook and feel they don't need it. Many of the villagers have never travelled abroad. They are just happy to stay in their peaceful little village. Those looking for a career end up moving away, but more decide to take what is available nearby and stay where they are happy. I myself have evolved to where I am enjoying a simpler life in New Zealand, though I am lucky with Wellington being a city with opportunities and still close to the sea and outdoor pleasures.

It is always wonderful to have happy folk around you. A German propensity for complaining about almost anything was one of the reasons I wanted to leave. Now that I live in New Zealand, I find that most Europeans – including the British, Dutch, Italians and French – are complainers, not just the Germans. I was glad that where I was right now, I didn't notice any of that.

People were curious about my life in New Zealand. How did I manage with a smaller salary and higher prices? It's true, I don't think anyone would immigrate to New Zealand looking for easy money or a great career. It is mostly for other reasons, such as life in the great outdoors, that it is so appealing. And in a direct comparison with my line of work, taxes in New Zealand are lower than the package of taxes, health and unemployment insurance or social security premiums you have to pay in Germany. So, the bottom line comes out to be the same.

## Insurance

Because of a strong need for personal security, Germans tend to try to cover every eventuality with insurance. If there was an insurance that would automatically insure what they might have forgotten to insure, it would be a bestseller and the entire populace would be on cloud nine.

I can't explain here in detail what New Zealand's insurance system is like. You must do your own due diligence if you intend to come to live here, since everyone's situation is different. I can say, however, that all

citizens enjoy subsidised health care, which is very good in international comparison. Depending on your type of residence or work visa, you might be eligible for this as well. The first year, I chose a private insurer and the highest cover possible. I paid a double-digit monthly premium, which was a far cry from the exorbitant rates in Germany. Two years later, I have dispensed with additional private insurance, preferring to dip into savings if I need to pay for something extra. All of the basics are covered: illness, accidental injury, surgery and hospital stays. Dental care generally is not. Even tourists benefit with partial coverage in the event of an accident, courtesy of the ACC (Accident Compensation Corporation).[32]

Screening programmes are not covered by any insurance in New Zealand, though some are provided free of charge to women above a certain age (please refer to the website of the National Screening Unit for information).[33] For certain procedures, it is actually cheaper to have it done in Germany, if you happen to be there anyway, and pay out of pocket, for example teeth cleaning or having moles or other lesions removed. I know quite a few New Zealanders who got their teeth done in other countries like Indonesia. The health service only covers skin screening if there is a suspicion of cancerous growth. Private insurance does ensure shorter waiting times for elective surgery. In the event of a serious illness such as cancer, I have purchased coverage for myself that will pay off the mortgage on my house with a lump sum, so that I could afford retirement through renting out the house. The insurance is a kind of mix of health insurance and disability, like we have in Germany. No matter where you live, being properly informed about insurance options, benefits and disbursement well before something actually happens is a must.

I do appreciate the comprehensive German health care system, even though it is easy to abuse. It also provides little incentive for people to be responsible for their own health and prevention. You can choose the insurance company, but insurance is compulsory. The government or private health insurance, respectively, stipulates which preventive screenings are included in the tariffs and how much is refunded. After emigrating from Germany, I now have the freedom to choose whether I want insurance or not.

Disability insurance, as we have it in Germany, is not offered in New Zealand, though the names of some insurance types may sound like it (this is why I kept mine in Germany).

Premiums are not stable in New Zealand. They keep rising and the services are often inadequate, so it pays to take a good look at the policy and arrange for a payment plan over its entire validity. You want to make sure the premiums aren't highest when you are most likely to have to make a claim.

There is also superannuation – essentially New Zealand's national pension plan scheme. Or you can sign up for private retirement savings plans like Kiwisaver, similar to the Riester-Rente in Germany, with which retirement savings can be topped up. Retirement in New Zealand is government subsidised. More or less the same amount is paid out to everyone, whether the person was a freelancer, employed or never worked at all. This sum is unrelated to the actual amount of money someone earns over the course of a lifetime, reflecting the egalitarian principle that governs New Zealand society. (Please refer again to the chapter *Hierarchy and egalitarianism* on page 137).

The upshot is that comparing insurance schemes in both countries is like comparing apples to oranges. The infrastructure, premiums, services and taxes are quite different, even if the products have a similar sounding name. A close look is crucial.

I arrived back in Germany just in time for two important birthday parties: a friend's and my mother's. As usual, my mother had been preparing for days. The invitation read 6 pm and of course the first guests rang the doorbell at 5.56. Amused, I told myself it's only because they can't wait to interview me after two and a half years of being away. My mother loves to cook for a crowd. My family loves good food. The people of this region are connoisseurs, as you will find if you visit the many wine and culinary festivals in the autumn. In New Zealand, on the other hand, you would never be expected to cater for a party all by yourself.

## Social events – and what they have to do with dependability

Dependability is a highly valued trait in Germany. Kaitiaki often told me how much he appreciates that he can count on me. He said also, 'Germans actually judge one another on their dependability. The cultural standard of "conscientiousness, or sense of duty"[34] is a very important German value. It is one area that often leads to conflict in international communication. You expect the same exactitude from others while they would never guess they are not living up to your expectations, and don't have the same of you.'

My Italian friend Renata once said she would love to go on holiday with me. I trusted that was true and waited for her to let me know when we could book our flights. And waited. She kept putting it off. The airfares increased. I was getting angry. Didn't she want to go travelling with me? Of course I do, Renata kept saying, but it's much too early to commit to a non-refundable flight. Something unexpected, *'qualcosa di imprevvisto'*, could still get in the way. This was not the first time she did this. I told her it hurt me that she was procrastinating for fear of something that probably wouldn't happen. I felt a bit hurt and like our friendship must not be worth much to her if she was more worried about the unexpected, which would probably never happen, than committing to a trip with me. That's when the penny dropped for Renata. She immediately booked her flight and since then our friendship has grown deeper.

I can count on most of my friends one hundred percent. There are two kinds of New Zealanders: those for whom dependability is as important as for a German and who admire this trait in us, and then there are those more like the Italians... No, wait. New Zealanders are dependable, as are Italians in their own way. Full stop.

Let me try again: New Zealanders rarely plan very far ahead of time. Their decisions are quite spontaneous and they can't say exactly how they want to spend their day or week until it is almost upon them in case something comes up. Germans interpret this as being totally unreliable – but it isn't.

**As a host in New Zealand, you will often have no idea how many people were at their party until it's over. A potential guest will decide at short notice if they will attend or not. In their leisure time, Kiwis live in *event time* (we will be discussing this in the section *The perception of***

*time – back and forward to the pas*t on page 82). Conversely, a New Zealander would never be upset if a guest cancels at the last moment, if they even bother with that. German immigrants forget this approach to things and complain about Kiwi unpredictability. To top it off, New Zealanders usually take their leave soon after dessert. They don't sit around talking and drinking for hours as we do in Germany after a fine dinner. Another sore spot in German–Kiwi relations.

Potluck get-togethers suit Kiwi spontaneity much better. And *morning tea*. Everybody brings something, so that there is enough for everybody. It isn't usual to provide all the food and drinks for the evening like in Germany. New Zealanders would feel very uncomfortable if they couldn't bring something. If somebody in New Zealand tells you 'bring a plate', you don't literally bring a plate. You contribute in your way. In other words, something to share, so that the host/hostess doesn't carry the full load of cost and preparation. Usually you bring your own drinks as well.

I wonder why we can't do this in Germany. Dinner parties get ever more elaborate as people try to outdo themselves or their friends. Some can't afford it and worry about serving food and drinks that are not good enough. I've heard quite a few grumbles about this. Sure, it starts as a sign of appreciation when we try to match an invitation we've enjoyed. Eventually it just spirals out of control. No chance for that in New Zealand. Kiwis would probably never get together if only one person had to do it all. With potlucks, you never have to worry if you have the means to throw a party. In the 1980s, potluck parties were popular in Germany, too. Luckily the practice seems to be making a comeback.

On the day after my mother's party, something else happened that I hadn't experienced in a long time. A huge thunderstorm. It even hailed! It rained so hard that I just stayed indoors and enjoyed German *Gemütlichkeit*. This is another word that has made it into the English language, representing a feeling that can't be described in any other way.

Thunder and lightning are rare in New Zealand. Grey skies for days on end almost never occur. You see sun and blue sky almost every day, even in Wellington, which probably has the most unsettled weather in

the country. I never miss German winters: four solid months of thickly overcast skies and maybe one or two sunny days in between. However, Aotearoa can be inclement too, and cities like Wellington often are. If you don't like it, you need to move to Australia. The weather and the beaches of New Zealand often remind me of Northern Germany, minus the freezing temperatures and the universally grey skies of winter.

I was thoroughly enjoying sitting in my parents' warm living room, sipping coffee and writing, not having to feel guilty for not being outside kite surfing or jogging. I suddenly remembered what my Spanish friend, César from Barcelona, once said in his perception of Germans: a collective migration, long lines of cars heading south, faces all turned smiling into the sunlight.

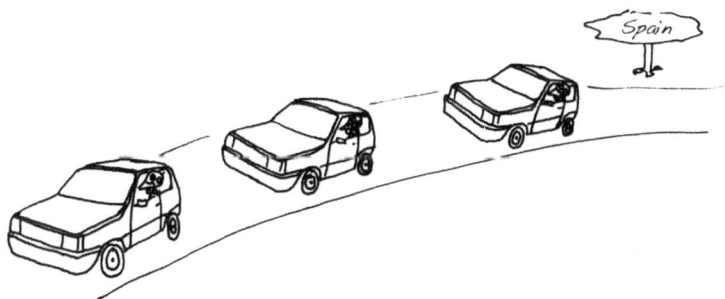

One evening as I was sitting with friends, the topic of expats and relocation came up. There are many stories of expats returning home and being unable to readjust. Many of my friends knew this from people within their own companies. The same topic came up the next day on a wine tour through the Palatinate. A friend who had lived for a longer time in Italy told me how difficult it had been to return and reintegrate into business life. It is normal for returnees to go through several phases until they are really and truly home again. Some are finally relieved to be back; others yearn for their life abroad.

Many of the people who contribute to the German–Kiwi internet forums have moved back and forth between Germany and New Zealand several times. The British have an amusing name for their own expats of this type: **Ping-pong Poms** (Poms being an epithet for the British), because they have ping-ponged between the United Kingdom and other countries.

In the following sections, I will describe the first and second phases of reintegration according to Hirsch's Three-phase Model of Reintegration.[34] The phases can differ in length at delegation or return, and also depend on whether the person has taken the assignment voluntarily or not. The third phase will be discussed later in the book on page 176.

*Common features of the first phase of reintegration*
The first phase is euphoric, also called the honeymoon phase, and usually has these characteristics:
– good mood, even euphoria, at being home again in familiar surroundings
– happily reconnecting with old routines and with old friends
– superficial acknowledgment of how things have changed.

I noticed my own honeymoon phase in Germany was on its way out when I was at the small local post office. I politely asked an older gentleman if he was queuing, and got a snarled at. 'What else would I be doing here?' was the reply.

It seemed to me that people were always aggressive, even angry, with each other in public. Was I so used to Kiwi smiles that the directness that Germans are famous for was actually painful? Or was it just a full moon, making everybody grumpy? Well, not everybody. My communications regarding prospective jobs were very pleasant. But I was beginning to miss New Zealand.

*Common features of the second phase of reintegration*
The second phase is distress, reintegration shock, and usually has these characteristics:
– the realisation that many things at home have changed
– the realisation that you yourself are different from before
– difficulties at work
– a certain arrogance from the returnee for having been abroad
– feeling misunderstood and unwelcome
– disappointment and dissatisfaction
– feeling foreign in your own country.

It was nice to hear from my German friends in New Zealand who asked if I was missing it, even as they were homesick for Germany. And as always, there was that feeling of being torn between here and there.

One day I got a call from my tenant in Wellington to tell me that the motion detector light in the front was not functioning. I knew this lamp well – it was definitely Kiwi, with an independent mind of its own. The radio-controlled clock I had brought with me from Germany to New Zealand, on the other hand, had literally spun crazily, searching for German time as it was programmed to do. Instead of the Sauerkraut frequency it was used to, it had located the Kiwi frequency.

## The perception of time – back and forward to the past

Kaitiaki loved my crazy German wall clock. It reminded him of the different attitude towards time I had brought with me from Germany. 'You Germans and other Westerners have an interesting relationship to time. You can steal time, save time, gain time and waste time. You can lose time and you can manage time. Time is money. Germans invest time. If a moment has passed, it will never return. The best way to frustrate a German in business is to be unprepared and come to a meeting without an agenda. Germans don't get together without a reason. Small talk is a waste of time. New Zealanders wear watches less often than Germans.' Kaitiaki snickered.

Indeed, our understanding of time has an impact on time management and how we work, and how we plan projects, etc. How do we deal with the past? Do we take the past into account when we plan for the future, or is it irrelevant? Can we clearly envision the future in front of us? And how far into the future can we make plans?

Dutch researcher Fons Trompenaars describes Western cultures like Germany as *sequential* or *linear*. Time can be measured and interpersonal relationships have less influence on our perception of time. Imagine the situation where we have an important business meeting and a friend calls for help. As a German, you would most likely explain that you can't do it right now and will call him later. Not going to the meeting is not an option because our reliability would be on the line; our sense of duty towards work would be compromised.

Trompenaars calls the opposite pole *synchronic* or *cyclical*. Several things can be dealt with at the same time. Relationships and the unexpected are integral to time planning. A friend in need might take precedent over getting to the business meeting on time. There is time for everything, time is flexible. Time breathes.[36]

Edward Hall defines the linear perception of time as *monochronic* or *sequential*, with a strong focus on planning and partitioning. The opposite pole is *polychronic*, where things happen and can be handled at the same time.[37]

In Italy it is an art to deal with the unexpected – '*l'arte di arrangarsi*'. It is considered a virtue to be able to take care of many things simultaneously. They can be driving, talking on the phone, twiddling with the radio buttons, checking the map and using a foot to open the glove box, all at

the same time. The point being that it is not necessary to do things in sequence.

Richard Donald Lewis defines time orientation in Germany as *linear-active*. There are to-do lists that you tick off as you go. Communication is based on a question and answer formula. A typically German reaction would be like this: 'That is not the answer to my question. What I asked was...' or 'Why don't you ever answer my questions properly?' This happens to us Germans abroad quite often because we are not used to indirectness or reading/listening between the lines. We feel misunderstood when we don't get a (for us) clear answer. In *multi-active cultures*, according to Lewis, the focus is on relationships and people. Time is handled flexibly and communication is a series of rambling dialogues rather than a series of questions and answers. When dealing with these kinds of people, a German soul can easily get frustrated if their counterpart constantly interrupts them, even though this signals interest and active engagement and is not considered impolite behaviour.

Lewis' *reactive cultures* favour a cyclical sense of time. A good example is Hindu reincarnation. Everything will come around again, so why hurry to get something done? If things happen again, the past and present have strong bearing on the future and making slow, well-thought-out decisions.[38]

The people of Madagascar have a particular sense of the past and future. They think of the future as being behind them, flowing through their heads into the past, which they visualise in front of them. Logical, actually. You can 'see' what has already transpired, whereas the future is uncertain and unknowable. Lewis wrote an interesting article on this subject: *How Different Cultures Understand Time*.[39]

If, for example, Germans, New Zealanders, Australians, the Dutch, the Swiss, Americans, the British or Scandinavians speak of yesterday, they will most likely point behind themselves, and ahead when referring the future. Interestingly, the Māori language reflects a similarity to the way Madagascans view time: the Māori word for past, *mua*, translates to front /in front of. History, the land, the people, the tribe, elders and events exist in a continuum. The Māori people live within time, whereas the Pākehā leave it behind. This contrasting relationship to past, present and future can lead to conflicts of interest, as can be observed in the example of the

Treaty of Waitangi. For the Māori, it was likely less a matter of what had happened in the past, which the Pākehā believe can't be changed anyway, but to secure a basis for future generations. *He pai te tirohanga ki nga mahara mo nga raa pahemo engari ka puta te maaramatanga i runga i te titiro whakamua.* It's fine to have recollections of the past, but wisdom comes from being able to prepare opportunities for the future, as this Māori saying goes.

The difference in the perception of time between Māori and Pākehā throughout history has been researched and published in an article by Kevin D. Lo. He distinguishes between *clock time* and *event time*. Do people organise their time chronologically (Pākehā) or circle from event to event (Māori)? Punctuality is the degree to which plans and deadlines are kept. How much deviation is acceptable? Five minutes? Half an hour? A day? A week? Cultures on clock time tend to have a smaller window than event time cultures. The Māori culture is governed by events and has a flexible window of punctuality. This doesn't mean that Māori people don't use clocks or wristwatches, but that the time the clock shows is subordinate to what is happening in its social, cultural and situational context. The past, present and future are not points in time strung up like pearls. They are interrelated in a complex, cyclical flow, featuring not only events, but ancestors, the tribe as a whole and Mother Nature.[40]

In the same article, Lo writes that punctuality for Non-Māori means, for example, arriving to work on time, taking planned breaks and to finish a task at an appointed time. If time was needed for something outside of work it would cause a disturbance and organisational problems. Māori work relationships start and end flexibly. If someone comes late, a Māori boss will assume there is a good reason for it. They can take time off to take care of personal things and it's understood that the time will be made up later, since they care about their jobs. As an opportunity for an informal exchange of information and ideas, tea breaks are important, too. They are usually part of a work contract, so time doesn't need to be made up (unless they go over the allotted time). A cordial relationship between manager and employee is more important than the money earned for the company. I experience this effect on my own work assignments on a daily basis in New Zealand, and I find it very pleasant. Nature itself had traditionally influenced the Māori sense of time. You

went out to catch eels when the wind was right and the water temperature prompted them to start migrating. Fish were caught, and plants were planted and harvested when the time was right. Natural events flowed according to its own rhythms. A wood carver needed as much time as was necessary to finish the carving. Though there was a structure and order to the work, each step was not pressed into quantifiable units of time. Historically, time wasn't an abstraction of hours and minutes for Māori culture; rather, a relative quality belonging to the task at hand. However, it has also been observed that when a piece was finished and ready to sell for their livelihood, the time spent making it was assigned a value in the same way Europeans do.[41]

Edward Hall is quoted in the same article in reference to his description of sense of time as a 'silent language' that gives meaning to people and their behaviours – our culture. The impact of our time orientation on what we do is tremendously underestimated, especially in business contexts.

A fair amount of the distinctive cross-cultural traits mentioned in the section *Efficiency, Planning and Organisation – or the Germans and their 3 Ps: Planning, Preparation and Process* on page 183 can also be explained by their understanding of time.[42]

New Zealand's society has greatly been formed by the Māori and Pākehā cultures, which traditionally have an opposing awareness of time. It is surely not a coincidence that many of my New Zealand seminar participants place their culture in the middle between the reactive and linear-active points on Lewis' triangular model.[43] Germans are clearly linear-active. So, it was a pleasant surprise to hear that schools in Germany were allowing classes to begin later the day after evening broadcasts of the European soccer championship. 'Work first, play after' is an adage that is much more often turned upside down in New Zealand than in Germany.

No surprise either when my wall clock spun around like crazy when it arrived in New Zealand. The motion sensor light was born in New Zealand and had no qualms about resting for a while whenever it chose. Praise and a little jiggling usually got it working again, but this time nothing helped. Maybe because I was gone? I remembered someone had recommended an electrician in the neighbourhood, so I contacted him. His reply came promptly with a **DIY solution**.

That is quintessentially New Zealand. Not only a nation of DIYers, but giving free advice so that someone else can save a bit of money. When my gas heater was giving trouble, the expert could have come by and charged me NZD200 to disconnect and remove it. Instead, he told me how to do it myself, saving me a lot of money. When I wanted to buy an electric garage opener, a friendly locksmith suggested I try first on Trade Me (the Kiwi version of eBay or Amazon). Programming it would be easy. He gave me all the details so I could find it online for about NZD29. It worked and I saved several hundred dollars.

My visiting parents were helped in the same way with their van, not to mention the replacement of a door handle. My house is from the Great Gatsby era with old art deco elements, among them high door handles which are not manufactured any more. One of them was loose, on the toilet door no less, which really needed to be able to be locked. I looked for help in an antique store. They had no such handles, but gave me with the telephone number of an elderly man in the neighbourhood whose hobby was fixing things. It was a landline, so I was passed from family member to family member until I met him personally and arranged to bring him the broken handle. When it was

fixed, he came by and insisted on installing it himself. Finally, as a goodbye gift, he gave me a little Allen key so that I could tighten it if it ever came loose again. He only wanted NZD29 for all that work, so I asked him if he would also accept a bottle of my favourite wine. He grabbed it, mumbled a thanks and disappeared.

I'm sure you can find this kind of support in Germany too, but to what lengths someone might go I couldn't say. Maybe it was more common years ago. Germany is geared towards monetary remuneration for service rather than trading a service for a service as is the case in Italy or New Zealand. I'll fix your car if you fix my heater. That sort of thing. It ends up being much cheaper for all concerned.

# Cologne – or the return to street-side cafés

The following weekend I decided to take a trip to Cologne and booked a Rideshare. Isn't it great? In Europe, you can be in another place with its unique dialect or language and culture in just a short time. This is what expatriate Europeans miss most. Europeans have a different **feeling for distances** than New Zealanders. When I was still a teenager, a 30-minute drive to H&M in Mannheim seemed like a world tour and was an event that happened maybe twice a year. New Zealanders feel compelled to travel overseas at least once in their lifetime. For their OE, overseas experience, they often choose Australia or Great Britain, though some do travel elsewhere. A flight to Australia takes a minimum of 3 hours, and other favourite destinations in the South Pacific take quite a bit longer. New Zealanders give no further thought to it. Europeans are used to the idea that they can be in a completely different world in just an hour or two. I am told that the main reason why they 'can't' come to New Zealand is because of the long flight. For me, it's like taking an extended bus trip. I love long haul flights and the 'me time' it offers. There's food, entertainment and a good book to read. I can leave the day-to-day demands behind. Kaitiaki added, 'Having children is no excuse. I see how New Zealanders take these long trips all the time with their kids.'

So, I arrived in Cologne after about 2½ hours with some time to spare before meeting my intercultural trainer colleagues. A déja-vu hit me as I strolled through town. You can get anything, in any colour, shape or form, in great quality and for a reasonable price. There are countless nice cafés in which to hang out. The concept of street-side cafés now took on new meaning. Germans can feel comfortable anywhere, even in rush-hour traffic. Were there cafés like this in New Zealand where you practically sit in the middle of the street? Only beach cafés came to mind, especially my favourite, Maranui Café in Lyall Bay. Did I miss the seating and view from the beach there? Not really. Maybe I was still in my German 'honeymoon' phase. Cologne is just different! The *Gemütlichkeit* on the street was so charming. I was staying with my friend, Ines, who I knew from kite surfing in Wellington. She

had a room in a shared flat. The first German flat sharing I visited since I emigrated.

## Flat sharing and German Gemütlichkeit

Yes, you can experience *Gemütlichkeit* during a thunderstorm or in a street-side café in Cologne. It deserves its own section in this book. If it is stormy outside, then we feel Gemütlichkeit sitting cosily at home with a cup tea. It's 'cocooning', feeling comfy and safe. You can experience this when you live in a shared flat as well. Flatmates do a lot of things together: cooking, chatting, watching a video or partying. Of course, flatmates are independent people with their own agendas, but there is an unmistakable homely feeling, of creating something nice together.

Kaitiaki thought about his home, and said, 'I think New Zealanders live in their own microcosm, and in a shared flat, they are loosely joined into a macrocosm. Flatmates live alongside each other, each doing their own thing, each creating a private haven. Of course, there are exceptions to every rule. New Zealand flatmates who choose the 'one big family' style, or Germans who share an address but little else.

Kaitiaki giggled as he continued. 'What I find really not gemütlich in Germany is compulsory airing out. You Germans have an almost paranoid fear of stale air and humidity in your flat or office! I know, you have explained to me that opening all of the windows wide for a few minutes several times a day is totally normal. However, in New Zealand, people might tell you that is exactly what lets the humid air *in*. We use dehumidifiers, or we just deal with the air as it comes.'

The next morning we went to a café for breakfast. We sat inside since it was raining and had a long chat. We were surrounded by Gemütlichkeit, even without the contents of our fridge on the table. While paying our bill, I almost forgot the tip. And even worse, I almost forgot to pay for the meal.

Kaitiaki just had to comment, 'My dear, remember that in New Zealand we don't have **tipping**. At most, the *koha*, which is a donation into a box at the counter. We normally order and **pay** at the counter or

cashier. The service at the table does not usually include the whole process from ordering through to paying. Often you can place your order with the waiter and pay at cashier when you have ordered and are ready to leave. This causes quite a bit of confusion with overseas visitors. Helga and Herbert will hypnotically stare at a waiter, who doesn't notice a thing. The stare then turns into the evil eye, garnished with a comment about the bad service in this place. They get up and leave, angry and hungry. As I said, it is very easy. Just order and pay at the counter. And by the way, in New Zealand everybody pays their own tab. Splitting it up is uncommon, so the patrons do it themselves at the table. Sometimes at private dinners, and often at business functions, it can happen that someone pays a round of drinks for all. Don't expect this, though. The occasional round-buying is a lot like in Italy where friends rotate with paying. The trick is to do it early enough, so that you don't end up looking like a "free-loader", rather a "fair-player".

# A visit to a sauna paradise

One Sunday, I decided I would visit a very dubious and exotic place (at least in a New Zealander's mind). I went to the sauna, which is not just a wooden box to sweat in. In Germany we have thermal baths featuring entire sauna complexes with various themes in terms of decoration and sauna experiences. In Northern Germany I had three favourites: the Bartholomäus baths in Hamburg, the Dünentherme baths in St Peter-Ording and the Ostseetherme baths at Timmendorfer Strand. In New Zealand there are a few saunas, and usually in a gym. Wellington has a Finnish sauna. The rates are normally per hour and can cost as much as an entire day in a German sauna complex. I visited a sauna with Manu in Hanmer Springs in the South Island once. We had a whole box to ourselves for one hour. Very romantic.

In the Cubo baths in the Palatinate city of Landstuhl, I paid the entrance fee and proceeded to the changing cubicles. Oh, it was a unisex changing room! I felt a bit uneasy and shook my head. What was going on with me? 'That's how New Zealanders feel when they are confronted with your – ah – natural attitude towards nudity,' Kaitiaki reminded me. Well, I suppose the contrasting experience for us Europeans is when New Zealanders walk barelegged and barefooted through super-markets, in the great outdoors or even at work. People wear jandals (flip-flops, as Europeans know them, or thongs as the Aussies say and slippahs in Hawaii). They don't have much more on 'down there', whereas Germans tend to be foot shy. They wear fuzzy slippers at home and often have a selection of guest slippers ready for visitors. The Goethe Institute of New Zealand has an entertaining Lifeswap video on the topic of fuzzy slippers vs jandals.[44] New Zealanders go barefooted to the sauna too. I have not been able to find out how New Zealanders avoid the horrible foot diseases Germans imagine they must have. In the German saunas I decided to follow the New Zealand custom, and my feet suffered no consequences.

Kaitiaki was a little audacious now in saying, 'In New Zealand we have the stereotype image not only of a rotund German in Lederhosen with a huge stein of beer in hand...'

'Which could maybe pass for a Bavarian,' I thought.

Our tui wasn't finished. '...but we also imagine a nudist couple standing

on a cliff staring out to sea. We think you spend most of your day without a stitch of clothing on,' he said with a giggle.

I felt I had to overrule that silly notion. 'There are unwritten rules,' I explained, 'that you can only know if you have had access to the German soul. Let me be clear. We Germans have a very clear sense of propriety. We don't just take off our clothes wherever we want. You will never see us without garments outside of a sauna, not even in a public swimming pool. In the sauna restaurant we wrap a towel around us and we don't enter jacuzzis without wearing a swimsuit unless it is specifically part of the sauna ethos. There are nudist beaches on the northern coasts, but they are properly labelled and flagged. Some baths offer late-night nude bathing as a special, but people put on towels and robes as soon as they come out of the water.'

A few years before, my Italian friend Renata came to visit me in Hamburg for a few weeks while taking a language course. We talked on the phone before her trip. I suggested we visit one of the baths, which she thought was a nice idea, and wanted to know what she should pack for it. I said, 'Nothing,' and she asked, 'What do you mean, nothing?' I suggested that she could bring her jandals if she wanted and she could borrow one of my towels and a bathrobe. 'What about my bikini?' she asked. I explained she wouldn't need one in the sauna. 'What? Everybody will be staring at me!' she squeaked. I had to laugh. 'No, they'll stare at you if you have a bikini on.'

She got used to it quickly and enjoyed the infusions. Over the years she brought some of her family and friends along to Hamburg for a visit, which often featured an outing to the sauna without a bikini. Her cousin Giada was concerned. 'Everyone will be staring at me naked!' Renata replied with a serious voice, 'No, they'll stare if you are wearing one.'

In the unisex changing room, I quickly wrapped my towel around me. I was used to covering myself up in New Zealand so as not to embarrass anyone. In the gym saunas I still refused to wear a bikini, but I did wear a towel. Now at the German sauna, it seemed like I had to relearn how to be naked around others. I studied the infusion plan. I really miss this ceremony in New Zealand. I took a seat between all of the other nudies, only to be admonished for not leaving my jandals outside. Of course, I has already forgotten basic etiquette!

The first infusion was spectacular. The sauna master is responsible for pouring water on the hot stones and waving a towel around to circulate the steam. This one poured ice cubes instead of water, and as they sizzled, he whirled the towel around in time to heavy metal rock music from the band Rammstein, which was playing on the sound system. Wait a minute... one of the sauna guests was sitting on the top tier, loudly singing along, and he was actually dressed! He wearing a Tyrolean hat with his birthday suit.

When the door opened some time later, I couldn't get out of there fast enough to jump into the cold pool. That is something which is always missing in New Zealand, just like the cold-water hose to rinse down with.

Looking for a lounger to rest on, I noticed that the stereotype of Germans insisting on reserving loungers with their towels at every pool and beach in the world was pretty much true. Sigh.

The next infusion was a plain one – just water. This was followed by the Robin Hood infusion, as I called it. Not one, but two sauna masters were involved – the previous master and a woman named Frau Müller. She was wearing a Robin Hood-style cap. 'Are people now wearing headgear in the sauna?' I wondered. 'Perhaps to offset the perception

of the rest of the world of Germans being too risqué?' At any rate, the rock music continued and the sauna masters dipped and whipped around a birch branch, just barely missing our faces. Both of them were having trouble repressing an obvious desire to head bang along with the music.

In spite of my initial trepidation, I enjoyed my sauna afternoon very much and went home with baby-soft skin. I felt that five hours had been too short, so I promised myself I would go again during my visit to Germany.

Germans, Scandinavians and probably Austrians and the Swiss are among the more open-minded cultures in this sense. However, New Zealanders love competitions, even if it means going au naturel. Notable examples are the Dunedin Nude Rugby Tournament, the World Naked Bike Ride, the Great Annual Nude Tunnel Run and the Nude Golf International. Naked bungee jumping is probably more of a touristy thing. Still waters run deep, as they say. Despite their bashfulness, New Zealanders frequent a number of nudist beaches. Here is a list (but check for any changes before you go): Ladies Bay (this is unofficial; you risk a fine if caught), Uretiti Beach and Matai Bay (both under DOC oversight), Pōhutukawa Bay Beach, Papamoa Beach, Breaker Bay (around the corner from my house), Peka Peka Beach on the Kapiti Coast, Waikuku Beach, Spencerville, North Beach, Orpheus Bay, Opoutere Beach, Five Mile Bay, Milnthorpe Beach, Little Palm Beach on Waiheke Island, Tapotupotu Beach, Henderson Bay, Waitata Bay (Donkey Beach), Long Beach, Kauri Mountain Beach, Ocean Beach, Whale Bay, Mimiwhangata and Tawharanui Beach.

## Down under in Germany, or a life in the dark: the German mole gene

By now I was in my fourth week back in Germany and it just wouldn't stop raining. There were a few sunny days now and again, but for the most part it rained constantly in that summer of 2016. New reports on flooding kept coming. Who says Germans can't do small talk about the weather? If you remember, Germans equate small talk with complaining, so the miserable weather was easily the number one topic. Personally, I didn't mind so much. There wasn't much I could do

outdoors around here anyway. I think it is part of our heritage, a kind of mole gene. Not even Gemütlichkeit can help you survive the four rainy -grey months of a German winter. It has to be something more, something making it easy for us to go 'underground' for so long. A mole gene.

We also have other grievances regarding the weather that are difficult to explain. *Feeling under the weather* is one the Brits and Irish know, but we also have *spring tiredness* and *foehn-wind-illness*, which is an adverse reaction to warm drainage winds, made responsible for low or high blood pressure, headaches or migraines and a host of other pains. We Germans often sigh a collective 'Tja' (which means something like 'oh well', but not quite) when we have finished listing our weather-related symptoms to each other.[45]

Enough of the weather. New Zealanders find that Europeans talk far too much about it anyway. I was mustering all of my New Zealand optimism, so I was able to continue enjoying Gemütlichkeit through thunder, lightning and rain.

## Frankfurt – welcome to the city of penguins

The next leg of my trip through Germany brought me to 'Penguin City'. No, I hadn't left Germany and returned to the southern coast of Wellington. Frankfurt is the city with probably the most penguins in Germany: poker faced and pale, wearing suits and ties.

I arrived at my new shared accommodation on a Sunday, having aced my interview on the Thursday, and was starting the new job on the Monday. I found this flat in no time and would be sharing it for three months with two young women; one from Mongolia and a German from Bonn. That is if nothing changed, which you can never count on with people from the other side of the world. The girl from Mongolia was really nice, spoke fluent German and had gone to university here, so she was fairly **germanised – *eingedeutscht***, as we say.

The grey clouds threatened rain, but it stayed dry, so I went out for a stroll around my new neighbourhood. Did I need to clean my glasses, or was it true that most of the people I saw were not your typical German faces? Most people I met appeared to have immigrated. I stopped to spy on a big African wedding that had spilled onto the street. They spoke impeccable German with one another, even the toddlers. How thrilling! They would have two hearts in their breasts, one for Germany and one for where their parents came from. They seemed to be happily integrated – germanised. I thought this was great. Speaking German in Germany. If you remember how my CV had to be in German for it to be even considered, it becomes clear that Germany still isn't very international these days and likes to speak German.

Speaking of germanised, one day I overheard an immigrant family playing in the courtyard behind our building. Suddenly, a little girl started yelling 'Nein', which is *no* in German. Her mother replied with 'Nein?' and the girl confirmed it with another 'Nein'.

Kaitiaki agreed. 'It should be normal for immigrants to integrate well into the new country they live in, and that they try to understand the culture and learn the language. I admire anyone who learns German, which is not an easy language to master, and who attempts to understand the culture. I found it rather difficult, myself, to look

past the grumpy, growling, super-efficient, evil-eyed exterior to find that Germans are actually cooperative, friendly, profound, reliable and very hospitable. You don't see it at first. It took me a while to understand you.' He winked at me.

## German bluntness – how to deal with it? How to say no without actually saying it.

I am guessing you already knew what *nein* means. We Germans use it unabashedly and fairly often, so people from other countries are usually familiar with it. My parents and I discussed this once over wine and a delicious Alsatian *Flammkuchen* (tarte flambé). My mother felt that *nein* could be understood in the same way as the word *well* in English. It's true, we do start many a sentence with the word *nein*. Does that cause misunderstandings? Or do we really often say and mean no? An entertaining how-to for New Zealand-style indirect complaint in comparison to a German's bluntness is showcased in the animated film *Lifeswap, Episode 2 – The Tea Towel Stinks.*[46]

Just for fun, I did a survey among my friends to find out how people from different cultural backgrounds would say no to the following message. It is an authentic one that a friend of mine received. 'Hello, my dear! What are you doing this weekend? Could you take my Saturday night shift from 6 pm to midnight? Many best regards!'

Here are some reactions and replies:

- An American woman who lives in New Zealand: 'Hey, thanks for thinking of me. Unfortunately I can't do the shift. Good luck getting it covered! Let me know if you wanna meet up for a glass of wine or kite surfing (for example) while I'm here.'
- New Zealand woman (jokingly): 'Yeah, naaah', which is often said when you mean no. In reality, she would have responded like this: 'I'd really like to help but I'm not free on Saturday.'
- A Spanish man from Barcelona: 'Sorry, I can't.' Simple and upfront.
- North German: 'It won't work, sorry.'
- Someone from the Palatinate (Ok, it's me): 'Hi. No, sorry. I don't feel like doing a night shift.' Kaitiaki rolled his eyes at this.
- South Tyrolean woman from Northern Italy: 'No. Unfortunately I can't because I already have to...'

- New Zealand man: 'Sorry, I would like to, but I already made plans with some friends.'
- British woman: 'Hey there, I hope you are well! I'm afraid I've already got plans for next weekend. Sorry I can't help you out. Big hugs.'
- Irish woman who lives in New Zealand: 'Ah well, I'd love to, but you see I promised my mammy I'd...'
- Scottish woman who has lived in New Zealand for years and then moved to the Cook Islands: 'Awfully sorry but I have plans.'
- Canadian woman who lives part-time in New Zealand and part-time in Canada: 'Thanks for thinking of me, however I'm not available.'
- Filipino man who lives in New Zealand: 'Sorry, I can't. I have something planned.'
- English woman who has lived in New Zealand and then moved to Fiji: If I don't like the person, I may not even reply at all! Otherwise I'd say 'Sorry for not being able to help out. I already have plans. I hope that you get it sorted soon...' while thinking: the message that the person sent is random and quite rude.
- A woman from Hamburg: 'Exactly.' (That is all. Do you know the German word *genau*? This is what it is. A very German way to show the middle finger in this context. Genau as such is an agreement, like 'exactly'.)
- New Zealand man: 'No thanks.'
- Finnish man: 'I've had a pretty rough week and just need to get some rest.' Or say politely the thing you're up to, straight up and honest.
- French woman who has worked in New Zealand for some years: 'Sorry, I have some plans on Saturday.'
- Tyrolean woman who lives in Munich: 'Not really. I am arriving very late from Frankfurt the day before and I need to sleep. Maybe another time.'

As the sun set on Frankfurt, a frog choir took over the evening's entertainment and croaked an a capella round. The first week passed quickly and I found myself at the railway station waiting for

the train home to Weilerbach. I was planning a shopping trip to the outlet stores – VAT-free, of course, since my tax home is now New Zealand.

## Tax-free shopping

As a non-EU resident, you can opt out of paying European VAT. It works in London as well as in Germany. The German customs website details how to have the tax reimbursed on your purchases. They also provide the necessary forms for download free of charge. You can ask the stores where you purchased items to fill this out. You add your address abroad, your passport details, credit card and bank account. Before departure, you have the export of your goods confirmed by the customs office at the airport, and the forms are sent to the stores as proof, so that the tax can be credited to your card or account. Some merchants or outlet centres provide this service through a third party for a fee so that you can collect all of your receipts and hand them in at the airport in exchange for immediate reimbursement. The German customs office has a service number, and the people on the phone are very nice and helpful.

Back in the world of work I was happy to discover that things hadn't changed all that much in my absence. The projects were as chaotic as ever; not at all German-efficient. There were the same obstacles to contend with as in New Zealand, no matter who the client was.

Though there were some new things that hadn't reached Down Under, like WebID[47] via Skype, or PostIdent (verifying your ID and address via the German post office), for that matter. The **banking system** in New Zealand is much simpler than in Germany, and often less bureaucratic, as is the case with many official things. The bank sends a letter to the address you give them and you return to the bank with it in hand to activate your account. These innovations had passed by us Germans in New Zealand. For immigrants and expats, the online WebID verification system can be very helpful.

After a week, I was already using the informal *Du* with 20% of my new colleagues, and things were easing with the rest of them. I guessed I would be on a great footing with everyone after a month. We chatted about travel plans, weekend plans and such things. As the days passed by, I got more smiles. The only exception was my first meeting with a British man who had lived in Frankfurt for the past 15 years and was terribly angry at the results of the recent Brexit vote. In the end, he did laugh about it, and we agreed to say *Du* to each other.

Another difference I realised was that this company had a canteen, something that is very rare in New Zealand.

I had sent my consulting outfit (a trouser suit and shirt) to Germany by post ahead of time, because I didn't want to travel with it all over Cuba. I didn't intend on taking it back with me to Wellington either, as I hadn't even worn it once in two and a half years.

Regarding **dress codes**: I have already mentioned that it is possible that in New Zealand people wear jandals/flip-flops at work (not in all work places, though). Naked toes and hosiery-free legs are generally not a problem, especially if dressy. It is pretty relaxed. Barefoot and in sports togs at the supermarket? No worries. You wear what you feel like wearing. No tie on at work? So what? Ties are not usually required business accessories, not even in banks or insurance company offices. Tattoos? They are an integral part of Māori culture and totally normal. There was one thing that threw me off guard: Jeans. Wearing jeans with a (more often than not black) T-shirt or sweater is pretty much a typically German outfit. If the top is stylish, it elevates any pair of designer jeans – in Germany. Not so in this part of the world. I was once dressed like that at a business event and quickly noticed that I was decidedly underdressed. Jeans on this side of the planet are only jeans, and no amount of fancy accessories will make them less casual. My English friends later confirmed this. Lesson learned. Even if jeans are worn at work, and not only on casual Fridays, it's better to ask beforehand if jeans are okay for an event. This applies to coloured jeans as well as blue ones.

At the Frankfurt railway station on the way to my tax-free shopping spree, I spontaneously spoke to a woman standing nearby. She had encouraged me to buy a herring sandwich without knowing it. I just felt like talking to her. Of course, she mustered me with a 'who-is-this-person-does-she-want-to-sell-me-something' look. I was lucky, though, because she replied, and a wonderful conversation ensued. She explained that she had lived in California for four years (which is why she was used to unexpected chats, I assume). At over 40, she quit her job and started something new, almost like me and my immigrant experience. She said she loved the atmosphere at the train station, and exclaimed, 'I feel like I am on holiday! There are people from all over the world here. A wonderful start to my weekend.' She had to go then, but she turned back to thank me for our conversation and added that she thought I was a terrific person. What a great start to my own weekend!

Germany welcomed me yet again. The Deutsche Bahn train was late. I was going to miss my connection, so my ticket was replaced for another one, on the fast train to Paris, which would take me straight to my destination in the Palatinate. Imagine! In the middle of Germany I was on a train heading for Paris on a Friday after work. '*Mesdames et Monsieurs, bienvenus dans le train à Paris.* Ladies and Gentlemen, welcome on board our train to Paris.' Who wouldn't enjoy hearing that? My mother had just told me that olives, Italian Parma ham with melon and my favourite French rosé wine – Tavel – were awaiting my arrival. My Dad was out playing boule with his tennis pals. Welcome to Europe! I thought to myself. Not only that, summer had finally arrived in Germany. I love summer in Germany, probably because you can't take warm, sunny weather for granted.

## London – the city where everything began

Remember when I was dragging my bags to the car and my mother was weeping because she was sure I would never return home? London was my very first big time abroad all alone. I had secured an internship in a London bank. Back in 1999, London was a cosy place where banks still did what they are supposed to do: lend and borrow money. Credit derivatives, which caused a crisis years later, were still in their infancy. In Soho, the streets were home to drug addicts. Okay, that part wasn't so cosy.

As I was sitting on the grass at Leicester Square, looking at the people around me, someone asked me where I was from. I said, 'From Germany,' and he immediately shot back with 'Oh, Hitler!' It only happened to me once; it never happened again on any of my later travels.

The pubs closed at 11 pm in those days, which was plenty of time for a drink after knocking off work at 5 pm. We walked out the door of the bank and into my favourite pub next door for six hours of drinks and dancing, so we still got enough sleep to be fit for work in the morning. The Lord Raglan was sparsely furnished with mismatched armchairs, which gave it an especially homely atmosphere. Nothing better than to sink into one with a glass of cider in your hand.

Of course, I stopped in at the Lord Raglan again on this visit to London. It is still a traditional pub with fairly good grub. They had, however, refurnished the interior. But you still got your pint at the bar. I didn't stay long enough to see if there was still the late evening dancing and socialising. Just being here with my memories of good times reminded me of parties in Hamburg where the Germans would either take over the kitchen or sit on the sofa in the lounge while everyone else, mostly southern Europeans, stood around making silly jokes or danced. But the favourite place at a party in Germany is definitely the kitchen. In New Zealand, the kitchen is reserved for the potluck food and people hang out everywhere else. Talking mostly. I miss **dancing** at parties when I'm in New Zealand.

At Frankfurt Airport, the bus from the gate drove and drove and drove... after 10 minutes we had reached the edge of the airport, surrounded by fields of grass. The British began joking. 'Do they have a new Brexit runway for us?' This was only two days after the vote and I had mixed feelings about it. And losing the European Soccer Cup to Iceland that year had apparently shot them straight into Brexit with finality. The pound was at its lowest since 1985. It would make the weekend a little cheaper for me, but I was uncertain what the vibe would be in London when I got there. Arriving at London City Airport, my favourite London airport, right in the middle of the metropolis, it was only a short Tube ride into the centre of town.

I knew the drop in the exchange rate was significant, but imagine my surprise as I inserted my credit card into the teller machine and it showed £0.61 for a Euro instead of £0.82. Amazingly, the banks were ripping people off this way! The screen had a large, colourful button you were to click on to accept this ridiculous rate, or you could choose the one that read 'Without conversion', 'I accept' or similar, which had the correct exchange rate in a milky grey, as if this option was not available. It made me feel almost criminal to click on that one. Dear reader, New Zealand enthusiast and world traveller: always, always try the 'criminal' button first. Do not accept any predefined rate offered by the bank! Do it! Enjoy the moment to do something forbidden. The bank will then have to exchange your money to the actual daily rate without the horrendous surcharges they try to sneak in.

## Laws, rules and supervision

Kaitiaki had to grin at my call-out for the ATMs. He said, 'For New Zealanders, what is not prohibited is allowed. Nobody asks "Is that permitted?" as often as Germans do. People in my country will only look surprised, and say, "Why not?" While you are still searching for the hidden "prohibited" sign, they just do it. If it's wrong, they will hear it soon enough.

'In general, New Zealanders are less rule-oriented. They are slower to hire a solicitor to litigate a dispute. Traffic accidents are settled

unconventionally. To insist on one's rights or to "get justice" in smaller matters is a very German attribute, as is "to be right (after all)". "Doch" is a singular German killer phrase, meaning "it's so!" Another killer phrase is simply "it's my right" to do something, allowing no further discussion or friendly debate. It is the line in the sand. If this is not understood, there will inevitably be trouble. In countries other than Germany, however, this argument is about as effective as butting your head against a wall. You will accomplish exactly the opposite.'

Yes, my tui often just flutters around and ignores me. At university in Toulouse I learned my lesson the hard way, running into many very hard walls, with bruises and bumps as my only reward. At some point I realised the only way I would get ahead is to adapt to the French way of indirect, even flowery, expression.

Here, Kaitiaki jumped back in. 'New Zealanders live by rules which reflect the idea of equality in a hierarchical sense. I will explain this more fully on page 137. Rules come into play when everyone is to be treated equally, and breaking this principle to the benefit of an individual is objectionable. I have noticed that New Zealanders tend to follow rules without question. They are confident that they make sense and are for the good of all. You Germans will look for and find a loophole somehow.'

An Italian friend says that Germans do their high standard of 'honesty' a huge disservice with this sneaky attitude. She explained that Italians at least freely admit to using loopholes, or, put more bluntly, cheat – it's part of the game! Germans do it, but they never talk about it. In addition, in an apparent contradiction to their attachment to rules, Germans despise supervision and monitoring, an attitude perhaps also relating to 20th-century history.

Geert Hofstede states that Germans have a direct, participative style of communication. Supervision is a no-go. Managers are expected to have expertise in their field, and their leadership is less likely to be accepted if expert knowledge is lacking.[48] I didn't realise this aversion to management control until I arrived in New Zealand in a British working environment. I felt somehow spied upon! And I had the same feeling in the USA. Now, in Wellington, I finally understand a long-past conversation with project colleagues from the US and Britain. Because

I adored London, I could never understand why they wanted to live and work in Frankfurt. They explained that they felt like they had more freedom in Germany. 'In Britain, your manager is breathing down your neck,' one of them told me. Although New Zealanders also have a certain aversion to supervision, this intense dislike of 'being managed' is a particularly German trait.

Is it then contradictory to say that rule-oriented control is a German cultural standard? There are two kinds of control in this cross-cultural context. One is person-related and the other applies to rules. Germans feel coerced by a person in control, but they happily abide by rules and regulations. The same applies to agreements and especially contracts, which are considered an immutable commitment to the rights and obligations of each signing party. This corresponds to the general adherence to laws, regulations and reliability, in turn probably leading to the high standards of quality that Germany is known and appreciated for. Without this particular combination of values, 'Made in Germany' would likely be meaningless.

Geert Hofstede also distinguishes between New Zealand and Germany by comparing the cultural dimensions of indulgence versus restraint.

German people are generally more restrained and they tend to be cynical and pessimistic, suppress their longings and have a diminished desire for free time. New Zealanders are more indulgent, following impulse and a desire to enjoy life. They tend to be optimistic and gladly spend money on entertainment and fun.[49]

I wonder if Germans would be more inclined to follow their impulses if they knew that they often break rules by doing things they never knew were prohibited. Some absurd laws, for example, strictly prohibit climbing on deerstands and swimming in sewers! Why would anyone ever swim in a sewer?

When my parents were visiting New Zealand, they especially enjoyed the sunset on the beach as they sipped a glass of wine. They wondered why the New Zealanders all around them kept looking over and laughing. When they got up to leave, they saw they had been sitting right in front of a sign reading 'No Alcohol Allowed on Beach'. I can just

imagine how Germans sitting around them would have reacted – certainly not by just giggling and remaining silent.

Back in London, I was still thrilled with my little irregular though satisfying victory at the ATM machine. Then I headed for the Tube.

I used to love the underground, its smells and even the rush-hour crush. The Tube represented a feeling of freedom, of belonging, and even London itself, as it was a significant juncture in my life. Whenever I flew into London, I felt as if I was coming home.

And this time? The skies were grey; the buildings were of stone. Too many small flats and not enough green space for so many people. Playgrounds squeezed in between concrete blocks. A few front and back yards. Are the vegetables growing there even safe to eat? Houseboats in small tributaries of the River Thames, directly under railway bridges. Boats in a small harbour that looked like a desperate attempt to put a sticker on a sprawling metropolis that read '**quality of life**'. There were so many cyclists now in the mornings, which would have been unthinkable – even dangerous – in the heavy traffic of a few years ago. I remember going for a jog back then and returning home feeling like I had sucked on an exhaust pipe for an hour.

Dragging suitcases in the Tube: How did mothers with kids manage it every day? An English woman I met the following weekend at a hens' party said it was easier with kids in London than in Switzerland, where they currently lived. You could always stop in for a chat with friends after kindergarten. The Swiss are much more anonymous, she told me, with everyone going their own way, doing their own thing. This conversation was proof again that it is worth changing your perspective once in a while.

By the way: there are special intercultural coaching and training sessions and many books on the subject of trailing spouses – often the wives of expatriates. The challenges for the stay-at-home mother and the children abroad should not be underestimated. There is some literature on the topic suggested in this book's bibliography.[50]

It was clear to me that my perspective on London had changed.

Well, it wasn't 1999 anymore. I was 17 years older and have had a life since. Yet I still felt like London was home in the way a smell reminds you of something dear forever.

On the first evening after my seminar I met up with Corny, my South Tyrolean friend who I had lived with for a while in Milan. She had spontaneously offered me a bed during a university semester break when I had a job at the Junior Enterprise. At the turn of the millennium, we lived in a courtyard-facing flat in the Navigli neighbourhood. We reached our flat through a large gateway, which was usually closed but had a miniature door in it that we could pass through. The door did not line up with the threshold so we always had to lower our head not to bump it. We named the courtyard Melrose Place after the popular television series in the nineties. Only the pool in the middle was missing. The flats were old and beautiful, with slanted floors and off-kilter doors and windows. Half the time we sat at the neighbours' gossiping, just like it was done on Melrose Place. During Milan Fashion Week, some models even stayed in neighbouring flats. It was more exciting than watching any cinema film.

One day, some carpenters came to fix the door seals, which they only partially finished. It was autumn and cold outside. Without properly closing doors, it was very draughty in the flat. Corny and I made the most of it, as always. We lit a fire in the fireplace, put on mud masks, roasted some chestnuts, drank red wine, nibbled on a bunch of grapes and talked the night away, wrapped up in thick blankets. It did get smoky in there as the flue seemed to be faulty. But because the door was essentially open because of the unfinished works and we couldn't have suffocated.

At the pub in London, we also had a lot to talk about. Corny was then living with her husband in London, and they had recently had a baby. As I had already heard in the product owner seminar, Brexit was really having an effect on personnel planning. People from the European continent weren't being hired because of new visa complications. Corny was married to an Englishman, yet her company was thinking of letting her go because of her Italian passport. There was no end to the things we had to catch up on. The

pub practically threw us out at closing, but we just continued talking until we reached a street crossing. It turned out we were headed in the same general direction, so we walked and stopped and talked, and walked and stopped and talked again. Finally, we came upon a taxi rank and said goodbye after what seemed like a century.

The next morning, I walked to the seminar location. On the way I stopped at a café – which could have just as well been in Paris – and enjoyed a lovely English breakfast with toast, smoked salmon and scrambled egg. And a good coffee.

In the nineties in London, I used to mix cocoa into my **coffee**, because it was not drinkable any other way. In the meantime, the English have caught up to modern coffee culture, just as New Zealand has. Especially Wellington, with its cafés, had brought the secret of good coffee to the country.

This time in London, my first coffee order was a failure. The barista didn't understand 'long black with a bit of trim milk'. After a bit of searching through my memory and help from the barista, I remembered how Londoners ask for it: an americano with a bit of skimmed milk. Visitors in New Zealand are probably unfamiliar with 'flat white'. This is a local version of cappuccino with a particular method of frothing the milk. Espresso is a short black. And filtered coffee refers to a particular roast or grind in New Zealand, not necessarily that you will be served drip coffee.

As I ate breakfast, I noticed two very nice-looking young men, and we got into a conversation. One of them was actually planning to visit New Zealand that very year. To him it seemed totally normal to travel to the other end of the Earth, and he wasn't at all awestruck that I had actually moved there. In England I felt altogether less 'exotic' when I talked about my life in New Zealand. The antipodes were clearly on the British radar and not so impossibly far away as for most other Europeans. The Brits have more things in common with New Zealanders too, in terms of mobility, and buying and selling their homes, also internationally. The dream of a German is to build a nest and settle in it forever.

## A cultural look at real estate

History plays an important role in the German attitude towards owning property when compared to the rest of the world. After two world wars, the real estate market is still mostly under government oversight and controlled by cooperatives. This keeps much of the infrastructure out of private speculators' hands. Houses and flats are meant to be a roof over one's head, rather than a means of amassing a fortune. Most of the German population pay rent all their life rather than buy property. Some cooperatives provide living environments tailored to the elderly, with delivered meals, for example, or to families with children with on-site day care. To ensure rent stability, regulations are much more tenant-oriented than in New Zealand. Capital gains from rental property is highly taxed in Germany, as well as any profit made by speculating on real estate if the property is sold within ten years. This is in addition to property transfer or ownership tax.

For a long time, buying and selling real estate was uncomplicated in New Zealand. A basic rates tax, or land tax, was levied on capital gains from rental properties sold within two years (as compared to ten years in Germany). The country is now attempting to stem the tide of rising housing costs and speculation. The new bright-line rule affords tax exemptions to home buyers who actually intend to live there as their main domicile if it is sold within five years, previously two years if the house was bought between 1 October 2015 and 28 March 2018.[51] Since July 2016, investors from abroad pay a substantial residential land withholding tax, in contrast to the tax that every real estate owner in Germany pays regardless of residency. On 22 October 2018, the Overseas Investment Amendment Act 2018 came into force, prohibiting real estate acquisition by non-residents.[52]

In an international comparison, there is far less real estate speculation in Germany. Due to sharply rising demand of rentals and properties to buy in the cities, it is nevertheless doubtful that the upward spiral can be curbed. There are opinion pieces published daily, arguing for or against regulation. It is also true that basically only foreign investors speculate on the German real estate market, which keeps that factor rather low.

Kaitiaki summed up. 'In any case, history and the regulation of the real

estate market has generated a culture in which German people don't buy and resell property as easily as in New Zealand. You tend to rent and live your entire life in the same building; even in the same flat. Regulations favouring the tenant support this. Tenants in New Zealand have fewer rights and the laws favour the landlord, even though regulations with regards to insulation have become stricter. What confounds me and German tenants in New Zealand is the fact that the area of a given property is not specified. I still don't know how big your beach house actually is.

'Germans don't usually get rich off property speculation. Their relative wealth comes from maintaining a good career or starting a business. Of course, it remains to be seen how the new laws regarding property ownership in New Zealand will play out. In recent years, de facto ownership numbers have gone down.'

One of the young Englishmen at the café asked me about my upcoming weekend. I told them I was excited about going to a hens' party for my good friend, Gemma, in York. They grinned and asked me if I even knew what I was in for to spend the weekend with girlfriends from Northern England. Laughing, I replied that I had seen reports on television about these wild parties, but I was sure it was going to be a quiet weekend among best friends. That's how it was indeed, though details shall remain secret. I can say, though, that Crayke Manor in York is a beautiful place and suited to such events.

Sometime during the weekend, I discovered that I had absent-mindedly booked the wrong train to the airport for my flight back to Germany. I would get there far too late. The ticket was fixed and non-refundable. Asking for advice at the railway station ticket counter, I was at first told that a new ticket for an earlier train would cost almost £100. After some charming, I was allowed to board the earlier train as a blind passenger; that is, without a seat. I headed for the restaurant car. To my surprise, it had no tables or seating like the trains in Germany. I ordered a bottle of water and stood around for a while until someone motioned me to sit on the floor. So I did. No sooner had I done that, a nice man came out

from behind the bar with a beer crate for me to sit on. Such simplicity, improvisation and uncomplicated assistance, served with a good-natured smile – it's obvious the English were the first European settlers in New Zealand!

By the way, the platforms in London train stations are only announced shortly before departure. Why arrange it ahead of time if you can't know what issues might unexpectedly arise with a train? Passengers can wait in the terminal for the platform number rather than having to rush up one long platform and down another if something changes.

The weekend in England was so wonderful. Two of my best, oldest female friends, Corny and Gemma, were there, with whom I have had great adventures even though we seldom lived close by. These friendships are special.

## Friendship

We Germans often yearn to have the same kind of deep friendships we cherish in Germany with people from other countries. In online forums, I repeatedly read about how this is often a reason for moving back. New Zealanders or Americans are so superficial, people complain. You can't get close to them. My own experience with New Zealanders tells me otherwise. It only takes longer, sometimes years. I tell my New Zealand friends, 'If a German calls you a friend, it means just that. For lesser relationships, we have the word acquaintance. That word – Bekannte – carries more weight in German than in the English language in which acquaintance is rarely used. Everybody you know a bit in New Zealand is a friend. Deeper relationships are close friends. The line between the two are not as clearly drawn as in German culture.

I once poured my heart out to a New Zealander I had mistaken for a closish friend. She retreated pretty quickly after that. I know others to whom this also happened. Germans often appear cool and hold you at arm's length, but there are moments when we feel a connection that bewilders New Zealanders. Those that embrace it are the New Zealanders I call my good friends.

I am not forgetting the phenomenon of 'out of sight, out of mind'. It takes a long time to develop friendships that stand the test of time and distance.

Another example is hospitality. New Zealanders are open-hearted. They easily invite people to visit or to stay for a few nights. However, longer visits, which can happen in Germany, are more seldom in New Zealand, and even good friends are expected to chip in for groceries and utilities during an extended stay. Of course, this is merely a pragmatic solution to the high cost of living.

I heartily recommend talking about friendship and relationships with New Zealanders. It is definitely a way to get to know them better. Who knows, you might find someone who likes the kind of loyal friendships Germans are fond of.

At the hens' party, Gemma and I reminisced about our trip to the Basque region when we were still living in Toulouse. It was a split-second decision and off we drove with our tent and sleeping bags. It was raining heavily when we got there. We pitched the tent anyway and crawled in, enjoying the French goodies we had bought during the drive. Well, the goodies and our rear ends had room inside the tent; our heads and feet remained outside under the edge of the tent to be able to enjoy the night. Years later,

Gemma sent me a postcard picturing a tent from the inside with two pairs of feet sticking out onto the grass. I still have the card propped up on my dresser in Wellington. Gemma tells her friends that she thinks our relationship is so special because we often dared to leave our comfort zone and try something new together. We've done so many things in our lives, tried this and that, and fell on our faces too. These are experiences neither of us regret having. Friends like that are priceless. And I miss them at the other end of the world.

With a heavy heart I left England to fly back to Germany. In the Lufthansa plane, a flight attendant marched up the aisle yelling, 'Cheese or salami sandwich!!! Cheese or salami sandwich!!!' The exclamation marks are not a typo. Welcome back to Germany.
We landed on the Brexit runway again, by the way.

# The world of fitness

Once again in Frankfurt, I felt I needed to do something about neutralising all of the delicacies I had been eating at my parents' and in England. I joined a gym and was surprised to find that this is about the only thing that is cheaper in New Zealand than in Germany.

There are several differences to note. You can tell where you are from when the group classes start. In New Zealand they are very early in the morning. This is a paradise for early birds. New Zealanders go to bed early and rise early in the morning. Sleeping late is overrated – better to get up at sunrise, grab your surfboard and catch some waves before breakfast. In Germany, ten horses couldn't pull someone out of bed early enough to go to the gym. There are classes instead on Friday afternoon, late in the evening and Sunday. This could never happen in New Zealand.

Next, in New Zealand the showers are single cubicles. Not so in Germany, where people freshen up in a common shower room, happily gossiping to each other in the raw.

This is a conversation I was privy to once: 'Guess what, Kirsten (all names are changed) actually bought Lisa a second-hand school backpack for 25 Euroshappily gossiping to each other in the raw. This is a conversation I was privy to once in a gym sauna: 'Guess what, Kirsten (all names are changed) actually bought Lisa a second-hand school backpack for 25 Euros.. Well, that would simply never occur to me. From the start, I knew that our Lilly would get the top-rated-number-one-super-stylish-busy-bee backpack for school start. You know, the one with 6000 five-star reviews on amazon!'

Why is this typically German? Remember, in New Zealand there is only a limited selection of anything and it's often lacking in the quality department. If you find a top brand, you can't pay for it. Normal to bad quality is expensive. I know I have been repeating myself on this topic. One of the things I notice over and over again in Germany is how we take the diversity of high-quality products for granted. I can most certainly guarantee that you will get into trouble with this in New

Zealand at some point. It's also a reason why some immigrants pack up and leave again. For others, it's just another piece of paradise to have fewer consumer goods to deal with.

Back to the world of fitness. I love to explore places while jogging. There are plenty of woods and fields in Frankfurt's environs, but the paths are almost all paved. Even so, I enjoyed the outdoors along the Nidda river, smelling the trees and listening to the birds. Soon, the path led me under autobahn bridges where traffic noise drowned out the birds, making me miss the running paths over hill and dale through the wilderness and along the coastline near Wellington. I looked at Kaitiaki. He declined to learn how to imitate cars. A bit further on, I passed the clubhouse of a local gardening club, followed by the clubhouse of the local angling club and finally another gardening club.

## Clubs

Germans look to connect with like-minded people through clubs. Bowling clubs, carrier pigeon clubs, Carnival clubs, soccer clubs, local history clubs, shooting clubs, women's clubs, tennis clubs, music clubs, environmental protection clubs, dog breeding clubs, motor sport clubs, choral singing clubs... If you immigrate to Germany, these are the places to start making friends. New Zealand has sporting associations, of course. Often it's enough to just go down to the beach and start talking to someone or to simply join in an activity.

Another time, I borrowed a bicycle and rode along the Nidda from Bockenheim to Höchst. This green belt is very nice, as there are lovely spots where you can stop and pretend you are out in the country, and others where you can take a swim in the river. I discovered a riverside café called the Alte Schiffsmeldestelle, the 'Old ship reporting station'. I lay on the grassy bank nearby, and as my gaze lost itself in the water, my thoughts wandered along my usual work route in Frankfurt: over bridges and along concrete walls, train tracks and underpasses.

One morning on my walk to work something bizarre happened. I was revelling in the summer temperatures. And in the middle of the walls all around me, I suddenly missed New Zealand's sandflies, those little biting monsters. I associate sandfly bites with being at the sea. Such

episodes were occurring more often. I felt like a comic book thought bubble was floating above my head and I imagined myself back in my own New Zealand world, scratching a mosquito bite, or sitting on a beanbag on my balcony over the ocean, or on my favourite jogging path, or on my scooter, riding to work along the coastal road.

On the other hand, I was totally happy to be in the less aggressive sunshine of a European summer, breathing in the familiar smells and being close to family and friends. The rain appeared to have stopped, and I, the cultural fish, was happily swimming in the river I was born in, while at the same time missing the Pacific Ocean and Tasman Sea I had grown to love in my new home.

## Barcelona – *pura vida*

Some things never change. When I still lived in Germany, I would usually fly every other weekend to visit friends who happened to live in famous holiday destinations. They met me and dove with me into the local culture in a way I never could have done as a tourist. I have always been a culture junkie. I love Germany, but I was positively hooked on anything that was harder to get. In keeping with the cultural fish analogy, I was often bored with my home river and longed for the open seas. Sometimes I managed to reach a cultural river delta to feed that hunger.

When I arrived in Barcelona this time, I used the Aerobus to Plaça de Catalunya, where César was waiting for me in proper style with his scooter. My carry-on fitted perfectly in the footwell. As soon as I checked in to my accommodation, I wanted to head for the beach, even if it was the most touristy place of all. César took me to a bar where there was less going on, located in front of the venerable building of Real Club Nautico and just to the right of the famous nudist beach. Listen up, New Zealanders! You can get publicly naked in Spain too, not just in Germany! After so many years, César and I had a lot to catch up on too, so we stayed in the bar with a drink and a view of the sea and talked.

*Relationships, gender equality, dating and platonic friendships*
Not only do we miss German-style friendships in New Zealand, my girlfriends and I agree that platonic relationships between women and men in New Zealand are rare. We German girls might think nothing of weekends hanging out with men, whereas New Zealanders hear wedding bells. Kaitiaki understood what I meant, since he has been living with me peacefully for years. So, it comes as no surprise that my New Zealand friends always ask me if I'm sure nothing is going on between César and myself when I talk about him. Of course, I'm sure. He has been a terrific friend for decades. Kaitiaki was very curious to see how things would unfold during my visit in Barcelona.

Everyone knows women and men have their own cultures. Are relationships in various countries different too? A few years ago in Hamburg, I talked with my friend Fiona about German–New Zealand

relationships and how they fare in each country. She told me that New Zealand never had the kind of feminism movement that Germany did in the seventies, following France.[53] She concurred that the division of roles in New Zealand is traditionally more equal than in Germany, be it out hunting or in the kitchen. This probably has to do with the fact that people are on their own in large parts of New Zealand. Where neighbours are few and far between, everybody shares the work. New Zealand's egalitarianism is probably a further indication. My couple friends, Māori and Non-Māori, confirmed that it was normal for women and men to just get on with what is necessary.

Imagine living in a world where *Emanzipation* (as the word used in German for the feminism movement) is a foreign word, something that only has to do with the rest of the globe. 'Oh, that. Yes, I heard that happened a while ago in your country,' is a typical comment if the topic comes up. The traditional differentiation of gender roles is a German cultural standard, according to Alexander Thomas.[54] I researched some further facts and opinions. New Zealand was the first country in the world to give women voting rights in 1893. Half of the representatives in government are women. However, a Māori girlfriend also verified that, just like in Germany, women's salaries are lower and leadership roles are mostly filled with men.[55] Kaitiaki agreed. 'In gardening, vegetables were a man's domain and women did the flowers. At official events, the women were responsible for the food with "Ladies a plate".[56] In Germany, suffrage for women was established in 1918, a quarter of a century later. The feminism movement – to the extent that we know it in Europe – never happened in New Zealand.

A friend from former East Germany, now living in New Zealand, reports that she had enjoyed *equal* partnerships in Germany. Indeed, there are significant differences in feminism between former East and West Germany that are heatedly debated today. In former Eastern Bloc countries and in Scandinavia and France, it is more common for mothers to work full-time than it is in former West Germany. And it appears that the younger generations throughout Europe are championing a more balanced division of roles.

Kaitiaki became thoughtful. 'There is another side to the coin in New Zealand: domestic violence, which is rarely openly discussed. But I don't

have any first-hand knowledge or understanding of this, so I cannot comment on it,' he mumbled.

One clue might be the safe house in the vicinity of my home. The Wellington Women's Boarding House[57] is situated in the bush above the next beach over from me. There is no question that domestic violence occurs behind closed doors, at odds with the so-friendly outward face of New Zealand. Does this have to do with the passive-aggressive behaviour that I will discuss later in this book, on page 162 in the section *Opinion – feedback – directness – low context – objectivity – honesty*? Or is it 'keeping face' as described in the theories addressing face-saving strategies? Alan Duff's controversial book *Once Were Warriors* is an interesting read on the subject, as is Witi Ihimaera's book *The Whale Rider*. Both explore whether gender equality is real or delusional wishful thinking. More on the subject of *egalitarianism* in a general context follows on page 137 of this book.

I wondered if a look at a 'stereotypical' New Zealand man and woman might provide more insight, well knowing that they are never quite right. Just as there are prototypes of a typical German, a Bavarian or the nudist on a cliff, there might be prototypes of New Zealanders.

Whereas they are harder to find for women, who seem to display a certain masculinity and independence, men, especially in earlier years, seem to feel and act like modern pioneers as they successfully wrangle with nature. Some sources say that New Zealanders are generally rural, not intellectually or culturally inclined, strong, unemotional, democratic. They know their way around machines and animals, especially horses, can make do with little, and can refashion useful things out of anything.[58]

I recall an example and a travel experience with my modern pioneer. I will never forget the time the world record distance kite surfer asked if I had some dental floss. Floss? Really? I mean I wasn't wondering because New Zealanders were known for their general negligence in the tooth care department, which has only just recently become a thing in health education. I was just confused. Why would this guy ask for dental floss? It turns out he uses it for sewing repairs to kites, as it is a very strong thread. This is what I like about Kiwi ingenuity and Kiwi men. They follow their instincts. They just do it, and don't waste eons of time thinking about it, as Germans do.

I was on one of our weekend trips with another New Zealand friend,

riding in his ute. Suddenly – I don't know how he could react so fast – a pheasant flew up in the road in front of us. Instead of braking, he sped up. The bird landed squarely on my side of the windshield and then ricocheted off. We got out, expecting to find it behind the car, ready to be taken for our barbie (BBQ), but it wasn't meant to be. We couldn't find it anywhere. Poof, gone! Like witchcraft.

Let us take a look at our German tourists, Helga and Herbert, again. Helga is dressed in safari shorts and oversized T-shirt, wearing Birkenstocks and fancy hexagonal designer eye-wear, and sporting a curly hairdo. Is she any more womanly than a New Zealand female? I doubt it. I've heard people say that you might see differences between rural and urban areas, and even between the cities of Auckland, Christchurch and Wellington.

In Germany, I was once sharing a ride in a car. One of the other passengers talked about his situation at home, how his wife worked to help with the expense of having kids. Naturally, he helped in the kitchen and around the house. Everyone in the car agreed that the division of roles in the family was more balanced than in the past, at least for the younger generation. Could I imagine such a conversation in New Zealand? I couldn't. To get to the point: was the situation in Germany so 'natural' if it was worthwhile talking about? In New Zealand, gender parity seems to be much more a given, so that no one feels the need to talk about it. Maybe that is the big difference, although I understand it could be either: true equality or a polite strategy to avoid the subject entirely.

And it's much the same for relationships. What about getting to know someone? A French colleague asked me once how I would know if a German man was interested in me, because Germans do flirt in much more subtle and indirect ways than in other cultures. Compliments that come thick and fast only scare German women away. What she will appreciate is English-style manners, such as holding the door open. Red roses are symbols of romantic love and conquest.

As I said before, my girlfriends and I find platonic friendships with New Zealanders are difficult. Perhaps it has to do with the different speeds in how relationships are initiated. This is true even with cultures that might seem to be closely related. A study discloses that during World War II, American soldiers stationed in England spread the word that English girls were easy, while the young women complained that the soldiers were too

impetuous. The study goes on to describe how this dichotomy was unravelled. Courtship patterns in both countries go through about 30 distinctive stages, from meeting through to sex. However, the proper sequence of the stages differ in each culture. For example, kissing comes relatively early in American courtship, while it comes at stage 25 in English culture! In practical terms, this meant that the English rose kissed by her soldier felt cheated out of stages 5 through 25 and had to make a quick decision on whether to 'go all the way' or break off the relationship before it had really even begun. If she chose the former, the American soldier found her behaviour completely improper and brazen. Such conflicts cannot be resolved by talking to each other about it, because what is happening is culturally anchored and an essentially subconscious action. The parties involved only know that the other person's behaviour is somehow not right.[59]

German dating patterns also differ from those of New Zealanders, English and Americans. Germans casually do things together and spend time getting to know one another as friends. It is far easier for Germans to just hang out with Germans because they are on the same page, culturally speaking. The same goes for Scandinavians, it seems. We Germans enjoy cuddling up together as a group on a couch to watch a movie, for example. In New Zealand, hugging and cuddling has sexual consequences, even as a couple. Simply cuddling for its own sake doesn't seem 'normal' to New Zealanders.

Kaitiaki was getting impatient, wanting to see what a platonic relationship was all about. So back to Barcelona. Nothing compares to talking about other men with a man, or about women with a woman. César and I had ants in our pants, so we left the café, chatting and drifting along through the streets. Having no plan is the best plan. At one point I was language-confused. I saw a sign that read 'Date un Chicken Break'. What did that mean? I was in my New Zealand brain, wondering, 'Date a chicken? Did the Spanish meet chickens for lunch?' We both had a good laugh. It meant you should take a break and have all-you-can-eat chicken. César wanted to know about New Zealand summers. 'It's at Christmas, isn't it?' he asked.

I giggled, because it sounded like the entire season was packed into a single day. César never liked to travel to places cooler than Barcelona. The weather was generally an important topic for him, making it difficult to charm him into coming to Germany or New Zealand for a visit. So, I grinned when I said, 'Yes, Christmas is in the summer in New Zealand.'

And I wondered, shouldn't I be having Christmassy feelings in this sunshine? December is a summer month in Wellington. There are wagons full of pine trees for sale on the beach. There are holiday decorations everywhere, but for us Europeans it is hard to get in the spirit when the temperatures are so warm. We yearn for freezing weather and mulled wine.

It's the Germans in particular, who miss their **Christmas**. After all, the tree with its lights, candles, angels and other decorations is a significant German contribution to the world's Christmas-making in the 19th century.

As an antidote, we host midwinter Christmas dinners or potlucks in July or August, because that's when we feel more like it. *Lifeswap No. 5, Christmas Special* by the New Zealand Goethe Institute hits the nail on the head.[60]

César and I finally landed in Barcelona's Barceloneta district, where Catalan tapas specialties are served up on plates. My favourites: Boquerones and sardines. Another way tapas can be served is on slices of baguette, as it is done in the Basque region. We enjoyed every mouthful. How I had missed this kind of European nibbling! For dessert, César took me to Gelaaati di Marco, the best Italian gelato place in Barcelona. Heavenly.

We ambled on until César's ears virtually snaked into a courtyard that music was coming from. It was vintage Rumba from the sixties and eighties from southern Spain, the kind that took César back in time, in the same way Nena's *99 Red Balloons* or music from the Neue Deutsche Welle (New German Wave) does for me. We followed it inside and saw a bunch of locals dancing dreamily to the music. It seemed to be playing from a balcony, so we peeked

around the corner. Sure enough, there was a band up there playing for the dancing couples below. César almost freaked and together we let the atmosphere carry us away. We danced, ate Mexican cornbread and a Spanish tortilla (potatoes and egg), and drank an Estrella. The bands changed at some point. The new one started playing something jazzy. It reminded César and me of our time together in Toulouse. Finally, the band came down and played among the dancers. What an evening! The band was joyously joking around, just as it spontaneously spilled out of them. Pure life – *pura vida*.

I remembered **one of the best days** in New Zealand. It did not start well, and at first I was sure it was one to forget as soon as possible. Everything seemed to go wrong and all I wanted was to get home from work and have some peace and quiet. My neighbour Brian texted me that he would like to go for a walk and a swim in Princess Bay. I decided to give the day a chance. At the end of the road above the ocean, we hiked down through the bush on half-hidden tracks. On the way, we ran into others, even some neighbours, who were out there jogging or hiking. Brian had his dog with him, so we couldn't go to the regular beach. We got all dirty as we climbed down a nearby cliff to the water. Later, on our way back, we took the regular road, passing a house that I had often seen and wondered about. It was a wooden house with sheds full of craft materials. So colourful! It looked a bit hippy-like and had a sign advertising organic honey. We followed the guitar music to the rear of the house. The musicians were playing, seated in a circle around a wooden platform that a girl was dancing on. Flamenco. We were served honey mead as we sat on the ground. My skin was salty from the sea. As I listened and watched the dancing, keeping time silently in my head, I felt so free. And this was a day I had hated when it started.

César interrupted my reverie. It was late and he had sacrificed his siesta for me. I smiled when he mentioned that. It's nice to see that some cultural traditions in Europe are still alive. European culture as a whole is quite different from Oceania.

The day was over. As César walked me to my Airbnb, he had his 'lighthouse gaze' on. This is something Southern and Latino people do when they are wary of danger. They demonstrate it like this: first, they point to their eyes with splayed index and middle fingers. Then, they hold their hand to the back of their heads as if they were punching eyes in that can see in any direction. I have always felt very safe in the company of César and his friends. Pick-pocketing techniques seem to be a part of standard education in some countries. Half-heartedly locking up your bike, like we do in Germany, would never stand a chance in Barcelona. Yet, since the financial crisis, petty crime in Barcelona had gone down. Before, pick-pockets had been tolerated as a way to earn a meagre living. After the crisis, this sort of income was 'removed', as tourism became the most important source of revenue for the city. You still have to watch out on Las Ramblas or at the beach, but César was much more relaxed. He didn't feel he had to keep my bag and the entire vicinity in view. Except for at night. Hence the 'lighthouse gaze'.

In the morning, before César left to visit his father in the Extremadura region, we met for a last cup of coffee. I was scheduled for a brunch with members of InterNations,[61] a great website for expatriates and immigrants anywhere in the world to connect with locals. In Hamburg, I had often gone to an InterNations meeting just for the international flair.

Brunch was great fun. Everyone was very welcoming. For me, it was a wonderful opportunity to taste Catalonian specialties like *Horchata da Chufa*, a kind of almond milk with sugar and water. I also had *esqueixada*, which reminds me of South American *ceviche*, as it is made of raw codfish called *bacalao*, mixed with paprika, onions, olives and tomatoes and seasoned with salt and vinegar. And I had my favourite Spanish bread, *pan con tomate*, which is toasted slices of bread spread with tomato and garlic.

During this wonderful feast, we had an interesting conversation. The immigrants in Barcelona said they felt not only tolerated but actually welcomed. I could feel this was true, especially for one of the group who said she felt more at home in Barcelona than in Singapore or the USA. She said, 'It's the feeling you have when you

land. Do you feel that you have come home? Or have you only returned and you feel basically neutral about it.' Oh yes, I knew it well. I felt it whenever I returned to London or Hamburg. For me, home is where my friends live. Even in Barcelona or Tuscany. I wondered what it would feel like to land in New Zealand when this long trip was over. And because this group was so warm and friendly, I asked myself why I didn't just station myself in Barcelona, this historic Spanish beauty on the Mediterranean, on my next trip to Europe, rather than in the big metropolis in Germany?

I joined the other snoozers on the beach for a little siesta. I heard the beach vendors yelling, 'Agua! Coca Cola! Cerveza!' A few years ago, the call had been more slurred to 'Cerveza Colagua'. I joked to myself, debating whether the EU could exert enough influence to make the call appeal more to the linear-thinking ears of Northern European tourists?

The sand between my toes took me to the beaches of the Land of the Long White Cloud. What were they like? Certainly not like Barcelona's **beaches** in the summer. New Zealand's beaches are emptier, due to the lower population, and also because people don't sunbathe as extensively. You go to the beach to kayak, to surf and kite surf, and to SUP. In contrast to Europe, being out in the aggressive sunshine for too long is not good because of the hole in the ozone layer over New Zealand. Lyall Bay, where I live, is one of the most popular beaches in Wellington. Lots of activities are offered and everybody is busy doing something different. Scorching Bay, Oriental Bay and Princess Bay are also favourites when the weather is good. I do recall beaches further north around Auckland that have more sunbathers, like Piha or the beaches on Waiheke Island. It's warmer up there too.

The next morning in Barcelona, I decided to let my New Zealand side out and go SUPing, which is standup paddleboarding. You literally stand up on a big board and paddle around. You can do this in shallow water or in the waves. People also do yoga or pilates on the SUP board.

I was thrilled with the empty beach and the gentle sea that morning, remembering how Louis had taught me to SUP. It was an unknown sport in Europe back then. Now it's become very popular. SUP harks back to ancient Polynesian fishermen. So yet again, New Zealand has pioneered an outdoor sport.

With New Zealanders being the pioneers in so many things like sports, no wonder the country likes to call itself 'Middle-earth', loosely based on Tolkien's *The Lord of the Rings* trilogy. When you used to land in Wellington, you didn't just land at Wellington International Airport – nothing that ordinary. No, a sign actually read **Middle of Middle-earth**, in *The Lord of The Rings* lettering, no less. A New Zealand-centric map will show the islands in the middle, with the Americas to the east and Asia to the west. By the way, Spain is the exact opposite of New Zealand on the globe. You can check this and find the opposite of anywhere else on the website Antipodr.[62]

In Barcelona, I found myself not only half way through my trip, but also at the other side of the world.

# Berlin – an exploding new world

Berlin, Berlin. What is happening to you? I used to be one of your greatest fans. Your variety and colours, your trees and parks, your throngs of people, your size. I could smell your history in every corner. Now your scent seems to be fading. So much is new and modern. I had the same impression in London, for example in Covent Garden. But why in Berlin, where recent and spectacular history was evident wherever you went? The population has recently been growing by a hundred thousand annually! The city is exploding. I wanted to take a closer look at today's Berlin.

Of course, it was still as green as ever. Before I moved to New Zealand, I thought Berlin's greenness was truly special for such a big city. I suppose it still is so, yet it's not enough for me anymore; I want more. Just as I had arrived at the opposite side of the world in Barcelona, I was now in the second intercultural phase of reintegration in the middle of Berlin. I realised how much Germany and Europe had changed. I equally noticed that I had changed a lot too.

As always, I toured the city on foot. A friend tried to warn me in a phone call: 'Silke, you can't walk around in Berlin. Everything is so far apart! Nobody does it. Nobody walks around here.' That didn't stop me, of course. I much prefer walking to the subway or the bus. As we walked, some cars made quite an impression on Kaitiaki, who picked up Berliner sass in no time at all, and squawked, 'Who are all these dopes in posh heaps, cruisin' and makin' all this ruckus? Why you here from Düsseldorf or Munich, hey? Wanna get yourself some Berliner cool? Won't happen, jerks! I'd sooner swear by an orange surfer bus with a kangaroo painted on it than what you blockheads are driving. I geddit, I geddit. A wagon like that doesn't show how much dough you got. So, you ain't any different to anyone else. Yeah, I almost forgot about **Germans and their cars**...'

I remembered a conversation about cars I had with a client in Stuttgart once. At some point, I was asked what kind of car I drove. Everyone

looked at me expectantly, since I was a consultant. 'Consultants have money', I could see them thinking. And a German with money drives a fancy car. I answered the question with relish, 'Well, that depends on what I'm going to be doing at the weekend. If I'm staying in Hamburg, I'll use a small city car. If I'm going out kite surfing, I'll use a station wagon that has room for all my gear and I can sleep in it if I have to.' They all just stared.

'You see, I don't have my own car, because it would just stand around unused most of the time. I just rent what I need, where I happen to need it, be it Hamburg or Tuscany. But if I did have my own vehicle, it would definitely be an orange surfer bus with a kangaroo painted on it.' That made everybody laugh as they pictured it. Kaitiaki couldn't resist adding, 'Everyone has their idea of freedom, wanting to try something different, even if it's something they've always wanted to. If only "different" was not so dangerous! German anxiety kicks in when a big step is being considered. Especially when it involves a car. Do you remember the evil eye you get when you lean on someone's car or even put something on it? A German's car is sacrosanct. A New Zealander would probably choose a good and sturdy SUV.'

It was the following morning and I really hoped that I would like Berlin more than yesterday. As I sleepily sipped my coffee in a café, I looked for signs of big city life around me. Berlin was still fast asleep, a late riser as it had always been. Without warning, a golden-brown, naked bottom walked past me. Phew, Berlin was still Berlin. Which other major city in the world had so little going on in the middle of town on a weekend morning? The wide streets and huge intersections without traffic lights were virtually empty. I was glad to see that some things had not changed. By the way, Berliners love to eat liver served and know well how to serve it in all sorts of delicious ways. It's a delicacy here. I'd forgotten about that.

In the evening, it was party time: the Astra Epic Fail Party. This kind of humour would go down well in New Zealand too. Let's get completely wrecked and laugh about it. Queuing in Berlin hadn't changed either. 'Sure, sneak right in between us here!' someone

said with a big laugh, making some room for me. I hadn't been wrong about the Germans queuing in Havana. They just hadn't been Berliners.

The music was eighties and nineties pop. I danced as if there was no tomorrow amid the confetti fluttering down. Just outside the door a Berlin-style redistribution was going on. Empty beer bottles were tossed straight into a shopping cart so that a few men could collect the deposit as their meagre earnings for the day.

When I put my beer down on the bar for a second to take a picture, the girls reminded me that I should never leave a drink unattended in Berlin.

Uh-oh, I had obviously turned into a country bumpkin in New Zealand, so I was glad to have my girlfriends as big-city chaperones.

I made it safely to my accommodation, but not without stopping for the obligatory 3 am after-party snack called a Döner. That's a gyro wrapped in flatbread and apparently invented in Germany.

After spending the next day sunbathing in a beach club by the Spree River, I sadly had to leave Berlin. It's still very much worth a trip, in spite of my impression on that first day. Obviously, it was my own transformation through life in New Zealand that made me feel less comfortable in a big city than I had felt before.

At the airport in Berlin, we were just getting ready to board when we were informed that the flight was cancelled. And of course the information desk for rebooking was at the other end of the airport.

Everybody rushed off in different directions, hoping to get there first. German efficiency, time is money, be faster or know a clever short cut to get ahead of everybody else... there was masterful planning at work here. I realised how German I still was as I hurried along. I failed and ended up at the end of the queue. I had missed some details at the gate and assumed things – 'shbireit' – and I would get to Frankfurt somehow. When I then started to sprint, everybody else was already in the queue.

Three hours later I finally had a hotel room and a rebooked flight for the morning. It wasn't so bad, because I got to know some nice people while standing in the queue.

In emergencies and through complaining, we Germans can rise to the occasion and make small talk with each other. I found that people had generally become more relaxed about such things. It couldn't be changed anyway.

I chatted with the woman just in front of me in the queue, a German with Bulgarian roots who lived in Brisbane, Australia, and worked at the University of Queensland. Her area of expertise involved endangered animal species and conducting studies that would help conservation efforts. She told me about a study about New Zealand, which originally had virtually no endemic fauna.[63] She specialised in the mammals of Australia and New Zealand. I recalled the possum. In Australia, the possum is protected, as they are caught and eaten by snakes and other animals. In New Zealand, however, it can be hunted freely since it has no natural enemies. Ha! One more reason for my pheasant friend to step on the gas whenever he sees one.

Behind me in the queue there were two very nice couples who graciously held my spot in line while I sprinted off to locate the checked luggage. I tried several times, since nobody could give us any information as to the location of our bags. It was in this way that a friendly group formed around me, cheerfully laughing about the situation and taking it in our stride.

Then suddenly there was a disturbance further up front. A young Asian man, who was at university in Germany, was so angry about the cancellation that he took it out on a floral arrangement. A member of the Air Berlin staff scolded him while the rest of us secretly named him 'the flower killer'. When we got up to the desk, things went quickly, because we only needed a flight to Frankfurt and had no connections to worry about. We laughed with the staff. They weren't having an easy day but were cheerful nonetheless. We all got rooms in the same hotel and the same rebooked flight in

the morning. As we were getting our hotel vouchers, we jokingly asked the staff if the champagne had already been booked in the spa pool of the hotel for us.

Our good mood continued through dinner at the hotel. We found out that the women of the two couples I had befriended actually came from a village neighbouring mine in the Palatinate! We had even gone to the same school. They now lived in Frankfurt. Then a Canadian woman with a German-Argentinian-Chilean background gossiped a little about the 'flower killer', whom she had stood directly behind in the queue. That got us started on a conversation about cross-cultural topics, which went on until late at night. As a group, we went to the airport in the morning. The 'flower killer' was on our plane, still unwittingly the catalyst for everyone's good mood.

## The day-to-day – museums, media, childhood, helicopter parenting and the world of work

I feel that Frankfurt is coming up short in this account, which is surely because I was away almost every weekend and the weekdays were full of work. When the IT project was scrapped, I had much more time on my hands. Higher management had cancelled the project and so there was no budget for my assignment.

I enjoyed spending time with more creative ideas and seeing lots of friends. Whether it was a visit to Café Siesmayer with a coaching colleague of mine followed by a stroll through the Palm Garden, or a lunch with a colleague from my time spent in London or other lunches with former mates from university who love New Zealand and reminiscing about the past, I got to know Frankfurt through people. I can recommend the Weinkontor, a wine shop in Bockenheim, which you would never know about without a tip from a local resident. Then there is Wacker's Kaffee Geschäft, one of the oldest cafés in Frankfurt. Leipzig Street is always worth a stroll. Just around the corner from where I stayed there was a wonderful Italian gourmet wholesaler called Venos. People also recommended Günthersburg Park and Lilu on the Lohrberg to me for fresh air and sunbathing.

I loved my visit to the Senckenberg Museum with all of its dinosaur skeletons. I hadn't been there since my childhood and was really excited. I was most impressed by the huge dinosaur eggs and fossil animals on display there. And they have Egyptian mummified animals like the mummified crocodile honouring the river god Sobek and the mummified falcon representing Horus.

In New Zealand, you can view dinosaur fossils found in New Zealand in the museum in Dunedin. There is no entry charge. Displays include fossils of the flightless bird the moa, the ancient ancestor of the kiwi. Moa eggs are at least as impressive as the dinosaur eggs I saw in Frankfurt. Fun fact: the moa has been immortalised as a brand name of beer, just like the tui.

There is also a lot to learn about the culture of Oceania in New Zealand's museums. Unlike Germany, where the **museums** charge an entrance fee, museums in New Zealand like Te Papa in Wellington have followed

the example of the Museum of London. They are generally free to the public as a way to interest people of all income levels in the sciences. Anyone who has ever applied for an immigrant visa knows how important education is. Germany is admired for its mostly free and affordable access to public schools and universities.

I visited my childhood home in the Palatinate several more times from Frankfurt. On one Sunday afternoon I strolled around with my best friend, Verena, who I have known since I was three years old. She was just recovering from chemotherapy for breast cancer and I was so happy to see her. We had so much fun together as kids. We used to ski down the hill behind our houses and skated on the frozen street in front. I remember a lot of snow and ice in the wintertime. As we walked, more childhood memories surfaced: we were outside most of the time, climbing trees and hiking through the woods. 'Remember when we climbed over that fence?' Verena asked. 'I still have the scar from where I cut myself on the barbed wire. We both still have the same scar in the same place. And do you remember where that pond is where we caught the tadpoles? And all of the frogs and worms and insects we kept as pets at home in jars with holes in the lids?' Our parents often had no clue where we were and no way to contact us. Why isn't that possible anymore, we wondered.

Has the world really become such a bad place? In England, my friends had briefly mentioned that children could not be left to play on their own outside, since everything had become so dangerous. An older lady did admit that she believed the country hadn't changed as much as the media said it had. I heard the same complaint from German parents too, though, that they didn't dare let their children roam freely. I had an interesting conversation about 'helicopter parenting' with my mother and my editor. In contrast to the 'helicopters' who seem to hover around their children night and day, in my childhood there were no cell phones or internet. My editor, Claudia, mentioned 9/11, as she perceives control mechanisms to have become more prevalent.

Kaitiaki said sadly, 'Has criminality really become so bad? Or is it only

the news we hear about in the media? It is possible that the fear of criminality and terrorism has risen considerably since then – in the media, on the internet and ultimately in how children are raised.'

He philosophised, 'There are quite a few immigrants in New Zealand who come back to Germany and then actually return a few years later, not only because their **children** are homesick for New Zealand. They believe that society in New Zealand is more conducive to personal development. The environment for children seems to be safer, they can be let go, are encouraged to experiment and spend lots of time outdoors. The educational style at home and in schools is based more on praise and encouragement rather than inhibiting rules and barriers. My friends also report that there is less bullying in schools in New Zealand. And yet, New Zealand has the highest suicide rate among teens in the world.' Kaitiaki sighed, and continued. 'The periods our kids sit at the computer are getting longer, though much of daily life still happens outdoors in comparison to Germany. Catching your own fish for dinner is not unusual. New Zealand has more opportunities and fewer restrictions. The rest of the world is very far away. That's why it can happen that a cat stuck in a tree is a local news headline for days.'

In the midst of all this I received a hilarious message from my friend Ray, who has an Airbnb in Wellington's Breaker Bay. He had just installed a spa pool, and wrote, 'German spa rules apply!'. I asked what he meant, and Ray shot back, 'No clothing allowed'. Ah, there we were again with a parallel stereotype that paraded around the world naked, oblivious to what the rest of the world saw.

In Frankfurt, I was starting to get annoyed with Germany's obsession with cash. Without it or – at most – without a local bank card, you can't go shopping comfortably. German merchants are charged higher fees for credit card operations than for debit card operations, so they don't really encourage their use. Since German consumers believe they can control their spending better if they use it, cash is still the preferred method of payment.

In New Zealand, my bank account is set up to move as much money as possible to my mortgage account for the house. I save a

lot of interest by using my credit card, so I was accustomed to having no cash in my wallet. At farmers' markets you can use your local bank debit or eftpos card. Otherwise, even small amounts, amounting to cents in the smallest stores, are paid with credit cards. Payments are immediately debited from and are visible in your credit card account in New Zealand so that it is a lot easier to manage your finances. You can always see your current balance online and payments are charged to the cheque account immediately in New Zealand. In Germany, payments show up much later in your online credit card account.

On a weekend visit to friends living in the Bavarian Forest region, I listened to their conversations about what and where they buy things for their families. I felt left behind.

They gave no thought to the fact that they could get anything, anywhere, anytime. When they asked me about New Zealand in this respect, I answered in a small voice that it wasn't that easy. The second time I mentioned it, they thought they understood. 'So, buy on eBay or Amazon!' they suggested. I had to explain that the shipping charges are prohibitive, if the vendors even ship to New Zealand. **For delivery to New Zealand**, the New Zealand postal service offers patrons a YouShop account[64] with a virtual address in the UK, the USA or China through which you can order things online and have them shipped to New Zealand, though there are additional charges. From Hong Kong you can get some electronics shipped for free, but as for any shipment coming from abroad, you are responsible for customs and import taxes. If you can't live without a free shipping consumer universe, New Zealand is not the place for you.

Kaitiaki was off on a tangent again. 'The hamster wheel is deceptive. From inside it looks like a career ladder you are running up. You have blinkers on, so you can't see the nice, relaxing things life has to offer outside. You don't have to be a careerist to be in a hamster wheel. Anyone can get stuck in one if your ambition is to climb higher, faster, better and get richer by trying to meet social standards. You can't please everyone and soon enough you are caught in a vicious circle you can't

break out of. Is it possible that people, in day-to-day life, are immune to this information? Perhaps because they have never gone off to see the world with just a backpack. Some only live, study or work abroad for a short time to be able to put "experience abroad" in their resumés. Travellers and commuters between different countries and cultures seem to be more open to the idea that you can't get everything everywhere like in Germany. They are thoughtful when you talk about it. If you travel with a backpack, you know what basic minimum needs are. You get to know places where things don't work perfectly and certainly not the way you expect they will. However –' Kaitiaki bowed his head '– let's not be pretentious. Not everyone has the chance or the funds to travel. In New Zealand, the wheat is separated from the chaff: do you love it in spite of limited commercial goods? Or is it a reason to go back to where you came from?'

Kiwi ingenuity is closely related to this. I remembered how a friend had brought special massage balls to our Bavarian weekend, and how my kite surfer friend had glued two tennis balls together for the same effect.

On that weekend in Bavaria, I received a message from a former colleague in New Zealand. He had contacted me a while ago about how to get a job in Berlin, and now he was writing to tell me he had succeeded.

He was surprised about the six-month probationary period. It's normal in Germany – anywhere from three to six months. In New Zealand, with the exception of 90 days for employers of fewer than 19 employees, it's only two weeks to a month.[65] The same periods apply in each country for giving or receiving notice. Be aware that notice in Germany is generally given with respect to the end of the quarter. Depending on the terms of your contract, you might end up with several more months before you can actually leave the workplace. This can be anything from three to nine months. Along with France and a few other countries, Germany has one of the most rigid **job markets** in the world. For the workforce, it safeguards their jobs, while companies benefit from less fluctuation. As a result, German companies tend to hire rather slowly. All of this fits into the cultural standard of security they ascribe to and

is mirrored in the way the real estate market works. Germans move less often, buy property less often and change jobs less often than people in other countries, who tend to be more flexible and mobile. Germans never cease to marvel at this perceived lack of stability and sustainability. To many Germans, losing your job feels like it's the end of the world and you do everything to prevent it. Because of this, my friends abroad think that Germans are subservient, basically kowtowing to superiors and dishing it out to subordinates. Curiously, in comparison with many other cultures, Germany's workplaces have rather flat hierarchical structures. This means that employees are allowed, even encouraged by management, to give an opinion and participate in decision making. On the other hand, great importance is given to academic and occupational titles. Isn't this an interesting contradiction?

## Hierarchy and egalitarianism

Our serious tui settled on my shoulder, looked into my eyes and embarked on another cross-cultural lecture. 'In Germany you can achieve much more if you have one of those titles. In Middle-earth, you would be laughed at. The janitor is respected in equal measure as the bank employee. In the 'land of poets and philosophers' up there in Europe, on the other hand, you enjoy status according to your level of education, particularly with a university diploma or a PhD. Many German parents would object to their university graduate offspring dating someone who had only gone to vocational school. In my country, a barrister can marry a carpenter and nobody cares.[66] Managers in New Zealand are respected as part of the team and are just as much hands-on workers as everybody else.[67]

'Geert Hofstede, the Dutch expert on cultural studies analysed the correlation between national and business cultures. He shows that national and regional cultural norms have enormous influence on how companies are organised and run. On his website, Hofstede states that New Zealand scores low on the power distance scale. Hierarchies exist for pragmatic reasons; leadership is highly accessible. Managers trust the expertise of individual employees or teams. Managers and employees equally expect to be called upon to take care of a task or make a decision. Information is disseminated regularly and the style of communication is informal, direct and dedicated. Germany is decentralised and characterised by a strong

middle class. Not surprisingly, it also scores low on the power distance scale. Employment is highly participatory, compared to other countries. Employees in Germany have many rights that are borne in mind by management. The communications and meeting style is direct and dedicated. Intensive supervision is frowned upon. Leaders are expected by their subordinates to have considerable expertise in their field and it should relate to the projects at hand.'[68]

Hierarchy is closely linked to the sense of order and to power structures. Most older cultures, which still place importance on this triumvirate, featured an aristocracy and a stratified social system. It is important to note that in Germany and New Zealand, the flat hierarchical structure has not evolved over time, but was brought about deliberately. It would reach far beyond the scope of this book to address the complex histories of both Germany and New Zealand that have led to these modern societies. In short, 'new' cultural standards as described by German cultural researcher Alexander Thomas were energetically instituted in Germany immediately following World War II to conform with Allied expectations regarding freedom of speech, self-determination, accountability, participatory government and the distrust of absolutist or dictatorial hierarchies. New Zealand has been shaped by egalitarianism that has become an integral part of the culture. Newcomers to New Zealand often have real difficulties dealing with this, even as they admire the principle. Only later generations of immigrants can truly espouse it.

'So, what is egalitarianism?' Kaitiaki cleared his throat, and added, 'Inequality is vehemently rejected. Boastfulness has its own word in New Zealand: skiting. A New Zealander has an opinion and will articulate it (please refer to page 162 in the section on *Opinion – feedback – directness – low context – objectivity – honesty* for more about this).[69] New Zealanders are adamant about democracy and prove it with the highest voter turnouts in the world. When the government called for a new flag, every New Zealander was invited to submit a design.'

In her book *Watching the Kiwis: New Zealanders' Rules of Social Interaction*, academic author Brigitte Bönisch-Brednich offers a bit of background history on the complexity of egalitarianism:

> 'So there are very good reasons for this carefully developed Kiwi system of playing down differences, denying hierarchies or at

least acting them out in a more backstage kind of way, applying various tactics of disguising difference and constantly creating a social plateau. All this makes working in New Zealand very puzzling for a newcomer, because you learn very quickly that all this is actually not true or, at least, it is only true on the surface. One soon realises that there are, as in every society, boundaries, social classes, status systems and signs and indicators for them; they are just harder to detect because these rules are written in a code. Often for foreigners they may as well be written in invisible ink. However, while Fox and others writing about England suggest the English are constantly acting out these differences, unconsciously and consciously reflecting on them and reassuring themselves of their validity, in New Zealand a whole set of crucial social rules and energies are caught up in doing exactly the opposite: pretending there are no class divisions and hierarchies. While distinctions are possible, they are understated and insignificant; the main thing is defacto equality and that everyone deserves a fair chance.

For anthropologists, the question is why this delusional behaviour makes sense. Why is this deep-seated need essential to a New Zealander's essential well-being? The search for an answer leads us back into history, to the conditions and promise of colonialisation in the 19th century. The bargain made in coming to New Zealand was that people wouldn't have to cope with the facets of the English class system anymore. While it did not mean the complete absence of class in the new country, not every aspect of daily life was ruled by it. Everyone, regardless of their original background, would be wearing similar clothing and have similar housing and provisions. Though employer and worker relationships remained, of course, the boss would have to treat you as his equal outside of the workplace. Over time, this understanding of equality morphed into a passionate egalitarianism that turns a blind eye to basic differences, talents, expertise and excellence. It has become such a part of national character that New Zealanders are quite unaware of it and are unable to recognise it in themselves. Short poppies are

encouraged to think themselves tall, while the tall ones are downplayed and deplored, and taught to bend and crouch down (tall poppy syndrome).'[70]

Therefore, it is better to crouch so you aren't cut off at the head if it is sticking out above the rest. Māori people have a saying promoting understatement: '*Waiho ma te tangata e mihi*. Let others sing your praises.'

I personally enjoyed working with Māori colleagues very much. Perhaps because they are very flexible with regards to 'how and when' (please refer to the section on *The perception of time – back and forward to the past* on page 82 for more about this). Compared to the Aborigines of neighbouring Australia, Māori people are fairly well integrated. They influence society in both business and private spheres. Many companies welcome Māori culture as indispensable to their daily activities.

Kaitiaki raised a wing. 'This was not always the case. It has only been in more recent times that places regained their Māori names.' And I have heard opponents complain that it is one on a never-ending list of further demands.

Something became clear to me. Flat hierarchies were an impression I had on my first trips to New Zealand. What I didn't realise was how strong other cultures figure in the background and how subtly they insinuate themselves into daily life. At my first job in New Zealand, I was surprised to find a hierarchy that I was not expecting, nor was I used to anything like it. Kaitiaki saved me by explaining that it was an English influence at play here. He flapped his wings, and said, 'Your impression of an upper class, big boy network sitting up there in their ivory tower versus lower tiers of soldiers and workers who endeavour to uphold principles of fairness and care can be explained with Geert Hofstede's theory. Great Britain has a low power distance index. It is a society which believes in minimising inequalities. This cultural dimension (power distance) looks at how individuals deal with the unequal distribution of power. Do they expect and accept it or not? A high power distance reflects greater inequalities in society, low power distance means power is more evenly distributed. It is interesting that the power distance index is lower in the higher classes of British society and higher in the lower classes. At first glance, the overall low index seems

incongruent with the historically established class system. It unveils the tensions underlying British culture between the importance of the social class you are born into on the one hand, and on the other a deep-seated belief that your origins should not impede your life's journey. A very fine sense of fair play leads to the belief that people should all be treated equally.'[71] Kaitiaki closed his summary, saying, 'In reality, it is virtually impossible to escape from the class you were born in.' His words reminded me of how perspective defines what you experience. Many of my colleagues were Asian, who perceived hierarchical structures as absolutely normal and didn't at all notice the nuances as I did. Cultures like Filipino, Indian, Chinese or Japanese are among the most hierarchical in the world.

The equality principle illuminates another experience I had in the same company. With respect to cross-cultural training, I was told by a manager that management regarded all employees as equal and actively played down differences. Kaitiaki criticised this by saying, 'The strengths that each culture brings to the table are ignored this way. Management is trying to squeeze everyone into the same set of conditions. The fish finds itself in a tree and the bird in the river. I'm not surprised that the kiwi has no wings and walks around in the lower ranks.'

I asked amusedly if he thought that egalitarianism played a role in the animal kingdom. I was thinking of a local news report of a cat who thought she was a sheep because she had grown up among them, or the sheep convinced it was a dog because they had grown up in another animal culture.

Kaitiaki grinned, but continued undeterred. 'In business, the same applies to risk taking or aversion. It additionally depends on the type of company and the industry it is engaged in. Company culture plays a huge role. For example, in a family-led company or a bank, you can expect to find a steeper hierarchy than in a small start-up. The bank will likely be the most stratified of the three. Government agencies are a completely different category, both in New Zealand and Germany.

'And here is the crux of the matter.' Kaitiaki squinted. 'In an international business environment, looking from the outside in, class distinctions appear non-existent, as Brigitte Bönisch-Brednich suggested. Take a look at family-owned companies where only New Zealanders work. Subliminally, there is quite a bit of comparing going on as to who went to which school and so forth. And there are titles in New Zealand's class system that only have different names. There are the SNAKS, or Sensitive New Age Kiwis, the foolishly trendy New Zealanders who live mostly in urban neighbourhoods with a strong focus on lifestyle choices. Then there are the TORKS, Traditional Old-fashioned Rural Kiwis all over the rest of the country, among them conservative businessmen or ultra-conservative 'redneck' farmers. The conservatives have a burning desire to inhibit change, and are often members of parliament or active in local politics. Particularly the younger generations of Māori call themselves IWIKS, Independently Willed Indigenous Kiwis. BENZERS, Better Educated New Zealanders, regard themselves as the elite and would never call themselves or others Kiwis.

'Some TORKS have ambitions to become SNAKS. Other SNAKS, finding IWIKS' demands too radical, might think of converting to the TORKS. To complete the confusion, an IWIK can simultaneously be a SNAK, TORK or BENZER. TORKS see themselves as the defenders of global agriculture. SNAKS – very much aware of the widening gap between Haves and Have-nots – see themselves as integral to global society in their roles of economic and social leaders. IWIKS consider themselves a sovereign people with all of the rights of other New Zealanders, though without all of the obligations. BENZERS believe the world would be an enlightened place, if only everyone was better educated. All of these groups have one thing in common: they feel they are also pioneers who can fix anything with Number 8 wire, and who can take on the entire world, especially in sports.'[72]

In some regions of New Zealand, hierarchies are more evident than in others. There is a pecking order according to whose family has been in New Zealand the longest. These are regions in which it is likely that immigrants will have a more difficult time than in the more multicultural cities like Wellington.

I flew to London one last time to take part in Gemma's wedding in York. I used the opportunity to expand my network by first attending a meeting of product managers. One of the participants was a German who had studied in Oxford and had lived in England for many years. He knew quite a bit about English society and its classes. He told me about his children and how British parents began early to position themselves for the kind of school they were aiming for by mingling with the 'right kind' of people who could later help with building careers. Titles like Lord, Lady, Reverend, Sir and speaking the Queen's English point towards a higher class in society. In British companies, however, class distinctions might be less noticeable and a newcomer might generally find working in England rather casual. Of course, each company and its specific culture is different, as is the case all over the world. The upper middle class in England for example is higher than the equivalent in New Zealand.

The inconsistency between class consciousness and the belief everyone should have a fair chance is aptly illustrated by the custom of

wearing **school uniforms**. In New Zealand, school uniforms are combined with Māori and local cultural elements to symbolise the principle of equal opportunity.[73] In Germany, school kids engage in fierce competition over trendy clothing brands. School uniforms in New Zealand are thought to undermine this behaviour, however there are contrary opinions as to its success.

Someone asked me whether I would root for New Zealand or Germany when the Olympics were on. I really had to think about this one. In the pub I was thrilled with a New Zealand win, and German athletes didn't capture my enthusiasm. I felt neutral about them. So I suppose my never-really-passionate-patriotism for Germany had imperceptibly been replaced by a new-found devotion to New Zealand.

In the afternoon, I went jogging from my friend Corny's house to Greenwich Park. Nice. If I had decided on London as my home, this would have been a favourite place to run. By now I was discontent with every city. Concrete all over the place and no horizons. York is a wonderful city, mind you, steeped in history, and the wedding in York Minster was extraordinary. But though the sea is not too far away, it still wasn't close enough for me.

What I love about Gemma is that she has remained the same, ready for any adventure. Like the time in the Basque country. A friend you can count on, always a good sport.

On the evening before the wedding, I visited her at her home. Then she brought me to my home exchange[74]. What a great concept: trading homes and sometimes even cars at no cost to each party. I had a good experience with this in San Francisco too. The house in York had a lock which was tricky to open, and we just couldn't get it to work. Luckily the owner had told me the secret way in, just in case. We had to climb over a fence at the back of the house. So the bride-to-be and I climbed over – with my suitcase – in the middle of the night. The courtyard was lower on the other side of the fence. I had to give Gemma a leg up to help her back over so she could get her bridal beauty sleep.

On the train ride back to London from York, the train suddenly stopped for no apparent reason. Wifi was made available to all

passengers, and a bit later, bottles of water were handed in through the doors. Such a difference to German service standards where for over a month a hotel couldn't manage to mail me an electronics cable which I'd left behind. After numerous queries, I finally received it via collect on delivery. Friendly communication and postage paid directly to them would have been the nicer and surely cheaper alternative. An Australian hotel sent me my diary which I had forgotten to pack halfway around the world for free. So much for Lower Bavarian service and goodwill.

After the wedding, I felt out of place in Europe. I hadn't found a new project yet, though I had had five offers. They all wanted to hire me until the end of the year.

Kaitiaki nodded. 'Germans plan long term, play it safe and reserve the right to cancel anyway, calling it flexibility.' I often confused interviewers on the phone at the placement firms. When they asked where I was registered, I said I lived in New Zealand. 'But where are you registered?' they insisted. I always had to explain that there are no **residents' registration offices** in Middle-earth like we have in Germany. 'But you have to be registered somewhere,' they argued. 'No one has to be registered in New Zealand. We just live there.' Dubious silence on the other end of the phone line.

The point is, I needed to be back in New Zealand by the end of October so I wouldn't lose my visa after nearly six months abroad. I had quickly become used to all the free time, filled with visits to family and friends, meeting old colleagues and making new contacts. Even so, I felt my sojourn in Europe was coming to an end. I often caught myself thinking, 'I'm ready to leave.' I even considered cutting the trip short and wrote two emails inquiring about new freelance job options in New Zealand. On the other hand, I hadn't seen some of my most important friends yet.

After returning from the wedding, only two days in the concrete jungle of Frankfurt had me heading for Northern Germany and I was drawn to the sea.

## My old home – Hamburg and Sylt

My old neighbours in the red brick building where I used to live in Hamburg-Barmbek are among the nicest, most uncomplicated people I have ever met. They were happy to welcome me into their home for the two extra days resulting from my hasty departure from Frankfurt. While I waited for them to arrive after work, I went to my favourite Italian place, Taormina, on Fuhlsbüttler Straße and watched the world passing by.

Not much had changed along this street. After lunch I walked past the stores I had come to know so well. Soon I reached the entrance to the building I had left two and a half years ago. I had stayed with these same neighbours on the last night before I emigrated. The hallway still smelled the same; only the postings on the notice board had been updated.

My former neighbours greeted me with joyful hugs at their apartment door, as always the most gracious hosts. They brought out a bottle of port from my former collection of fine wines and liquors, which I had given them before my grand departure to New Zealand. Of course, I wanted to know everything about everybody. Who had moved out, who had moved in? Things had changed in the building a lot. Not many of the group of neighbours who had partied and watched soccer games together in the garden were left; there were fewer spontaneous chats in the stairwell. There were not many of those left who had given the house a particular vibe. The next morning, I couldn't wait to get on the train to the island of Sylt and breathe in some sea air. I had a day ticket there and back, intending to stay the night in Hamburg again. The scenery on the three-hour ride inspired me so much that I wrote more than I had managed in two whole days in Frankfurt. The highlight of this train ride is the Hindenburgdamm, the rail track across the tidal mudflats between the mainland and the island. The causeway the rails are built on is so narrow that it is invisible to the passengers. You feel like you are literally flying low over the flats, or the water if the tide has come in. Having arrived in Westerland, I walked the shortest route to the shore and inhaled deeply. White

sand, the sea, the wide horizon... How I had missed them since leaving Barcelona! I had only just made the train in the morning, so I decided to walk along the beach to find a place for a leisurely coffee. Along the way to the Beachhouse, which locals had warmly recommended, people greeted me with the standard 'Moin' – meaning hello in the dialect of this region up north.

*Moinmoin* is the curious contraction of *Guten Morgen*, and it still slips out of my mouth sometimes in New Zealand when what I want to say is 'Morning'. When I got to the Beachhouse on the North Sea, I waved across the oceans to my own beachhouse in Wellington at the other end of the world. I would have loved to buy some of the glassware branded with their Beachhouse logo. Unfortunately, they didn't ship them Down Under.

My original plan was to take a bus to one of the ends of the island and buy some fresh North Sea shrimp to peel – there is a particular technique to do this – and pop right into my mouth. It was just as nice to sit here on the beach and look over the ocean, letting my thoughts roam. I thought about how nice it would be to have a genuine North Sea Strandkorb in Wellington when the wind blows hard. These are heavy, boxy wicker chairs for two, with a roof and a striped shade you can pull down to keep out the wind or midday sun. They are everywhere in northern Germany, and you can rent them hourly or daily on most German beaches. They are ubiquitous all along these coastlines, a marvellous invention.

Much of the North Sea coast reminds me of New Zealand: dunes, sheep, the tides, the screeching of the seagulls, lighthouses and sea animal sightings from the beach. The waters around Sylt are home to porpoises that sometimes swim up the Elbe River towards Hamburg. Around New Zealand you can see orcas and humpback whales. Orcas are plentiful in the Cook Strait, which is basically in front of my house. Often their hunt for stingrays will bring orcas speeding into Wellington Harbour to Frank Kitts Park, along Oriental Bay[75] and even right under my balcony.[76] Orcas might accompany you as you stand up paddle in Nelson. While jogging along the coast near my home in Wellington, I have even seen southern right whales. Both countries also have

unpredictable weather. Asking for packing advice before my first trip to New Zealand, I was told that **it can be four seasons in one day**.

On the way back to the train, a man with a huge cardboard box ran straight into me, as I couldn't get out of his way in the narrow lane filled with people. No apology. A few metres further on the same thing happened again with a suitcase. Very aggressive. There must be a nest of total idiots here.

I was angry, and then irritated at myself for even getting angry. I almost didn't know that feeling any more since I moved to New Zealand. The only time I felt this anger was the vibe sometimes apparent at Germans in New Zealand Facebook forums. I don't need it; life is much better without it.

As we know too well that Germans are notoriously reticent about small talk, a statistic that says that people on the island of Sylt flirt 11,000 times a day is very surprising. Had I misunderstood cardboard-box-man's intentions? Perhaps the Sylters' communication style is more the silent type. I doubt it: in 1970 there were 6,064 telephones on the island – 5,349 in the town of Westerland alone – which was more per capita than in West Berlin at that time.[77] Surely it was just a cross-cultural misunderstanding between me and the jostling men and I had missed my chance to meet my prince just because a cardboard box and a suitcase were in the way!

I moved into a new home exchange flat the next day in Hamburg. This one was in HafenCity (Harbour City), which is Europe's largest innercitydevelopmentproject, as Germans would write it (it *is* really called *Innenstadtentwicklungsprojekt*). Such long words in German.

Though the Māori can easily hold their own. Here is an example: *Taumatawhakatangihangakoauauotamateaturipukakapikimaungahoronukupokaiwhenuakitanatahu*, which is the name for a hill in New Zealand. Translated, it means something like: The summit where

Tamatea, the man with the big knees, the slider, climber of mountains, the land-swallower who travelled about, played his nose flute to his loved one.

At the home exchange flat in Hamburg, we reiterated that the daughter of the owner's partner, Dorit, and her family would be staying for a weekend in my house in Wellington. She was planning to live in Nelson, New Zealand, for about six months. My host excitedly reported how Hamburg had replaced Sydney's ranking on the list of most liveable cities in the world, and that Auckland came in at eighth.[78] It's not surprising to me that New Zealand's cities often rank near the top. Anyway, after exchanging this and other information, I was shown around the apartment. I told my host that I would go out for a while and be back for a nap in the afternoon before my jog. Outside, Hamburg grabbed me and pulled me in. I spent the day drifting around, first through HafenCity and the Speicherstadt, the spectacular 19th-century warehouse district built on timber piles which are hammered into the silty bed of the Elbe and is intersected by canals. An absolute must-see, if you ever visit Hamburg.

After a while, I reached my former optician's store. I could see his mind searching for where to place me when it clicked. 'What are you doing here?' he yelled as he hugged me. We chatted while he tested my vision. He had lived in Brazil for a while once and he told me how it had taken him nearly a year to settle back into life in Germany.

When arriving at Altona train station, a young blind man got off at the bus stop with me. For a moment I watched as he groped his way along a wall with his cane. Nobody else seemed to notice. There were stalls all along the street blocking the way, so I asked him if he needed help. He wanted to get to the suburban train station. He took my elbow and gratefully allowed me to guide him to the escalator where he said he could manage alone.

**Riding the bus** in New Zealand is a joy. Passengers greet the driver as they get in, and they say 'Thanks, Mr Driver' when they get off. School

kids get up to offer their seats to older passengers, even if they appear healthy and fit. Kaitiaki poked me, sniggering. 'Look at you, believing you aren't that old in spite of some grey hairs!' New Zealand bus drivers are a treasure trove of information. The best spot in the bus is in the front where you can chat with them. A friend of mine once had no cash, and as there was no ATM nearby, he was allowed to ride for free. The driver gets off to help people with disabilities, and most passengers will jump up to help.

Medical aids such as crutches are standard in both New Zealand and Germany. I offered a friend of mine in New Zealand the crutches I had from when I fractured my knee in Brazil, but she had already got some prescribed, just as she would have in Germany. People with disabilities can live relatively autonomous lives in both countries. Not the case in so many others.

I looked forward to a session with my acupuncturist, who I have known for over ten years. In New Zealand, acupuncture is quite a bit cheaper than in Germany. Some of the acupuncture training schools there offer a session for a koha, a donation. I thought my Filipina acupuncturist in Hamburg was still the best, though. For an hour, while she worked on my stiff neck, we chatted. She was thinking of visiting me in Wellington. Of course, I would love to have her visit.

Instead of a nap in the afternoon, I rented a bike along with Dorit and we rode to the Alsterperle, a little jewel in the heart of the city. Long ago it was a public toilet; however, since the late nineties, great food and drink is served here, and it has a magnificent view. We each bought a glass of wine and sat on the edge of the Alster river (which is as wide and calm as a large lake, smack in the middle of Hamburg) and dangled our feet in the water. A swan showed us its bottom as it fed, and behind it the skyline provided a stunning backdrop for the standup paddlers and sailboats. I quickly slipped into my summer dress in the bathroom nearby.

Dorit's husband jogged by. He stopped to say hello for a moment and we started talking. For a few hours, the topic was my life in New Zealand, emigrating, travel tips and their own plans. Late in

the afternoon, and two glasses of wine later, we parted ways.

I strolled up to Mühlenkamp Street through the park along the Alster. There were lots of people who had just let their bikes fall on the spot and were sitting in the grass for a spontaneous picnic. Everyone's faces were turned towards the sun, enjoying this gentle summer evening.

The area around Mühlenkamp is lively with cafés and restaurants. I had looked at a flat around the corner when I was moving to Hamburg. Now I was meeting former colleagues for dinner. I hadn't heard from them for years until they called me, asking if they could visit me, two days before they arrived in Wellington. Well, of course they could! In the past few years, I had more visitors in New Zealand than all of the eight years I lived in Hamburg. My parents were also visiting when these colleagues arrived. When I got home from work, they all sat chatting as if they had known each other for years. What's more, their paths had crossed several times already in New Zealand at campgrounds. Imagine their surprise when they heard that we had worked together in Hamburg. Kaitiaki was happy to see them here in Mühlenkamp again. 'This is so like New Zealand where the world is a small place despite its physical size. Everyone knows one another, even distantly related.'

One of them told me about how she was training for a marathon. A story about my 50-km ultramarathon came immediately to mind. I had run it accidentally! I had run several half-marathons but never had the plan to run a full one, until the time a colleague told me about the **Tarawera Marathon**. The route fascinated me: past gushing geysers, through the thermal and volcanic landscape surrounding Rotorua, through the bush, farmlands, over hills and along the shoreline, ending at Lake Tarawera's Hot Water Beach. Wow. I looked all over for a half-marathon along this route, but only the full was possible. So I registered. And I prepared as best I could by running up and down a few hills, which isn't too hard to do around Wellington.

Well, I tried. Running was my favourite way of getting to know places, so I'd get to the end somehow. At some point there was a sign pointing

151

left that read 'Marathon' and pointing right it read '50 kms'. I thought, why not, if I'm already here? I didn't think about it, I just ran, or walked fast. I didn't have a finishing time I wanted to achieve. Just be a part of the run and enjoy the scenery, I thought. How often would I have this chance?

Near the finishing line I passed an older man who was jogging back and forth, waiting for his friend because they wanted to finish together. Some amazing people ran through the finish, fulfilling a lifelong dream. Kaitiaki was moved to say, 'This too is New Zealand. A place where you can live your dream.'

The return transport from the marathon finishing line by boat wasn't fancy. The boats couldn't dock directly at the shore, so we had to cross an improvised bridge made of wooden boards. There were too few boats for all of the participants. The darker it got, the fuller the boats got. We could finally board when it was pitch dark and we were frozen to the bone. Our tui had to be a smart aleck: 'Stop whining. You know what? In New Zealand you can learn how much the human body can take. Only a German would complain about supposed bad planning. You, who say you love that things aren't as perfect here. It's an adventure! Shbireit! You can handle the jandal!'

Since the catering had been so good all day, it didn't matter that the restaurants were all closed when we finally arrived back in Rotorua. So this is how I ended another great day of my life.

As we talked at the restaurant in Muehlenkamp, my colleague and I were reminded yet again of how much we enjoy travel and adventure. She told me a little about her current life in the hamster wheel – one that I knew from my former career as an investment banker, with a maximum of two weeks of consecutive holidays. As an employee, I had a pretty good contract for New Zealand standards: 20 days' leave and ten days' sick leave. Anything above and beyond was **unpaid leave**. Kaitiaki commented, 'That is why New Zealanders will also use up their sick leave. Some bosses actually encourage it. Though I know yours didn't. Compared to Germany, it's almost never a problem to take unpaid leave, be it on the spur of the moment or for a longer period. For Germans, this is a scary concept. By the way, the German word "Angst" has also been adopted into the English language.'

Hadn't I planned an afternoon nap before leaving this morning? As I returned to HafenCity after 14 hours, I was tired but happy. I took the next morning slowly. That is, until friends arrived with their new baby. After I had left for New Zealand, they had got married on the island of Sardinia, where a friend we had in common lives. Because of regular visits to see her, many of us are now fans of Sardinia. For me, its many sheep and the varied landscape remind me of New Zealand. There is a saying about both places: When God created the world, he still had pieces left over, so he stuck them together to make Sardinia in the Mediterranean and New Zealand in the South Pacific.

As usual when friends meet up after a long time, we had many things to talk about and catch up on, mostly about writing, writing styles and all of our personal projects that never seem to find an end. It was great sitting there together, but we got peckish and decided to go out. We stopped for a drink first at the Oberhafen-Kantine, owned by the parents of one of Germany's top TV chefs, Tim Mälzer. It's a very old little building with sloped walls, surrounded by the waters of Hamburg's industrial harbour. The floors slant so much that you have to stand at an angle to feel upright. Later, at the authentic Japanese restaurant we chose for dinner, I couldn't contain my curiosity and ordered soy cream cheese with fermented soy bean, raw squid and tuna sashimi, and washed it down with a Japanese beer. When Kaitiaki pulled a face, I reminded him how I love ordering unfamiliar food. Discovering a delicacy can make an average day into a special one.

After dinner, I had to hurry along to a 40th birthday party in my old Barmbek neighbourhood. My neighbours from my former apartment were there too. I brought along a bag of purple potato chips, something I knew well from New Zealand. These were the first I had discovered here in Germany.

One of the guests was a young woman who had just spent three months in Barcelona and was confused about the work culture there. We talked about time orientation and German organisations. She spoke about how the Spaniards came to work later, took a long lunch

and siesta in the afternoon and then were surprised that they had to work at the weekend. Germans work through lunch more often than not, eating at their desks. Punctuality also came up in conversation. Germans can take someone's unpunctuality as a personal offence. Kaitiaki listened closely as I described the soul of the German perfectionist as seen by my Italian girlfriend Renata. 'Germans plan things. They know each and every hurdle well in advance. When they reach one, they already know what it is and how they can jump over it, which they do with ease. Italians just take off. At the first hurdle, there is a lot of gesticulation, talk about the situation and calculating the advantage or disadvantage of jumping over it this way or that way. After this great commotion, they jump, run on and arrive at the finish just the same.' Kaitiaki added, 'Rigid planning makes you inflexible. What if an envisioned hurdle never comes? Or one comes as a complete surprise? Italians, Spaniards and New Zealanders can deal with the unexpected much better than Germans. In many countries, uncertainty is a feature of daily life and it's considered a virtue to be adaptable.' I agree. Nowadays I really enjoy coming up with creative solutions and trying something new.

The party got lively. Long after midnight, I finally managed to break free and head for the subway. On the way, I overheard this conversation between non-Germans in front of a Döner (gyro) place. 'I don't like ties. If "tie", then it is "bow tie" anyway.' Kaitiaki stuck his beak in the air, not pleased with this exchange. He muttered to me that his bow tie is definitely not a tie. As we continued on our way, I had to think of all of the business suits I would be leaving behind. I was in bed around 4 am, worried about how I would manage brunch with friends in just a few hours.

We met at the Wasserschloss (castle on the water) in HafenCity. I needn't have worried: Anke had also had a very long night and short sleep. Meeting again felt like we had just seen each other a few weeks ago, not years. Anke and Nils had come to visit me in Wellington for my first Christmas there.

People from Hamburg are BBQ junkies, just like the New Zealanders. Nils was our designated 'beach house barbie master'.

There were a lot of tourist sightseeing boats in the harbour. We seemed to be a favourite subject for the boatloads of mobile phone photographers chugging by, so we waved majestically to everybody. A couple I knew well also stopped by with their baby to visit us. The mood stayed light-hearted and I reminisced about the time I had worked with many of the people I had met over the weekend. The project we had worked on back then had been a bit like a start-up: young, dynamic and – in this case – unfortunately unsuccessful, but the contacts I had made were still thriving.

We strolled around HafenCity, trading travel stories while taking a closer look at the huge cruise ship docked just behind the building I was staying in and the never-ending construction project of the Elbphilharmonie.[79]

Anke and Nils had travelled around Namibia for a long time and told me about the badly researched travel guide they had relied on. Planning to stay overnight at an ostrich farm, they followed the directions given in the guide, drove through the countryside, turned here and there, and ended up at an abandoned house. It was nearly sunset when they finally found somewhere to stay in a small village. It was one of those times when things go wrong and you still end up having one of the best evenings of your life. In the bar of this hotel in the middle of nowhere, they met other stranded people. The owner had only just won the hotel two weeks earlier at poker. A few others were there waiting for spare parts, as their car had broken down. Anke and Nils had nearly got lost searching for a non -existent ostrich farm.

Anke and I each looked forward to an evening on our own couches, both still feeling the effects of the night before. My home exchange flat was a beautiful place to just hang, and I enjoyed it very much. I woke to rainy weather, which they call Schietwetter (shitty weather) in Hamburg. The people who live here don't let inclement weather keep them from being outdoors any more than New Zealanders do. I jogged around the Alster, surely one of the nicest urban tracks in the world. It was just the right thing to do after several days of eating and drinking. I extended my stay by another two days at the warm invitation of my former neighbours

in Barmbek. Taking my time, I drifted through the days with no particular plan and no idea what I'd be doing the next day. I was happily bobbing on the waves of life in a country where otherwise everything is scheduled and timed.

I started my day with a stop at the nearest Globetrotter outdoor outfitter store. It's a must-visit for any new New Zealander or new German of New Zealand origin. Then I had breakfast in another favourite restaurant in Barmbek called T.R.U.D.E., an acronym for Tief Runter Unter Die Elbe, meaning: deep down under the Elbe River. It was once a factory building and is named after the largest tunnel borer in the world, T.R.U.D.E., which is stored behind it. It was used to dig the fourth tunnel under the Elbe River in 1997. To explain: the first Old Elbe tunnel was built in 1911 and is 426 m/ 1,398 ft. long, the other four vehicle-only autobahn tubes followed in intervals through the seventies and nineties. They are 3.1 km/ 1.9 mi long, have two lanes each and an estimated 130,000 vehicles pass through them daily. The machine is monster-sized. The food in the restaurant where it is kept is great too. My motto for the day was doing only my favourite things.

After a short meeting, I took a public transport boat (with the same fares as Hamburg's buses and subway trains) to Oevelgoenne on the bank down river on the Elbe River. I enjoyed walking along the line of wonderful, old, captain's houses, ending up at the Strandperle café (beach pearl café). The river is very wide at this point and home to Hamburg's harbour, one of the largest in the world, 110 km upriver from the North Sea. There I sat, with white sand between my toes, looking at fascinating industrial scenery. Container ships floated by into the harbour, and other ships travelled the other way. The water glittered in the afternoon sun like a valuable carpet, cut through by the waves of the passing vessels.

A conversation began with a gentleman sitting near me. It turned out that he would have ended up in Australia if it had not been for family and friends. In the end, the worry about retirement funding became the main reason for staying put. Originally from the Rhineland, he had moved to Hamburg instead. He needed the sea nearby, just like me. We said cheers to that, and after what seemed

like two hours, we thought to exchange names. Of course, the *Du* question came up immediately. He maintained that the formal *Sie* was still very much en vogue in Germany to demonstrate respect. Where appropriate, he was always for understated restraint. 'Oha,' said Kaitiaki, trying out his Hamburger accent.

## Peaches and coconuts

My conversation partner now took notice of my companion. Kaitiaki pointed to this nice man who lived in Hamburg by choice, and asked me, 'Is he a peach or a coconut?'

This question introduces a simple yet very effective intercultural model to demonstrate Alexander Thomas' theory of Interpersonal Differentiation. When comparing peaches to coconuts, we find that the peach is soft on the outside and easy to deal with until you reach the smallish, hard stone in the middle. Advancing further into the seed is very difficult. The coconut is very hard on the outside and you can only see inside if you somehow manage to crack that hard shell. In an international cultural comparison, Germans are coconuts. There are of course individual differences within cultures. For example, a person from Hamburg is more like a coconut, while someone from Cologne will tend to be more peachy. That being said, Germans are indeed coconuts when compared to most other cultures.

Naturally, Kaitiaki had to speak up. 'Peaches have thick, juicy flesh, coconuts a hard shell,' he repeated. 'If, for the sake of this model, we assume small talk is in the public realm, it is not surprising that you German coconuts are bewildered, perhaps even irritated, at how friendly and open-hearted Americans or we New Zealanders seem to be, as this behaviour only happens after a long time and much effort in German culture. Having traded what you in your coconut culture feel is private information (and you take this very seriously), you soon believe you have started a deep and lasting friendship in an astoundingly short time. What you have not understood is that I, your peachy counterpart, am still in the public realm of peaches, where all kinds of help is offered and promises are made (according to our cultural character).

'Not long after, you discover that the peach was not at the threshold of friendship at all and you think that peaches are liars and our friendliness

and helpfulness is a sham. Your German coconut feelings are hurt. You feel betrayed –' Kaitiaki rolled his eyes and sighed '– and suddenly we peaches are considered superficial, irresponsible and deceitful. You think we New Zealanders are incapable of real friendships. That is not fair! You never think about how I as a peach must feel! First you are so unapproachable and all of a sudden you crowd me and want to get at what is in my peach stone. What should I think of someone who is so presumptuous and pushy? You stand at my door, though when I said you should come by sometime, I only meant to signalise that I like you. A serious invitation always has a date and time, do you not know that? I am so tired of being called superficial. I have no idea what to make of it.'[80]

As coconuts do, the waiter at the café on the shore of the Elbe River came out to demand that we sunbathers move our loungers back to where they belonged within the beach café's imaginary boundaries. 'Oha!' Kaitiaki said again with a perfected Hamburger accent. 'It sounds like those Stuttgart sweeping rules. It is supposedly a no-go to sweep your neighbours' stretch of sidewalk, only your own. Though I do not understand why. I would never mind if someone wanted to sweep in front of my door. No problem at all!'

I wouldn't have minded sitting here chatting in the sun forever, but I had a ticket for my favourite musical *Die Heisse Ecke* (The Hot Corner) in a theatre in St Pauli on the Reeperbahn (street). It is the most successful musical in Hamburg, running for over 25 years. As I walked along the passenger ferry and pleasure boat jetties and through Hamburg's famous red light district, I found it was a perfect warm-up for the show. I saw an inline skater leaning against a windowsill to catch his breath and check his phone to make sure he hadn't missed anything important in the world in the past 20 minutes. On the other side of the street, construction workers set up a wooden board on the side of the street with Greek- or Turkish-looking snacks. The men were standing in a circle around the tapas, smoking together with an after-work beer in hand, enjoying the end of the working day. A guy came out of Herbert Street (famous for its prostitutes), looking satisfied. An older lady with a silver hat on and a bottle of Astra beer in her hand

was pulling along a shopping trolley decorated with a garland of flowers. She was obviously having a serious conversation with herself, judging from her facial expression and impressive eyebrow acrobatics. The bar next to the David Wache police station was already open for business. St Pauli and the Reeperbahn were getting ready for a busy night.

The musical is about what happens in 24 hours at a food stall in St Pauli and all the people who stop by. There are characters from the red light district and all manner of people who come to visit the Reeperbahn: an arrogant marketing dude, a bunch of girls from the suburbs on a hens' party, a pimp and other red light luminaries, 'exotic' prostitutes from a town north of Hamburg called Itzehoe and young musical actors on their way to an audition, hoping to make it big. Then there are the conceited yet naive tourists from Bavaria who ask a gambler if he would take a selfie of them (!), a man from Stuttgart on his grand tour with hitched up pants wearing Birkenstocks with socks and asks for Swabian specialities from his home town because that's all he dares to eat, and, finally, an old couple looking for the café in which they met 50 years ago. The show is about tragedies, tough guys with a heart, and the angel of St Pauli who saves people and lets them hope for a better future, though things will probably be the same tomorrow as they were today. I won't say more so I don't give too much away. What I like best is how the musical has adapted to the changes outside on the streets over the years. Especially at Christmas the world in St Pauli is very different to normal.

In the audience, I sat next to a couple with Austrian passports, though they were originally from Hamburg. The man had a well-cared-for pair of overalls on – absolutely acceptable attire for a musical show in Hamburg. We had such a grand time that we decided to finish off the evening together with a drink at the Ritze lounge, where you could easily run into Olivia Jones or take a peek at Muhammad Ali's former studio in the cellar. The bar's walls were covered with pictures of all of the celebrities who had partied here. A roaming flower vendor offered us roses on credit. Buy now, pay in two weeks. The barkeeper handed out chocolate-

covered marshmallows called *Negerküsse* (Negro kisses) to all of the ladies. A man at the bar reminded everybody jokingly that it was nowadays politically incorrect. Negros are now called Moors. Then I told everybody how Black people in Cuba are proud to be called Negros. 'Why not? I am a Negro,' one had said to me. 'Why shouldn't I be called Negro? I'm black-skinned.' Someone else suggested an even more PC option: Marshmallows with an Immigrant Background. The bar served Hacker-Pschorr, a Bavarian beer. Did that mean the owner of the Ritze was secretly from Bavaria? Or maybe Austria? There was that rumour going around… We will never know for sure because when I asked him, he retreated into his shell like a good coconut.

It was unfortunately a weeknight, so we couldn't follow the Saturday night tradition of partying until dawn and then going to the famous St Pauli fish market to try to sober up. Hamburg's red light district, along with Amsterdam's, is one of the few in the world where you can go out and meet regular folk having a good time. If you ever make it to the fish market in Hamburg early on a Sunday morning, be sure to drop in at the auction hall (Altonaer Fischauktionshalle). That's where Saturday night parties in the district always continue. Among the diehards you will see here are St Pauli's taxi drivers – who had fares all through the night – dancing away their stiff backs to a live band. Whether adult or child, woman or man, conservative or modern, young or old, everybody loves the Miniature Wonderland[81], which is continually expanding. Kaitiaki nodded. 'After these few days, I know why you love Hamburg so much and gush about it all the time.'

Back in Frankfurt, I locked myself out of the flat. Not on purpose, of course; I had only gone down to check the mailbox. As it turned out, it was a good opportunity to get to know the neighbours. Though all of them had foreign backgrounds, they all spoke perfect German and were eager to help me. I was reminded of a trip through Mozambique with a 4x4, although it really wasn't one. On the way to a kiting beach on the border with South Africa, we got stuck in the sand. In the end some Mozambique locals pulled us

out. A lot of white drivers had just ignored us and driven past.

I didn't know if my flatmate would be returning anytime soon, so we tried to think of other ways I could get back into the flat. It was pointless to try to get in over the balcony, because I knew that door was locked. The credit card trick they all seemed to know didn't work either because the door was too modern. It's so interesting that these 'techniques' are basic education in other cultures – especially Southern Europeans know quite a few (please refer to page 117 in the section about *Barcelona* for more about this). Obviously, knowing these tricks comes in handy sometimes, but using them to one's own advantage or to harm others is not okay. I swore I would take a crash course in Barcelona next time and see how I could include using Number 8 wire. I waited six hours for my flatmate and then had to summon all of my German efficiency to be packed and ready for my departure the next day.

## A former stage in life in the Rhineland – Düsseldorf and Cologne

On the way to another meeting with my intercultural trainer colleagues in Cologne, I took a detour to Düsseldorf to visit some friends. Düsseldorf was the scene of my main hamster wheel career days, which is no fault of the city. In fact, the couple I was visiting had just become parents and they loved Düsseldorf, as opposed to Berlin from where they had moved. The differences among the regions of Germany became our topic of the afternoon. We came to these conclusions: Rhinelanders are superficially more polite than others, but it's difficult to build and maintain strong friendships with them. My friend found people in the Hessen region, where he grew up, to be basically rude, while I thought people in Frankfurt (also in Hessen) were welcoming. You know what's what with Hamburg coconuts and have no clue why Berliners seem so insulting. People from Hamburg can be very welcoming if they want to be; sometimes they just don't want to be. Compared to the English or New Zealanders, we Germans are blunt, direct and brutally honest when we voice our opinions. My friend also confirmed that the feeling of respect for each other seems to decline with the use of the informal *Du* in the workplace.

*Opinion – feedback – directness – low context – objectivity – honesty*

In New Zealand it is regarded a virtue to have your own opinion about things. It's basically irrelevant what it is; the main thing is that you have one. New Zealanders appreciate it. They also do not find it difficult to say no or to take a contrary position or precedent, which they will heartily defend with political, social or technical arguments. Above all, New Zealanders are not bound by tradition.[82]

Still, I remember an episode in a restaurant in New Zealand with my friend Manu and her New Zealand boyfriend, Tim. Manu and I were unsatisfied with the service and wanted to comment accordingly – give our honest opinion. To this, Tim remarked, 'Why? It's not my place to tell them how to do things,' confirming that New Zealanders usually keep their thoughts to themselves because they don't assume they can tell

others what to do either.[83] This is clearly the exception to the rule of voicing your opinion.

Kaitiaki certainly had an opinion on this. 'I like this mindset. Let people do what they feel is right. You Germans should look in the mirror before criticising others or insisting your way is the correct one. However, feedback is valuable. You think, "How will hosts or owners know what I as a guest want or need if I don't let them know?" I also know that you like your own guests to give you a fair chance to make their stay unforgettable rather than leaving a negative comment publicly on the website. Feedback in New Zealand is challenging. We tend to praise and accentuate the positive more than you do in Germany. In communications training anywhere in the world you learn that feedback is most effective in sandwich format: the negative comment is sandwiched between two positives. It really works in cross-cultural scenarios, as it builds a bridge between the conflicted parties.

'I know that my fellow New Zealanders are not great at giving negative feedback. Disapproval might pile up for a while and end in a silent explosion that you would characterise as passive-aggressive. Indirect hostility, suppressed frustration, sullen and stubborn behaviour, and tasks repeatedly not performed are the result.'

It's not a secret that Germans are very direct in their communications. They are so honest that it sometimes hurts. Alexander Thomas emphasises this penchant for honesty in relationships as a cultural standard.[84] Edward Hall equated directness with a low context communication style.[85] Germans tend to disregard aspects of communication that are important to some other cultures, such as the surroundings and the emotions, intonation, facial expression, age and status of the person they are speaking to. Conflicts are carried out openly in the interest of clarification. Germans view conflict as an opportunity for problem solving. The English, on the other hand, are very good – even more so than New Zealanders – at saying just the opposite of what they mean. The way the English speak 'between the lines' is extremely puzzling for Germans, who tend to pick up on only what is specifically said.

Kaitiaki took up the reins. 'German objectivity, the way you argue only facts and disregard other factors that might be at play, is at direct odds with the more relationship-focused New Zealanders. German honesty

can be hurtful, especially if we do not realise that you actually mean well and that honesty is so important to you. Your motto is "Why not tell it like it is?" Germans and the Dutch are at the furthest end of the directness scale in international comparison. We New Zealanders do mostly appreciate this, finding it refreshing how you bring everything into sharp focus and straight to the point. We will laugh it away, though, and make fun of you in the same way we make fun of ourselves.'

Oh yes, how well I knew this myself. In a project, a client of mine presented wireframes for a new website, essentially its basic structure. I looked over what Sonya had presented, and burst out with, 'Is that it?' The entire room laughed uproariously. I had outed myself as a German. While on this trip to Germany, Sonya wrote to me about a new colleague who was busy preparing wireframes. 'I think I will ask him first: "Is that it?"'

Continuing his discourse on New Zealanders, Kaitiaki said, 'Why do my compatriots like your refreshing directness? We also hold honesty as a most important value. You can lose respect so quickly if you are dishonest to Germans or New Zealanders. Germans will accept a little bit of cheating; New Zealanders less so. You would run the risk of losing face (see the section on *Facework/face negotiation theory* on page 220 for more on this).'

In addition, Germans interpret not looking straight into someone's eyes when speaking as dishonest. Direct gaze shows interest and respect. In other cultures, such as in Gabon in West Africa, or in some Asian countries such as Japan, direct gaze is rude, disrespectful and read as a direct challenge to the other person.[86] Sometimes it seems to me that New Zealanders would like to absorb a little more German directness to honour their high esteem of honesty and are hindered by their instinctive British-style politeness, which we Germans admire so much..

Next morning, my Düsseldorfer friends left for a camping trip on the Dutch coast. The Dutch share this passion for the outdoors with Germans and New Zealanders. I headed off to Cologne for the evening with my intercultural colleagues. Ten of us had signed up. Because of the unusual heat, illness and planning mishaps, only four of us showed up. I thought I must be dreaming that I was in New Zealand where you never know who will attend your party.

I spent the night with my trainer friend who is a specialist in the cultures of Gabon and Uganda. At breakfast, she gave me another perspective on immigration issues in Germany. Her fiancé is an African from Gabon. He had lived in Germany for over 20 years. His father was a cabinet member in Gabon and so he was encouraged to come to study at university in Germany through a programme of the Goethe Institute. He speaks German with a French accent, is polite and intelligent. He says he used to experience courteous service in stores. Nowadays, most people treat him as if he was 'one of those asylum seekers'. My friend told me how it was totally normal for people to stare at her because she was out with a dark-skinned man. I felt caught out. I admit that I think I would have stared too in Germany. Less so in New Zealand, Barcelona or London, simply because it's more common there.

As I was leaving Cologne, I felt that the honeymoon phase was over. I felt insecure at the Cologne train station, the same as I had the day before in Düsseldorf. Now I saw all of the security police that hadn't been there two and a half years ago. At least not so many. And how is it that clean-freak Germans allow their train stations to get so filthy? I had to think of the spotless station in Dunedin. In New Zealand, I couldn't imagine seeing any of this dirt, the stench of urine and other bodily excretions, or the many homeless. I couldn't remember seeing this kind of scene, whether inside train stations or anywhere else. Dog owners always pick up the droppings in a bag and throw them in the next rubbish bin. You can safely walk around barefoot in New Zealand.

Unfortunately, my arrival at Frankfurt Main station did nothing to raise my mood. I was unhappy with myself because my spirits were at a low point. People everywhere, everyone thinking they had the right of way, running around cutting people off, rolling suitcases over toes just to get somewhere a few seconds faster.

In the evening, I looked out of the window over the trees to the skyscrapers towering above the busy streets full of cars, blinking traffic lights and neon signs. I watched the aeroplanes take off and land. I heard the fireworks they were letting off for the *Museums-uferfest*, a summer party sponsored by the museums along the

banks of the Main river. I missed the ocean view from my house. I was homesick for New Zealand. I thought about trying to get projects in Hawaii or Sydney or someplace other than Germany next time. Kaitiaki pulled me back to the present, reminding me that everything will happen when it is the right time; when it is meant to be. So this was the last weekend of the German leg of my European trip. I was looking forward to what I had planned for Southern Europe.

# My old love – Tuscany

A visit to my good friend Renata always reminds me of the time I worked at a French Club Med in Tuscany and another time when I lived in Milan in a shared flat with my friend Corny. In Tuscany, I was a GO, a *gentile organisateur*. I guess that would translate to holiday entertainment guide, at least that's what people thought. Friends and family were worried that I would ruin my career with this job, whatever career meant to people.

Anybody who works for Club Med is a GO, whether you are in administration, a cook in the club restaurant or a salesperson in a club boutique. The single entertainer at this club was a guy whose job literally was to be the clown.

I worked in the currency exchange office. There was no Euro yet. The Italian lira had many zeros. My boss told us to just round the thousands off and put the difference in the staff piggy bank. Only once did a German lady insist on the exact change.

Besides this job, I was the complaint and comment box for Germans who were dissatisfied with something. Of course, 'something' happened every day. My job was to deal with the letters forwarded to me from the German office in which my compatriots complained about all kinds of things, hoping to get a partial refund for their discomfort. Believe it or not, I was familiar with every single one of the letter writers from their stay at the Club and so was able to react appropriately. One morning, I was the first in the administration hut. I pulled out a fax from the machine with a request for a specific Polynesian hut. The fax had been sent just before the guest started his long overnight drive to get to Tuscany, obviously expecting that no one would read his request in time and just as obviously hoping for a reason to complain and get a refund. He was a guest twice a year, so he was quite familiar with our office hours and how things worked there. We were familiar with him too. It was a Saturday. New guests were arriving and my colleagues were busy over in the reception area that moved quite a distance away from where it was during non-arrival days. There were no mobile phones in those days, so I sprinted through the pine trees and informed my colleagues of the fax. Imagine his face when he got the key to his favourite hut!

Dinner was at 7 pm, and every evening the Germans charged into the restaurant to make sure they were first at the buffet, piling their plates high. The Italians enjoyed a leisurely aperitif at the bar before going in for dinner.

I had met Renata years ago on a flight from Pisa to London. Her family has a home improvement store in Aulla in the Lunigiana region.[87] The store is very popular with the British and Germans who own holiday houses in Tuscany. Renata had taken some leave from the store and booked an English course in London. After landing, I helped her choose the best Tube ticket to her accommodation. This was the start of a life-long friendship.

As it turned out, Renata often meets people who turn into friends in aeroplanes. Years later, we flew to Brazil together. Perhaps you remember the back and forth about booking a flight and Renata's worry that something could come up? (please refer to the section *Social events – and what they have to do with dependability* on page 77 ) Well, on the flight to Fortaleza in Brazil, we met Luca. Luca is now Renata's partner and the father of her child, whom I would see for the first time.

On the day of my departure, it was chaotic at Frankfurt Airport.[88] There were endless queues everywhere, since everybody had to check in again. Apparently, a woman had somehow entered a security area thinking she had already passed through the checkpoint. But she hadn't. A discussion ensued in the press on whether the security guard had overdone it or not. His swift reaction to the situation had caused dozens of flights to be cancelled or delayed and the airport to slow down to a crawl. My flight to Italy wasn't until the afternoon, so it was no problem for me.

En route to Italy, things seemed to slow down and waiting times increased. In Vienna, where I had to change planes, the Austrian flight attendant announced the onward flight in a decidedly relaxed manner. After landing in Bologna, the stairs were wheeled up in slow motion and the crew took its sweet time opening the doors and letting us out. They had to have a good chat with their ground crew colleagues first. Everybody was in my way it seemed, or, rather, I was in too much of a

German rush. I had to remind myself to take a deep breath and readjust to a Southern European pace. The bags took forever to appear. The staff took their time until they finally showed up at the car rental counter.I had definitely arrived outside the zone of German efficiency and punctuality. Once I reset my inner sensor, I was able to relax and enjoy watching things happening around me.

Driving away from Bologna airport in my rental, I was overwhelmed by the number of police officers and vehicles flashing their lights everywhere. To this day, I have no idea what was going on. The more my rose-tinted honeymoon glasses faded, the stronger my impression of heightened security and police presence in general became.

The pace picked up considerably in the only setting it ever would in Italy: on the highway. I felt I had totally lost my driving skills in New Zealand. Years ago as a student, an Italian riding with me in my overstuffed Fiat Panda in Milan asked me if I had got my driver's licence in Italy. I took this as a compliment. Italians drive fast though carefully, reacting to traffic with lightning speed. They have a lead foot similar to Germans, except for those elderly German couples driving Opel cars with bobble-head dachshunds and toilet paper rolls in crocheted slipcovers decorating the back window.
My New Zealand tendency to max out at 100km/hr was taken over by a taste for speed. The snail started zipping around in traffic like an arrow. Kaitiaki was a little panicked at first. 'Are you suicidal?' he squawked, seeing how the cars were manoeuvring around each other. However, once he found his retro aviator glasses and put them on, he settled down on the headrest and leaned into the turns, thoroughly enjoying himself.

At Renata's, there was one family specialty served after the other, featuring the best of Italy: *Testaroli with pesto à la mama* and all kinds of other pasta dishes, hams, the world, tiramisu and espresso, which is simply called *caffè* in Italy, with sambuca instead of sugar. In the evening, we had a specialty flatbread called *panigacci di Podenzana*, which is named after the village. Time

flew by. A leisurely walk with Renata and the baby through Lerici in the evening, a day trip to Cinque Terre with Renata's brother, Simone, on his Vespa, and my obligatory visit to hairstylist Franco Corotti, who ended up in Aulla by way of New York, Rio and Tokyo, or so. He taught all of the region's hairdressers. You should know that cutting hair in Italy is not just a tradecraft. It's an art.

So is crossing the street in Italy, as I remembered on the way to Franco's salon. Since I had supposedly learned to drive in Italy, if you recall, I still had trouble remembering to stop at the **zebra pedestrian crossings** in Germany and New Zealand. In Italy, it is pointless for pedestrians to wait at the pedestrian crossing for a car to stop. You have to carefully weave your way across, much like in Asia. In New Zealand, drivers somehow sense a pedestrian a good 100 metres before reaching the pedestrian crossing and screech to a stop just in time. This is very distressing for all visitor drivers who might be following close behind.

On our outings, my Italian friends were in constant mobile phone contact with friends and relatives, checking on who was where, doing what – and would plans be changing?

I used the time to chat in Italian, French, English and German with people from all over the world sitting at neighbouring tables, at scenic points and while sunbathing. Simone made fun of me, telling his partner on the phone that I chatted up everybody in every language. And if there was no one else around, then I spoke to *la tavola*, the table. Kaitiaki snorted. 'In Tavolese, of course.'

More and more refugees were coming to tiny Aulla. I couldn't remember having so many people beg money from me. So, this was a topic that not only Germany worried about. Discussions turned heated; everyone had an opinion, gleaned from different sources and polarised media reports. No one really knew what was going on. I mentioned earlier in this book that people from all over the world ask me about how **German history was taught in school** and what we thought of it ourselves. To understand how the Third

Reich happened – and it wasn't the only dictatorship that the world has seen, even since then – I highly recommend a book entitled *The Wave* by Morton Rhue.[89] We read and analysed this at school in English class, comparing the story to what had actually occurred and why it could easily happen again. I think the book is just as topical now as it ever was. It is a true story about what happens over one week in an American high school when a class begins re-enacting the rise of the Third Reich as a teacher-led project. Strong stuff.

Just before leaving for Italy, I had rebooked my flights via Nicaragua back to New Zealand for an earlier departure date, since I wanted to get home sooner. Sure enough, I received a call from a client in Bonn, Germany, that they would like me to work for them until October. At the same time, I was negotiating a contract through an agency for work in New Zealand. What can I say?

My communications with my chosen home were easier, friendlier and quicker, with a can-do attitude instead of making everything seem problematic. Just phoning New Zealand made me feel liberated and freed from a web of rules and regulations. As if the fish was finally swimming ahead with the current to its favourite pool. I didn't want to turn around again.

## Close to a former study home – Nice, France

The crowning weekend of my trip in Europe was a visit to my friend Sebastian in Southern France. He is originally from a neighbouring village in the Palatinate. We hadn't seen each other for 25 years. As children we played outdoors with others from the villages every afternoon. When Sebastian graduated from university, he moved to Nice for a job and has stayed there ever since. He feels very much at home there. The flight to Nice was from Frankfurt. You can say what you want about the French, but one thing is true: they smell nice. The captain finished his welcome on board the flight to Marseille by encouraging all of us passengers to take the time to chat with our seat neighbours. I happily looked to mine and saw that he was juggling three mobile phones while copiously texting with someone called 'My Love'. Sigh. So I returned to reading the paper and sniffed at all of the lovely scents floating around me. Kaitiaki wasn't used to this at all. He seemed a little high, and as he settled on my shoulder for a little nap, the captain assured us that we were indeed en route to Nice, not Marseille as he had mistakenly said earlier.

Sebastian and I recognised each other immediately. We both hadn't changed very much over the years. We wondered whether it was possible to know early on which lifestyle truly fits to you. How had it happened that the best friends from my childhood all lived somewhere other than where we grew up in the Palatinate? Only four years ago I had finally found my friend Felicitas in Cape Town, where she lived with her husband and children. Maybe we all had an extra live-abroad-gene and had recognised each other by a secret code.

Sebastian and I caught up with our life stories. He had also bought a house in France. Our parents couldn't just ignore this. His father came to check everything out and butted heads with French culture over building design and execution. It was the same with my dad and his dissection of New Zealand construction work. He threw up his hands in despair when he saw the building report. No central heating! No

double-glazing! Barely any insulation! Nothing to German standards... And why should it be? It's a house in New Zealand. Life is never dull when your children take up residence abroad. Our escapades keep them young, or so we'd like to think.

Sebastian introduced me to the **expat community** on the Côte d'Azur. One of his friends had a house with a pool where everybody's kids were welcome. It was amazing how differently they were growing up here compared to the kids I had seen in Germany. They did back flips into the water, their heads not two handbreadths from the edge of the pool. The host of the 'pool house' was from Berlin and was showing them how to do it. Then they dived in and climbed out again, over and over, just like we did as kids at the Rodenbach public forest swimming pool. We used to climb up the three-metre tower and jumped or dived, and then did it again and again, all afternoon. How else would we have learned to perfect our technique if we hadn't been allowed to make mistakes?

These kids are growing up bi- and tri-lingually. They mix up all of their languages in a single sentence and understand each other just fine. Their parents are from various cultures too. It is not unusual for each family member to have been born in a different country. The children I met here are very polite. They ask questions that demonstrate their broad horizons and understanding of how the world works. 'Do you speak New Zealandish?' they asked me. 'What does it sound like when New Zealanders talk? Do they play this game in New Zealand too? What kind of games do kids in New Zealand play?'

*Third Culture Kids*
I had a pool full of Third Culture Kids here, children who each had hearts attached to several places in the world and who have often grown up in completely different cultures to their parents. They have some very special talents, for example intercultural competence at an early age. They can quickly adjust to unfamiliar surroundings and unfamiliar people. They have the ability to make and maintain deep friendships in a short time. They also have difficulty answering questions about where they come from.[90]

Kaitiaki interjected. 'It is indeed not easy. Do you remember that you found that the students who had mixed backgrounds like that conceited? Third Culture Kids have fewer problems if they can stay among themselves. If they have to move to a place where most of their classmates have never left their village, they feel out of place. They feel they don't belong, even if rejection is hidden beneath the surface.'

Sebastian and I had both inherited a passion for outdoor activities. We went on a hike inland of the Côte d'Azur, to Brec d'Utelle. At lunchtime, we stopped to admire the mountains around us as we broke off pieces of baguette and ate them with slices of ham. In the evening, we met up with his girlfriend for supper. She was also a mix of several cultures. She was born in Ivory Coast and had Austrian-English parents.

We talked about German culture and how she felt that Germany was still in post-war mode. According to her, Germans are still getting up in the morning feeling obliged to rebuild a nation. Their diligence and earnestness leave no room for fun and the beautiful things in life. It might be true that younger generations are feeling less obliged, yet the description fits most of the population. Some regional exceptions are perhaps Berlin and the Palatinate.
The French have elegantly solved the issue of dirty public toilet seats, by the way. There are no toilet seats at all. Also, French hygiene standards in public toilets being what they are, perhaps you might want to think twice about going on holiday there. Another French peculiarity is definitely more inviting: you can't order less than half a litre of wine from a restaurant menu. However, the French haven't adopted the *Dubbeglas*s yet.

I felt the warmth of the Southern European sun on my skin and revelled in memories of my university days in Toulouse. I had gone on many adventures from there – to the Lot region, to Barcelona, to the Pyrenees for canyoning, or for weekends at the Atlantic coast or in the Mediterranean.

My first Christmas in Toulouse was warm enough to wear a T-shirt. I admired the city's passion for rugby – of course I didn't know anything about New Zealand and the All Blacks back then.

Nice is paradise for outdoor sports fans. You can go kite surfing, hiking, climbing, paragliding, kayaking, skiing, diving, sailing and canyoning. These attractions made me consider spending a working summer in Nice. Sebastian knew of shared accommodation in a coastal villa not far away. Kaitiaki squawked, 'Where else are you planning to work in the summer? It sounds like you are back to your old restless habits from before you came to New Zealand. I think it's time for both of us to get back. I want to go home.'

### Hello Germany – or, what is it like to return home after a long time abroad?

There is a joke that says the best couples are those who have split up. My European tour ends here. I knew I would return to New Zealand in a dual sense. It's become normal for me to find and talk with people who have travelled a great deal and have lived in other countries. Some people belong where they were born. Others are still searching. Some find their place in the world; some commute between several places. And some reintegrate into their original locale. A description of the third phase of the Reintegration Model by Hirsch follows.[91]

### *Common features of the third phase of reintegration*

The third phase of reintegration is often characterised by:
– adaptation to the changed circumstances.
– feelings of success, joy to have returned, familiarity and well-being.
– the feeling of having profited from the time abroad.
– a strengthened self-awareness.

Here are some stories of friends who have returned from one or several periods abroad and are happily living their lives in Germany.

*Susann, global wanderer in Belgium, Canada, USA and Singapore. She now lives in a small village in Saxony, Germany, and works as head of the Central and Eastern Europe section of the personnel department in a multi-national corporation. Her studies as an intercultural trainer are a great asset, as are her winning smile and welcoming demeanour that no coconut can resist. She tells her story:*
'I spent a total of three years abroad in Belgium, Canada, the United States and Singapore. It all started with my wish to work as an au-pair after I graduated from high school. It was a wonderful opportunity to see some of the world before I started university. I needed to know if I could stand on my own two feet. I was always interested in languages, so I was looking forward to everything that would come my way. I was an open book, completely unaware of what I was letting myself in for. I was an au-pair in Brussels, where I first began learning French. This year was unbelievably important groundwork for my next stops abroad. I saw such an open and culturally varied world, one that I had never experienced before. I was so

impressed with how different lives could be. It was liberating to be around people who shared a completely different perspective than me on things I had taken for granted. I could feel there was so much more out there than what I had known, and it burned.

Shortly after my return to Germany after my stay in Brussels, I realised I needed to go abroad again. It wasn't that I had a problem with coming back – I was happy to be home and I felt the time in Brussels was complete. Still, I was restless. I wanted to explore more of the world and to learn about different cultures and daily life in other places. I wanted to find out if there was some place that was a better fit for me. I soon realised that friends who hadn't gone abroad couldn't relate to my experience and didn't understand what I was looking for away from home. The thought of never being able to go abroad again frightened me. I feared stasis, narrowmindedness, falling into a rut I could never get out of.

That's why I spent the next years studying and working in Canada, the USA and Singapore. There was so much that I learned! Most importantly, I found myself. The most significant lesson of these years was that every culture provides opportunities for people to lead exciting and successful lives while continuously opening up new avenues to discover. In each of these countries I reached the point where the quotidian – the day-to-day – takes over and cultural curiosity shrinks into a smaller frame of reference. I saw that life elsewhere is not inherently more exciting because the culture or the people are different. We find the excitement within us, strange as that sounds. And it stays with you, wherever you go. Living abroad kindles that flame of curiosity because of all the strange new things you experience. But it is nevertheless a personal, internal thing you carry with you at all times. This was a crucial and wonderful discovery for me. It helped me overcome the restlessness that was wearing me down, because until then I never felt that I had actually arrived anywhere.

'My friends often tease me about how a global wanderer, such as I was, could now live in a small village in rural Germany. Admittedly, I would never have guessed it either. My neighbours and colleagues are so wonderful. And I have all of my memories to remind me to keep my curiosity burning. Life in the smallest village isn't restrictive at all, if you live it your way: make it as exciting as possible and as boring as necessary. The best part is, it makes me very happy.'

*Katrin, global wanderer in Sweden and Canada, married a Peruvian and now lives in Cologne with three children. Katrin and I met at our train-the-trainer for intercultural competence course, and I was impressed with her keen ability to see things from different angles. She tells her story:*

'I knew for a long time that I wanted to live abroad. I wished for it during my school years, but that wasn't possible. After graduating from high school, I left for Sweden, where I had the opportunity to volunteer in a European social service programme. I enjoyed every moment of it. It was the time between school and university where you are not yet tied down and everything seems possible. A feeling of freedom. Some might never find the freedom to try to succeed in an unknown place and in a job that very possibly will never have anything to do with your later ambitions in life. For me, it was wonderful.

'When I returned to Germany, I fell down a hole. I couldn't imagine staying here. Everything seemed so tight and narrow, so ordinary. I pined for the wide spaces of Scandinavia. My circle of friends hadn't changed, and I thought I hadn't changed much, yet I felt different.

'My experiences in Sweden had impressed me greatly. My first culture shock and living in a strange culture that I eventually began to understand... These were topics that interested me deeply and I wanted to learn more about. So, I chose to study intercultural communication at university. At first, I was not really happy with the first few semesters or with my life in Germany. When I started planning my semester abroad in Québec, Canada, the tangible perspective of leaving Germany made it easier to stay until it was time. My courses got more interesting as well.

'My time in Québec was even more enjoyable than Sweden. Perhaps I had a better idea of what to expect, cross-culturally speaking? Perhaps because it was university life, meeting people and making friends was much easier than during my volunteering in Sweden. I seriously contemplated staying in Canada to finish my degree. In the end, I returned to Germany. At least for a while, as I told myself.

'As it turned out, I was able to go on several internships abroad, among them to Paris for a stint at the Swedish Cultural Institute. I also met my future husband at university. He is Peruvian. This was a bit strange at first. While I had often thought that I would end up with a partner from another culture, South America had never been on my list of places I found

interesting. Through him all of that changed.

'We live in a suburb of Cologne with our three children. We have been fortunate enough to be able to regularly spend several months at a time in Peru so that I have been able to calm my restlessness. We are settled here in our little community near Cologne. We are growing roots and expanding our network of friends. My family is nearby, an aspect that has growing importance for me.

'The most significant thing I learned from my time abroad is how German I actually am, and that I like Germany much more than I expected. We have so much to be grateful for: a working social system, regulations that serve all of us, security and seasons – all things I missed in the other countries I have been to. I appreciate all of these much more now.'

*Anke, a retired kite surfer and former colleague who stopped at my beach house in Wellington with her husband, Nils, on their world tour. They shared my first Christmas in New Zealand with me, a BBQ, and the best view in the world. Anke and Nils are global wanderers with strong roots in Hamburg. A day with them is like a day at a spa – chats between likeminded friends. Anke says about her experience:*

'That there would be changes when I returned to my life in Germany after our six-month sabbatical was clear to me. I only found out exactly how things would feel different when we got back, in February 2015. On our world tour, I found I was missing my friends, even though my husband was with me. I am a person who needs my social network. Thanks to modern technology I could connect with family and friends when I got badly homesick.

'I saw eight countries and soaked up the different cultures and landscapes. I met locals and other world travellers. I have never since experienced positive energy as intensely. Back in Germany, I had to get accustomed again to the long queues in the supermarkets, the hectic activity everywhere, the complexity of life arranged according to your appointment diary. On my sabbatical, I learned how to sharpen my senses and experience things more intensively, like cloud formations, colours and landscapes. I am very grateful for that.'

# En route to New Zealand – Nicaragua

Managua. My departure date arrived as suddenly as Christmas seems to every year. As soon as we were airborne, I realised I had forgotten to pack a *Bunte* and a *Gala*, two favourite German gossip magazines for long haul flights. I managed to survive the flight without them.

The plane arrived late at night in Managua, so I had pre-booked a hotel and shuttle. We drove through dark, unlit streets. Where was the driver taking me? Did I get into the wrong vehicle? I secretly fixed him with the evil eye we Germans learn almost as soon as we are out of nappies. I thought this was the perfect time to deploy this weapon, though I took care not to anger the driver. Of course, I would give him my best, most charming smile as soon as I felt a little safer. The drive dragged on and on. I survived this too.

In the morning, my accommodation looked much friendlier, with a few tropical plants decorating the grounds. I had purposely escaped the capital because I wanted to explore the countryside.

Granada is situated directly on the shore of Lake Nicaragua and is a popular starting point for various outings. I took the 'chicken bus' to Granada, checking every few minutes to see if my luggage was still there.

The people seemed friendly and the fares were the same for locals and tourists. At least that was different from Cuba, land of the parallel world of the tourist, though in this bus, the other passengers weren't going to give up free seats next to them easily. They placed their bags there just as cheekily as people do in Germany. In New Zealand I was used to keeping my shopping bags on my lap or squeezed between my legs so that others could sit down without asking me to move my stuff.

The hostel in Granada had lockers in the dorms. The staff were very nice. I was starting to feel at ease and decided to trust my surroundings. I spent the rest of the day looking around, checking out the prices and offers of various tour operators. Unfortunately, I wasn't able to book whatever I wanted, because the tours all had minimum participant requirements. Very few tourists came here

in the rainy season. It was the lowest of the low season. As I started walking back to my hostel, the only tour operator I hadn't spoken to ran after me, offering me a special price for a seat on the evening bus tour to Masaya Volcano. This was the one I was most interested in because the lava glow is much more fascinating in the dark. So, of course I accepted.

A fellow German in the bus was visibly nervous. Rain had prevented the tour three times already. It still looked good; the day had been sunny and dry. We passed the gate, and everyone sighed in relief. Then suddenly the line of vehicles stopped. We held our breath. It started to pour. Our hopes sank, and finally the announcement came: we were turning around, the tour was cancelled.

Back in the office of the tour operator, we brainstormed and were offered several options. An American woman who lived in Panama, two Germans and I decided to take the tour in the morning. To sweeten the deal, we were given an extra, free bottle of water, some fruit and the promise to visit the Masaya Market. This was supposedly the best place to buy Nica gifts. The Nicaraguans give the nickname *Nica* to anything that represents their country. Coke and rum is called Nica Libre, not Cuba Libre. Makes total sense, especially since it is mixed with Nicaraguan Flor de Caña, not Cuban rum.

The tour was as good as advertised. We were able to see the lava flows from the 1772 eruption down into Masaya Lake. The road cut through it. Lava boiled dangerously in the caldera while clouds of sulphur puffed into the air. Green parrots live in the caldera walls; their flight above the glowing red makes a striking contrast of colours. Our guide told us about the fauna around the crater and how armadillos are considered a fine Nica delicacy. I asked where we could try one and got a horrified look from the two other Germans! We learned about the different kinds of volcanoes. An effusive, or shield volcano, such as Masaya, features relatively gentle eruptions and slow-moving lava flows. The dangerous volcanoes are the ejective, or explosive, kinds. Some volcanoes can be both.

Back in Granada, a boy tried to give the two Germans on my tour

something handmade as a 'gift', hoping for a few dollars in exchange. The woman jumped to the side, apologising to us. 'Sorry, I don't like it when they come too close.' Kaitiaki mumbled under his breath, 'Of course not. You are a German.'

## Personal Space

Kaitiaki often sat on my shoulder now. He now felt comfortable getting close. Cultures have different sensibilities regarding personal space and the distance people keep between each other. Edward Hall considered this aspect one of the most significant factors in cross-cultural misunderstandings. They are part of the unconscious 'silent language' that influences our behaviour and manners.[92]

When my Italian friend, Renata and I were in Brazil together, chatting and strolling around in the dusty lanes of the villages we visited, I noticed how we started on the right side of the road and soon ended up on the left side. I would then trade places with her and soon the same thing would happen again, from left to right this time. And so on. What was going on? Even though Renata was one of my very best friends, it irritated me that she kept closing in. She unconsciously invaded my personal space, which is clearly wider than hers. As I moved away to correct this, she moved closer to compensate.

Everyone has a culturally defined circle of personal space, which we wish to keep inviolate. If someone comes too close, we feel uncomfortable and hassled. People in some cultures seek closer proximity to each other, like Italians. Others, like the Germans, feel more comfortable at a certain distance from each other. New Zealanders tend to need even more of a bubble around them.

We all went to dinner together after the volcano tour. Not everyone in the party had visited New Zealand, citing the usual reason: too far away. My own opinion on the matter was immediately shot down with a lecture on the enormous carbon footprint the flights generated. I wondered if th had swum to Nicaragua from Europe.

Three of us planned to visit the island of Ometepe next. The travel guidebook said that we would have to book a shuttle service through

accommodation in Ometepe, since taxis were very expensive. I didn't like this idea, because I prefer to be spontaneous. Rather unwillingly, I emailed a guest house, and while they gave me answers to all sorts of questions I didn't have, they pointedly ignored the one about a shuttle. I took this – difficult for Germans to decode – silence to mean that I should take a taxi. What a relief! No fixed schedule, just go and see what comes next along the way.

The two other Germans asked me about my plans. I told them I had none and would just take off in the morning. They were sceptical and tried to call the same guest house. To no avail – the connection broke and the reception at our hostel in Granada couldn't help them either. They gave up and made a new plan: not to have a plan. Kaitiaki shook with laughter, crowing, 'You Germans. Even on holiday you plan to not have a plan.'

## Efficiency, planning and organisation – or the German 3 Ps: planning, preparation and process

Kaitiaki turned on his harmonious voice. 'As strengths, they are also challenging for you Germans,' he said. 'Once you start analysing, planning, organising and thinking, it might happen that you only see results later when the planning phase is over. For New Zealanders who have never worked with Germans, it could look like all you do is analyse and plan and never get to work.' Kaitiaki is right when he says that this methodical decision-making process seems very slow and obscure to non-Germans.[93] At these times, he often pecks me in the behind, and says, 'What are you still thinking about? Get on with it!' We Germans like to stick to the 'do it once and do it well' principle. Decisions are made when we have seen all of the facts and pertinent information. We want to feel we can make a sound decision that will stand the test of time.[94] The other factor is the cultural standard of time orientation,[95] which has been discussed in the section of the *The perception of time – back and forward to the past*, on page 82.

New Zealanders are conscientious and diligent; they work hard and a lot, starting projects with great zeal. Urban planning projects are adapted to the current situation, for example. Of course, in comparison, you could say that people in every culture are passionate about their work. Kaitiaki

interjected. 'Yet you often think that New Zealanders like to look busy, whether there is actually something to do or not – from your German perspective of course.'

We Germans are unhappy when things go wrong or get delayed, especially when we are not immediately informed about the situation. We feel left behind on the opportunity to adjust the plan.

Kaitiaki remembered the analogy my Italian friend used: 'Germans plan first. They are aware of any hurdle that might come up in the next ten years. Italians just start running. From a German perspective, New Zealanders are closer to the Italian way of thinking, though they spend less energy debating and waving their arms about. The analogy fits fairly well. At the same time, New Zealanders are work horses, like the Germans.'

However, generalisations are not always applicable. Examples where German planning has gone spectacularly wrong are the Hamburg Elbphilharmonie building, the Stuttgart 21 railway and urban development project and the new airport in Berlin; these three large-scale, partly publicly funded projects have gone many, many years longer than planned and massively over budget. It also depends on the eyes of the beholder. There are no doubt people in many countries who view much of the world as very organised and efficient – compared to their own – and might not even notice the nuances in behaviour I have just described.

'In New Zealand, you recognise quickly if you are expected to "just get on with it". You have two options: comply and act busy, even if you are still thinking and planning, or, you can try to convince your New Zealand colleagues to do it the German way. Be careful! Germans do have the reputation for confidently presuming they have the only viable solution.'

Kaitiaki had really warmed up to this topic and continued with a stern air. 'If you don't mind me saying so, you Germans are never shy about telling someone what is "right". I will admit that you are not bad at many things – please excuse the understatement. But if you self-confidently list your accomplishments and tout your expertise in New Zealand, you will very likely crash head first into a wall. A bit of understatement is more effective. Listen to what the others have to say and why. Ask more questions. You can carefully weigh in and list contingencies if you disguise them as suggestions. Don't be the elephant in the china shop. You Germans are very good at that.'

Kaitiaki had even more to say: 'Germans are champions at planning and organisation. In an international comparison, it is a skill that seems to come naturally, and you are admired very much for it. That is why you need not explicitly mention these in a job application. You are a German,

enough said. However, reality is very often different from what you expect. You are a guest in New Zealand. Show your skills in clever doses. A Māori saying goes like this: *Ka mate kāinga tahi, ka ora kāinga rua*. There is more than one way to achieve an objective.'

You might be asking yourself why you shouldn't live up to your true potential, no matter where you are. I agree with you, and I crack my head on it every day. It's a part of living and working abroad – and it will more than likely never end.

Kaitiaki was still not finished. 'One of the main reasons people give for emigrating from Germany or England is to get away from the pressure at work. If you import your methods, are you not ruining what you came here for? Perhaps you could embrace "shbireitmeit" more often.'

Friedemann Schulz von Thun's Value and Development Square[96] demonstrates this shift in perspective with the example of thriftiness and stinginess. Thriftiness is a positive attribute; stinginess is not. You need a bit of generosity to balance stinginess, and a bit of thriftiness to avoid extravagance, always depending on your point of view. Resolute Germans could adopt some New Zealand equanimity. Otherwise they appear hectic and career-crazed, while the German is convinced that their New

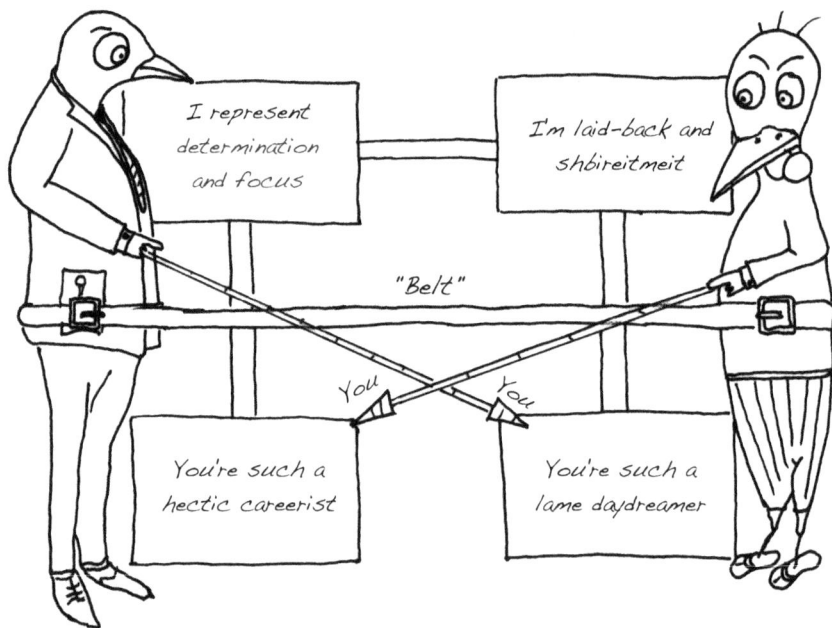

I represent determination and focus

I'm laid-back and shbireitmeit

"Belt"

You

You

You're such a hectic careerist

You're such a lame daydreamer

Zealand counterpart is a lethargic daydreamer and completely inefficient. The Value Square is an excellent tool for finding solutions in international teams. Identifying team members' strengths, the positive attributes, by reframing perceived weaknesses can help distribution of tasks to the most capable people.

After more than two years in New Zealand, I am less of a schedule fanatic than before. Even before I emigrated, I noticed that I felt overwhelmed by my mother's questions as to my plans for the second Tuesday after my arrival, or the following Wednesday. She had ideas that I was supposed to agree on – now. I reluctantly responded with, 'Great ideas. Can I please decide that on Tuesday and Wednesday morning? I have no idea what I will feel like doing in three weeks.'

Since I came to New Zealand, I have no personal calendar. I don't know why, really, but I've been managing just fine without. For me, this randomness is a large part of the feeling of freedom I have gained by moving here. I follow my flatmate's example of checking my mailbox only once a week. There is less bureaucracy, hence less paper mail. Houses don't have name plates and doorbells and everything still works fine.

In the evening I got a message with the news that New Zealand's volcanic White Island was highly active.[97] You might recall mention of White Island from the cross-cultural content at the beginning of this book. This volcano is the explosive type.

Isla de Ometepe. In the morning, I decided to walk to the chicken bus station for the bus to the Ometepe ferry in order to save some money.

I couldn't find it and stopped a taxi. We agreed on a good price. The taxi driver merely drove 20 metres around the corner to the station. Grrr. Of course, I was there much earlier than the two others joining me on this trip. As I waited for them, I discovered that it was a national holiday and the buses were not running. The three of us shared a taxi to the ferry, thinking we would still easily make the early one. Wrong. The gangway was up two minutes before departure, so we couldn't get on. So much for German punctuality.

On the next ferry, I sat down next to a young girl. Her arm nestled up to

mine on the armrest. When I moved my arm, hers moved in the same direction. I tried again, and there was her arm, as if it was glued to mine. Sigh. I got up and recaptured my personal space by sitting somewhere else.

The view of the volcanoes Concepción and Maderas was spectacular from the ferry. They are both active, and together they form an island in the middle of the enormous freshwater Lake Nicaragua. The three of us booked a guide for a hike up the 1,394-metre-high Maderas the next morning. The guide led us through impressive terrain and identified local fruits for us.

A bit higher than halfway, we hiked through a storybook forest of mossy trees. They reminded me of some tracks I knew in New Zealand, like the one through the Tararua Forest and around Lake Waikaremoana, which is one of the **Great Walks**[98] – the most famous trails in New Zealand. Further along we met a family with a little boy. His father told us that his son adored the volcano and insisted on hiking up twice a week. I thought he could just as well be a little New Zealander. **Outdoor activities** are a part of the **school curriculum**; dragon boat paddling, climbing, trekking, kayaking, mountain biking or skiing are all integrated into the educational system in New Zealand.[99]
The hike was quite an undertaking. At some point I gave up trying to keep my boots clean and tramped through the mud like any New Zealander would do. Soon I was muddy all over, as if I'd just finished a track in my favourite country.

One of the others quickly pushed on ahead, and I noted that all of the good food I had eaten in Europe was slowing me down. I wished I was more fit, though I was in the middle rank; the other of my two companions lagged behind.

When the fast one remarked on our slower pace, I retorted that that wasn't nice. She did apologise, I'll give her that. In my head I heard the encouraging voices of New Zealanders who would have said something like, 'It's not so far now, my dear. You can do it.' There was

actually no reason for her to say anything at all. We weren't tired, only slower. Why do Germans have to be so painfully outspoken? My intercultural trainer, an American living in Germany, once said that she was hurt like this every day and kept her spirits up by reminding herself that 'they don't mean it like that'. It did hurt! I wasn't used to this behaviour anymore.

In the evening I escaped them for dinner at the Margarita, a restaurant that appeared to be the locals' living room. I felt better right away. The evening before I had met a resident American who introduced me to some Nicas. In the course of the next few days, I was introduced to some of the village's secrets. Kaitiaki listened closely too. The construction of what was now our guesthouse, Hacienda Mérida, was commissioned by Somoza, the former dictator. It was one of the most important farms of the influential Somoza dynasty, which governed with an iron fist and amassed considerable wealth in the process. The hacienda now belongs to an Argentinian, whose brother supposedly murdered Somoza in Asunción, Paraguay, in 1980 before he built the farm; the Greek restaurant wasn't really one, but was supposedly a front for drug dealing. There was a German from Hamburg who immigrated here at the tender age of 18. He travelled a great deal and garnered considerable respect from the villagers because he often had two women living with him at the same time. Whether the gossip is true or not is irrelevant. While travelling, you hear an interesting story and you listen.
This is how I came to know about La Omaja guesthouse, featuring the only infinity pool of Ometepe, where a few locals and I dined in the restaurant.
On our last evening, my new American friend invited us to his home for a glass of wine. His roof terrace overlooked the breathtaking panorama of Lake Nicaragua and the volcanoes. Directly before us was the – still imaginary – waterway that was going to become an alternative to the Panama Canal, backed by the Chinese and newly interested Iranian investors. Our friend would be able to see the ships passing from his house. The project plan

includes cutting a swath through the jungle, resettlement of the affected population and dredging up sand from the lake bottom to make a few new islands. It has many supporters but also much opposition. My German companions were also critical of the plan.

## Environmental awareness

Conservationism is an important German cultural value, which it has in common with New Zealand. Environmental topics are nevertheless controversial and often divisive. The German expat community likes to complain that New Zealand's rubbish sorting and recycling efforts are not good enough. In Germany, towns and counties are responsible for organising waste removal and recycling schemes, so there are differences from region to region. Paper is separated out everywhere, but not every town has the famous yellow sack for collecting plastics and cans for recycling. Kaitiaki described the other side of the coin: 'German fussiness concerning rubbish sorting makes New Zealanders living in Germany shake their heads in wonder.'

When I remarked that New Zealanders have no worries about using weed killer, Kaitiaki countered this by saying, 'Environmental awareness is a big issue in my country. Many New Zealanders are conservationists who live as sustainably as possible and passionately argue their views on the subject. They are proud of their land and want to preserve its natural bounty. The Māori people believe that nature is of equal importance to humans. New Zealand was the first country in the world to award a national park, Te Urewera, full citizenship rights with the Te Urewera Act of 2014. The Whanganui River has the same.'[100]

By the way, in the language of some Māori tribes, the letter combination wh is pronounced f, so that Whangarei becomes Fangarei, and Whanganui is pronounced Fanganui by the locals.

New Zealand's dairy industry is routinely the target of protesting conservationists who criticise the amounts of manure that is slurried into the country's rivers. Kaitiaki added: 'New Zealand is nuclear free. It came as a huge shock to the United States when, in 1990, New Zealand prohibited nuclear-powered ships and submarines in its waters.[101] The Department of Conservation (DOC) is a present and successful organisation.'

Environmental awareness is one of the German values I have consciously upheld abroad. It is something we can be very proud of, especially as it is integral to our education.

The discussion on the new waterway through Nicaragua reminded me of the ever-lasting debate on the extension of the runway at Wellington Airport. The runway is adjacent to the surfing beach Lyall Bay where I live. The upgrade would allow bigger planes to land. It would benefit tourism and the economy while destroying a great deal of pristine landscape. It is seen as a potentially disastrous situation for the underwater world in Lyall Bay, as it might affect the wave action of the tides. Critical voices are water sports enthusiasts and organisations like the Surfbreak Protection Society or the Wellington Boardriders Club.

On this last evening, after discussing the future Nicaraguan Canal, we descended to dinner at the Margarita. We danced until past daybreak with the locals. The two other Germans weren't killjoys, at least, even though they often sat there with pressed lips and a serious expression as they commented on things. I started liking them after all. They weren't purposefully mean. We ordered one *más* beer, which is not a litre of brew, as a German would understand it, but simply means 'one more beer'. As we drank, we pondered why the otherwise precise Germans would host Munich's Oktoberfest in September. We decided that the arrangement was at least extra punctual and thus in keeping with German habits in general.

San Juan del Sur. I met my new American friend's brother in San Juan del Sur. He had married a Nica there. Her claim to fame was landing in a palm tree during a tsunami. Who else could say the same? So, in this surfer's paradise I was invited to a wonderfully local dinner at their farm outside of town. The other guests were close friends and family. A true highlight for me. He had built most of his house himself using a machine called CINVA-Ram, which compresses blocks of earth into very strong bricks. I was also told that you can build your house anywhere you want to in Nicaragua.

If no one claims that land within ten years, it becomes yours.
I spent most of my time practising my surfing technique. Playa Hermosa is a beautiful, wide beach.

There were some New Zealanders there. I enjoyed listening to their banter again. How I had missed that accent! We casually chatted about surfing and possible common acquaintances; we parted ways just as easily, as I had only just worked my way under their peach fuzz. It takes a few more chance meetings over a longer period to get closer to that peach stone.

In the afternoon, there was a sudden downpour while the sun still shone brightly. A mystical experience. The rain was warm, something that is very rare in New Zealand. I didn't need to put on anything over my bikini. I enjoyed the rain very much.

The next day, new experiences awaited at Playa Remanso, a popular surfing beach, just south of San Juan del Sur. I saw a few non-German guys drape their towels over some sun loungers. When a Jeep-load of young tourists arrived, I did the same, hoping no one would notice that I was German.

I was hungry and went off for a bit of lunch. Upon returning, I saw that the other towels had disappeared with their owners, while an English girl had sat down on mine. I felt my private space had been invaded. A little later when I retrieved my towel, the girl apologised profusely, explaining that she had thought the guys had forgotten it.
Then there was the 'shark attack'. After a surfing session, I rode a wave to shore. I like to call this 'taking a wave taxi'. I came out of the water, dripping blood from scraping a rock. It wasn't bad but it looked awful. So I made fun of myself by joking around that I was attacked. There are sharks even in the remotest waters of the world.

Once I hiked on Steward Island – the third island of New Zealand, south of South Island – and spent the night in a DOC hut. There were a

bunch of guest books and pamphlets on the table and among them one about protecting sharks. Were they making fun of me out here in the middle of the forest? The closest body of water was the water tank. It did rain a lot... but sharks? No, the reason was simple: the waters around Stewart Island have a significant population of great whites.[102] Surprisingly, though, few sharks attack around New Zealand (though there was one not long ago at Muriwai Beach, north of Auckland). That night on Stewart Island I wasn't bothered by sharks, but I did have a surprise companion.

A New Zealander showed up in the early evening. We collected wood for the fire. He generously shared his feijoa tea, his food and his knowledge of New Zealand with me. He even gave me a short massage for dessert and soon peeled off to bed in his own bunk. I heard from him once more and then never again, as is often the case with travelling contacts. Perhaps I will run into him again in a different DOC hut.

In the evening of the 'shark attack' in Nicaragua, I received a message from my former English colleague in New Zealand, who had finally given up looking for a job in Berlin. He had quit one after a week because the Agile project management method that the employer said was implemented hadn't been after all. I had to smile. Changes in Germany take time. The country banks on stability and has done very well with that approach. My friend's greatest wish had been for a job in Berlin.

Now he was looking for one in England, not least because of the high taxes and other levies in Germany. He was not really interested in the social benefits that mean so much to average Germans, and traded the shock-proof health care system for free choice of what he could do with an ungarnished salary. There is a price for everything, and to each his own. Whether he would survive in the other system was the question. I assume it is possible to survive outside of the German system, even if it's not gold plated. When I emigrated, some people said I was making a mistake, especially those who knew 'everything from experience', although they had never left home.

## Tradition and change

Kaitiaki whistled at me, reproachfully shaking his head. 'You are contradicting yourself. On the one hand you welcome change, and on the other you wish that cultures would hold onto traditions and remain true to themselves.' he said. He was right in that change – and the willingness to embrace it – is important to me. I feel most comfortable in an environment full of possibility and few restrictions, but one that also values tradition.

Changes take place everywhere in the world. We can't look at developments in New Zealand from only one angle. Even though it is a thoroughly open society, tradition is highly valued, particularly if we look at the influence Māori culture has regained in business practices in many companies and organisations. I personally believe that change is more easily implemented in New Zealand than in Germany, precisely because of how New Zealanders recognise and embrace traditions in both private and business life. At the same time, the pioneer spirit of 'giving it a go' is deeply ingrained in the New Zealand psyche.[103]

I myself have greatly benefited from the opportunities offered to me in New Zealand. New ideas and approaches are encouraged rather than blocked because of too many perceived obstacles or because it seems too risky. Over the last 20 years of my travelling and business life, I have managed to expel 'Can you even do that?' from my vocabulary. 'Why not?' fits much better into my new lifestyle. Most significantly, I have been successful in generating genuine interest in (cross-)cultural training for IT projects in New Zealand, especially for Agile schemes. In Germany, there has been some interest, though no understanding, for intercultural topics.

A traditional, non-Agile IT project unfolds pretty much like this (simplified):

1. The requirements for a system, a website or software are analysed, collected and documented. This is done by business analysts, who interview the future client, customer or user.
2. Developers program these requirements into the system, website or software.
3. Testers test whether the requirements have been met and whether the system, website or software works as intended.

How often have I seen that the requirements themselves have been incorrectly diagnosed and documented? How often has the developer

misinterpreted the specifications and programmed incorrect solutions? How often has it occurred that the testers 'test' for the stipulated requirements without questioning them? A cascade of errors. Two professionals talk about what they believe is the same thing – even using the same vocabulary – and each hears something completely different. Posing the right questions is crucial – not only for IT projects. As in cross-cultural communications, if you don't understand why your negotiating partner appears impolite and distanced, interrupts constantly, isn't listening... We usually hear and see what we know or want to hear or see. Remember the allegory of the natives who only noticed the tall ship when it was right in front of their noses because they had never seen such a thing before? In Germany, nobody understood intercultural training in the context of IT projects. What can be misunderstood in a world of zeros and ones? It's either A or B. If not A, then it's B, or otherwise C. How can this go wrong? But it does. Deadlines are not met; timelines are off by months because the communication broke down and the basic assumptions are wrong.

New Zealand could be a role model for Germany, in my estimation, because of how the culture interweaves both innovation and tradition. Kaitiaki was happy to hear this. He reminded me of his nest and that he had incorporated Number 8 wire to strengthen it instead of more branches, as had been the tradition since, well, almost forever.

San Carlos/Islas Solentiname/Rio San Juan. I took the chicken bus back to Granada and spent the night as the only guest of the hostel due to the low season. I was off to the jungle in the south-eastern region of Nicaragua the next morning. The bus was supposed to leave at noon and drive around Lake Nicaragua to San Carlos. I had this information from three different people. I was at the stop at ten minutes to twelve. The bus was there, but I was the only one waiting to get in, whereupon I was told that the bus at 11.30 am had already gone and this one would depart at 2.30 pm. I felt lucky anyway, because these buses only leave once a week from Granada. I had nearly missed the bus back in Ometepe too, having heard only at the last minute of an earlier departure time. What was that about German punctuality? After

these experiences, I made sure I was at the stops an hour early, like the Nicas.

I arrived late in San Carlos. A friendly local helped me find my accommodation. The guesthouse had no internet and no shower. I showered myself with a cup out of a pail. It works surprisingly well. I'd had the same setup three years earlier on the Guajira peninsula in Colombia, where I stayed in a fishermen's hut in El Cabo. I was there to kite surf. Supposedly, I was the only woman who had ever arrived there, alone, with all of my gear on top of the about 5-metre-high pile of stuff on the roof of the bus. That was a genuine chicken bus (not just by name like the ones in Nicaragua) and I sat between bags of rice, chickens and pigs. The driver stopped at every hamlet and hut in the desert along the way to deliver provisions. He was thanked at each place with a bottle of beer and a good long chat.

In San Carlos, I woke to the sound of rumbling wheeled suitcases. More guests had arrived? Half asleep, I heard something that sounded like a lawn mower. Were the guests being picked up by a lawn mower? A heavy rain started. What time is it anyway? A rooster crowed off in the distance, so I thought it must be around 6 am. I turned around and slept some more. When the rain stopped and the village came to life, I got out of bed too.

Exactly an hour before departure, I was seated in the boat going to Mancarrón on the Solentiname Islands. On the way, we stopped at every islet with a house on it and people who were waiting for something or someone to be delivered. The sea was choppy because of the wind. The captain tried to dock at the concrete landing at Mancarrón. Bang! And reverse. He tried again, missed again. After a while we made it and we could finally disembark, but not without my luggage almost falling into the water.

Mancarrón is an artist colony, which I immediately fell in love with. I was the only tourist there. Mancarrón provisions itself, so the circumstances were somewhat better: I had a mosquito net above my bed, a towel and running water. The trade-off was no dairy products and virtually no lighting at night.

A parrot lived at the guesthouse. Her name was Martina. She

danced to a music box, peeked under my skirt and played cleverly with a ball. Then it looked like she was doing yoga, but who knows? If she felt watched, she would disappear into a dark corner. She despised children, I was told. I ignored her and was rewarded with her following me into my room. She acted like she had known me for ages and tried to open my backpack. When I returned from a walk, she was waiting for me in front of my door. She tried to destroy my *Lonely Planet*[104] with her strong beak, obviously intending to make me stay there. She hid and peeked around the corner to see what I would do.

The owner of the guesthouse said that Martina was actually a Martin, and didn't like men or children. He was crazy about women, though. Oooh, Martina... probably the best flirt I had ever encountered. Kaitiaki finally had enough. 'Are you intending to break up with me?' he squawked. 'We are not taking Martina to New Zealand, just so we are clear on that.' Okay, I got it.

As in most places in Nicaragua, on the Solentiname islands you ate what the island offered up. I had to pay for my fish up front, because the islanders had no money to advance it and collect from me later. I knew how this worked because of the trip to Guajira peninsula in Colombia I mentioned earlier. Back then I'd ordered a fish but had not paid for it, so there was no fish for me that evening and I went without.

The natural surroundings on the Solentiname Islands are unique. One time I was sitting outside the library where there was a Wifi signal when I heard a rustle. I turned to look... and saw a tarantula slowly moving towards me. So I moved to another chair. It was only later that I realised the place was crawling with tarantulas. At dusk something fell into my lap. I tried to stay calm. Was it another one of those spiders? I reminded myself not to make any sudden movements. The thing jumped off and landed on the ground. As it flew away, I saw that it was a baby bat which had apparently lost hold of the eaves on the roof.

There were other parrots in the area which were just as clever at flirting as Martina. They could yell 'Hola', which they did constantly. Kaitiaki was a little envious of their vocal talents and

secretly practised 'Hola' after that, hoping he could beat Martina and the other competition.

On the return trip, I met a German woman who had been staying in San Carlos for the last three months. She told me all kinds of things she had observed about the Nicaraguans. She said that they are not even close to being as punctual and reliable as they are with bus and boat departures.

## Meetings, hui and decision making

I was curious about how meetings are held in different countries or companies, and how decisions are made.[105]

As usual, Kaitiaki had a lot to say on the subject. He started with a few reflective questions: 'Is there an agenda? Do the participants adhere to it? Are decisions made before, during or after a meeting? Are meetings like they are in France where every attendee has the opportunity to contribute and where resolutions are actually taken at a different time and place by superiors charged with review and decision making? Is a *hui* (the Māori word for meeting) a time to collect opinions and then vote democratically on a course of action? Must a decision always be made at a meeting? Or is it customary to hold a series of meetings until all of the stakeholders are ready to agree on and support a consensus?

'Understanding the principles of hierarchy, individualism, collectivism and how time is dealt with can help to explain a hui from a Māori perspective. *Marae* – the traditional Māori meeting places – illuminate the values behind the activities that take place there. Marae are a cultural icon. They are where issues regarding the iwi are discussed and decided upon, but also where other hui, as well as funerals, celebrations and political events are held. The meetings are organised in event time. In other words, the manner in which you arrive and leave is more important than when. There is enough time for everyone to be heard for as long as they need. The agenda and time for discourse are adjusted as necessary. It is very bad manners to hurry a speaker along or to set time limits for presentations. To be insistent, direct and worried about the agenda is considered very impolite. This adaptability and accommodating behaviour guarantees fairness.'[106]

In New Zealand, it is generally common to separate private affairs and

business spheres of life. Team dinners are strictly business. Colleagues tend to go immediately home to their families or circle of friends after work. New Zealanders tend to work to live, and not to live to work. They also value family life very highly.

In Germany, meetings with external business partners can be very formal. There is a strict agenda and the meeting has a declared goal. There is very little informal exchange of information. All discussion is taken very seriously. Coming late to a meeting, showing emotions, surprises in general, and voicing opinions not based in factual data, can all endanger future business relations. Negotiations are factual and analytical. Titles as status symbols must be acknowledged. The business partner with the highest status and title is the host, unless calling the meeting was specifically delegated. Decisions are made 'at the top', following a very thorough, detailed and long process. Once a decision has been made, it is engraved in stone.

Joking in German meetings is often viewed as unprofessional. Small talk and personal exchanges are expected to be kept to a minimum. The agenda is worked through in a timely and orderly fashion. Avoiding eye contact can be construed as dishonest. An oral promise and/or a handshake is binding. It is considered good form to send a note and follow up with a phone call after a meeting. The minutes are considered accepted if there is no immediate objection. After-work drinks or a dinner are usually reserved for existing and potential business partners; they tend to be formal and professional.[107] Meetings within companies or among peer colleagues might deviate from these generalised practices.

While I was thus reflecting on meetings in Germany, Kaitiaki chatted with the locals. He broke my reverie, excitedly shouting in my ear, 'Sexuality in Nicaragua is difficult to understand with our Western sensibilities. They marry early and have children. However, it seems extra-marital affairs are allowed, even encouraged, by family and friends, who will see to it that the lovers have a room to retire to.' I myself had heard in Ometepe that Nicaraguan men are open to relations with both sexes in a kind of omni-sexuality that has very little resemblance to what we know as bi, hetero, trans or any other kind. It takes place quite freely. I also found that Nicaraguan men find women

beautiful simply because they are women, not because they fulfil any particular ideal. This reminded me of what I had heard about the polygamous culture in Gabon. For Westerners, this is morally unacceptable. Yet it is easily explained through Gabon's history. The slave trade severely decimated the population in colonial times. Later on, the rural exodus at the start of industrialisation further expedited gender imbalance, particularly in the challenging rain forest areas. Single women, penniless widows and abandoned children would have had no chance for survival had a polygamous family structure not arisen to provide for them.[108]

I took a speedboat back to San Carlos and then continued on by boat along the beautiful Rió San Juan to El Castillo, a Spanish fortress halfway to the Caribbean Sea. As always, we stopped often along the way to pick up or let off people at their homes, often only a few huts and cows on the river bank.

Just before we arrived in El Castillo, everyone quickly put on safety vests. Were we in danger? No, we were just around the bend from the landing jetty. We were all to pretend that we had worn the vests the entire trip. On the return trip, we wore the vests until the bend, where everybody took them off again for the 3-hour cruise until we were close to San Carlos.

The Caribbean: El Rama/Bluefields/Corn Islands/Pearl Lagoon. Most tourists to this area fly to the Corn Islands. I chose the land and sea route: 7 hours by bus to El Rama and from there a speedboat, called *panga*, to Bluefields. This was followed by a further 5 hours on a large ferry to the largest of the Corn Islands and finished off with a short 30-minute speedboat ride to Little Corn. Though they are officially called *Islas del Maís* in Spanish, almost everybody refers to them as Big and Little Corn Island. The further into the Caribbean I got, the more people were wearing Rasta locks and speaking local Créole. According to the Nicas, this is just very badly spoken English with no attention to grammar.

When asked where I live, New Zealand only confused people. In a Bluefields hostel, a group of men bunched around a computer trying

to find New Zealand where this *chica* (Spanish for girl, and meaning me) lived. On the ship, Nicas asked where in Europe New Zealand is located. When I said New Zealand is not a country in Europe, they nodded and said, 'Ah, USA.' I admit it felt good to say I live in a place that is so far away from current distressing geopolitical events: in the South Pacific, at the beautiful end of the Earth.

Robinson Crusoe's spirit lives on in the Corn Islands. At the time I was there, its pristine beaches were mostly empty and we had better weather than even the busy and expensive tourist season usually enjoyed. A large hurricane further north was sucking up all the wind and heavy rains, the locals explained. Some travellers I met on the boat and I spent most of the day in the water watching fish, while a nurse shark swam peacefully around our feet.
A few days later I left paradise on a freighter heading into the sunset, where the Nicaraguan mainland lay. A Nica was swabbing the deck. I sat on a sack of coconuts and inhaled the warm, salty air. The tranquillity was deceptive. Little Corn is being slowly swallowed up by the sea. Six years ago, the seashore had extended 10 to 20 metres further. Some huts had already been swept away. A fellow guest's cell phone was stolen as he briefly turned away from his table. On Big Corn, a Nica tried twice in one night to break into our room by removing the windowpane! Backpacks were routinely stolen out of buses on the Caribbean coasts. Bluefield has a reputation for danger after dark, so I stayed in my hostel after sundown. In Bluefield's harbour I ordered a coffee and placed the 20 cordobas on the counter as payment. A man you wouldn't want to argue with, grabbed them and ordered a coffee for himself, while the woman desperately tried to retrieve the coins.

I had finished all of my reading materials. Now I recalled that there were only books to trade at the different hostels. I had seen newspapers but no magazines or books anywhere for sale. Many Nica can't read or write, so bus drivers and boatmen write up personal ID data on a list. These occur frequently, especially in the border regions of Nicaragua.

These were the times I wondered what I was actually doing here. Kaitiaki reminded me not to be arrogant, and I retorted that I actually meant it in praise of New Zealand, a land of good education and low crime rates. Even its physical beauty and nature could easily take it up with the Caribbean, I thought. This trip was feeling more and more surreal. I considered travelling to some Pacific Islands next time instead. Or maybe I was just getting old.

I inquired as to when, *quando*, the next panga was departing for Pearl Lagoon. *Mañana*. Tomorrow. Ah, I had asked the wrong question! I should have asked '*A qué hora?*', what time? These are language nuances that my translated German often doesn't correctly compute. In English, as well as in Spanish and many other languages, you get a time of day if you ask 'At what time?' rather than 'When?' Trust a German to answer 'When?' with the exact date and time. Well, it was my own fault. If you don't ask precisely, you won't get a precise answer, either.

Pearl Lagoon was tourist free. I feasted on my last Caribbean meal, which featured lots of coconut. The next day, I took the bus back to El Rama. The trip was normally scheduled to take about 90 minutes. Because of the rain and terrible road conditions, I was told it might take maybe three hours today. Six hours later, after a trip crawling along at what seemed to be 10 km/hr, splashing through rivers of rainwater and around other obstacles, we finally arrived in El Rama. I stayed the night there because I wasn't keen on the capital, Managua.

The distrust and suspicion the locals in Nicaragua often had for each other was starting to get on my nerves. I wanted to live in an atmosphere of trust and dependability, like I knew it in Germany or New Zealand. Though just then I remembered my sublet shared flat in Frankfurt, where my Mongolian landlords actually sealed up the cupboard in my room and nearly locked my flatmate and me out of the lounge for fear that we would touch or steal their things. The lounge was the only room with good daylight and access to the balcony. I was

hurt by this behaviour. My German flatmate found it strange too. I complained to the Mongolians that we Germans are generally trustworthy and that I would certainly not even think about touching their private things. Am I an exception? Were Germans less trustworthy than I thought? Or had more distrust come into the country, which other cultures were used to from home? During this time, I wanted to sell my computer through eBay, which had worked perfectly before I emigrated, however it was now impossible, since only questionable buyers contacted me. Whatever. Then better New Zealand, where people trust one another, for the most part.

In Nicaragua, the crude advances and wolf-whistles started to bother me too. I've experienced worse, of course. At first, I tried to whitewash them into compliments, like my Italian girlfriends do. They find it irritating in Germany when – after hours of primping – they go out and pass by a construction site, for example, and they get no male feedback on whether the effort was worth it or not. Well, I failed miserably. It seemed that I was turning into one of those Teutonic naysayers who garnish *No!* with an exclamation mark. I was really and truly at the end of my long trip, I felt.

Kaitiaki chided me. 'If you can only complain and feel uncomfortable, then maybe you should stay at home. You are acting like the immigrants who move to a foreign country expecting to find the same standard of living and complain all the time.'

León. Back in civilisation, I felt better. As I read a newspaper in a café in a colonial building, I was pleased to find that 5 weeks in Nicaragua had improved my language skills. During my time in Léon, I conjured up the last remnant of adventurous spirit and went volcano boarding. We hiked up the volcano and slid down, mostly sitting and sometimes standing, on a thin plywood or metal board. The pitch-black Cerro Negro is still active and its flanks are so hot you could cook eggs on the ground.

Back at my hostel, I jumped in the pool and relaxed with a glass of cool, white wine and brushed the black sand from my skin. I was the solitary guest, thanks to the rainy season, and suddenly thought that I could imagine working here after all. Or in Costa

Rica? Colombia? All admirable countries. I think my frustration towards the end was because I couldn't get past being a tourist and a superficial view of this culture.

On the last day, I took a local bus to the market and then another to the seashore. I waved to New Zealand across the Pacific. I was glad to be going home.

## En route to New Zealand – San Francisco

What can I say? The restaurant service was exemplary. Wait! Didn't I complain about it a few sections back? After four months of Europe, it seemed that people were anticipating my every wish. The first time I passed through, en route from New Zealand, I had certainly been underwhelmed by American service standards. Had my perspective changed with the direction of travel?

While I was in San Francisco, I found out that one of my favourite friends in Wellington was moving to Auckland. Kelley was American and a guaranteed laugh generator. I would really miss her, even though she said she would be in Wellington once a month. I felt like a stick-in-the-mud next to her: she had bought a house in Wellington about the same time as I did, and loved it. Then she decided to rent it out and moved into a flat with flatmates. Now she was planning to buy another house in Tauranga and work in Auckland. I admired her mobility. My friend Manu in Christchurch simply commented that she knows a lot of New Zealanders who are sedentary, so what did I want? Good question. I seldom missed my travelling years anymore, the search for my spot in the world. Was it my age or experience? I don't know. I felt it was time to come home and just be there.

As I was leaving San Francisco, I received the message that my former colleague had found a job in England and had definitely turned his back on the security and stability of Germany. Back to his roots. He also wrote that his wife was homesick for New Zealand and they were starting to think of coming back. To that I can only say: Ping-pong Pom.

## Arrival in New Zealand

Kaitiaki was happy to be among his own again. 'On the last flight to New Zealand you could feel how the vibe changed – the crew's humour becomes lighter. The safety video makes you smile. People look more casual. Everybody seemed relaxed and did what they needed to get settled, though not without their New Zealand politeness. If you step on their toes, they say sorry even before you can open your mouth.

Onboard entertainment includes trivia quizzes. New Zealanders are crazy about them. Quizzes are a favourite past-time at work breaks or in the pub. You will often see some colleagues or mates bunched together, betting on who knows the most answers.'

Kaitiaki shook out his feathers and settled on the shoulder of the child who had been chosen by the crew to hand out lollies to the passengers.

In Barcelona, someone had told me about the feeling you get as you land that tells you if you have come home or not. As we approached Auckland, I was really excited. The plane touched down. My heart was hammering.

All you could see were Air Zealand aircraft. And then came customs and immigration. The accent! The smiles! The offers of help! The friendliness! Did I just repeat myself? Doesn't matter – I had arrived in the land of friendly people.

Kaitiaki greeted everyone with 'Hola!' A customs dog sniffed keenly at my carry-on. I hoped a tarantula hadn't stowed away. Kaitiaki tucked his head under a wing, squeezed up against my neck and pretended he was invisible. The customs official asked if I had fresh produce? No, I had thankfully remembered to eat my banana and the orange on board, somewhere over the Pacific. The dog had apparently smelled their lingering odour. Good dog. The tarantulas had stayed in Nicaragua where they belonged. Everything felt so familiar, so good! I was teary-eyed with happiness. It was an amazing feeling, really heavy and feather

# Middle of Middle-Earth

light at the same time. The sun was shining and the air was clear and smelled of springtime. On the walk to the domestic terminal, I passed only three people going in the opposite direction. In Frankfurt and London, there would have been hundreds of people and trolleys to dodge around.

Arrival in Wellington. The windiest city in the world greeted me with the usual bumpy landing on the runway along the shore. Pilots to Wellington must have special training to land here, one of the world's most difficult runways. So here I was finally, at Lyall Bay. My home waters. Kaitiaki screeched excitedly at me. 'Our Lyall Bay! Our home waters! Our ocean view!' It was overwhelming to be home again – for both of us.

When we arrived at the house, I felt German *Gemütlichkeit*. Have I already said that standing on my deck feels like sitting in the basket of a hot air balloon, or on a cloud with a panoramic view 'over three seas'? I was home.

Kaitiaki had flown directly up to his nest and indulged in that newly learnt Gemütlichkeit. Our tui was thrilled to see that his Christmas tree, the pōhutukawa, had just started to bloom.

On the last leg of my trip, I had clearly felt that on several levels my journey was ending. My connections to New Zealand became more intense the nearer I got: messages, invitations to small adventures like hiking trips, dinners, movie nights, etc. My incomparable social life was waiting for me in a way I had never experienced in Germany.

I was driving to such an invitation when a window washer stepped up to my car at a stoplight. Normally I try to hide by looking in another direction and pretending I am not there. This young man was sporting an irresistible smile. In this kind of situation I usually pretend not to be seen. He grinned even wider, and as he passed, he said to me, 'You're awesome.' Can you imagine the smile I drove away with?

That evening at dinner, my friends reported on the real estate market in Wellington, which was recently on the up. I regaled them with stories of my adventures. They were keen to hear more about the sauna and communal showers at the gym, asking me how we could properly wash ourselves when others were around. I dug into my brain. Very good question. I realised for the first time that we turn the part of the body we are presently washing to the wall. The New Zealand women said they couldn't begin to imagine sharing a shower like that, and they shuddered.

My friends were also curious about the refugee situation in Europe. It certainly was a paradox of globalisation. Kaitiaki spun the thought further. 'You would think the world would become more colourful, culturally speaking, more open and accommodating. What happens in reality is that people moving to foreign countries simply feel misunderstood. The harder we try to explain ourselves, the more stereotypically we behave. For example, Germans are more direct, more insistent in these situations. After a while, you naturally seek out people with a background similar to yours. They also tend to embrace stereotypical behaviours and traditions, just so that they can feel a little more at home. You become companions in a foreign place. For example a German might finally find someone to pour their heart out

to in a land where the local population is generally too polite to say out loud what they really think.

'Cross-cultural competence means that you engage with not only foreign cultures, but also your own. If you live abroad, you might find that your expat group is "stuck" to traditions and even vocabulary that have changed since you left the home country. For example, the concept of helicopter parents was coined after you left Germany.'

Here, Kaitiaki held up a wing for emphasis, and then continued. 'Expats might interpret local behaviours and occurrences from only their own perspective. Negative interpretations easily get blown out of proportion the more often they are repeated. Sometimes it can lead to extremism and aggression towards the "foreign" culture they now live in. In countries like Europe and in the United States, wings or groups have formed that have led to sometimes explosive situations. 'As an immigrant, learning the local language is essential, as is learning about and understanding their culture and your own. Māori is being taught again in New Zealand's schools and the language is actively used in daily life. The names of many locations and towns have been returned to their original Māori designation.'

Perhaps Europe can learn from New Zealand's approach. Tradition and change are not mutually exclusive.

A parcel was on the way to New Zealand full of things I couldn't get here, for example a milk frother from Italy that made the best froth I had ever had. My friends agreed that they would come by as soon as the parcel arrived to test Nicaraguan coffee with frothed milk, fresh from a New Zealand cow.

'And then we'll have coffee on the "dick".' Oh man, I had totally forgotten how curiously New Zealanders pronounce the word *deck* and even make fun of themselves saying *dick* several times in a video advertisement about deck construction.[109] New Zealand humour. How I had missed it!

## Three weeks later – home in New Zealand

There are days when it does rain non-stop in Wellington. Today was one of them. No blue peeked out from between the clouds. It didn't matter. I sat by the window with a cosy cup of tea and looked out at the ocean. Three weeks had whizzed by. Neighbours had welcomed me with a hug. Over the last six months, a jungle had grown around my house that I had managed to tame a little, remembering how a neighbour had once shown me which plants were endemic and which were weeds not worth protecting. I was glad to be among my neighbours again.

## Neighbourliness

In small towns and in rural areas everybody knows everybody. In New Zealand, this is called 'being neighbourly'. You know your neighbours in the cities too. It dates back to pioneer days when such contacts were valuable for keeping up with the news. Māori people are strongly connected to the marae their tribe holds dear, which they visit regularly. Non-Māori nostalgically follow this tradition. Many locals take regular weekend trips between the cities and countryside.[110] Neighbourliness has found a new home on the internet with a website called Neighbourly.[111]

My house was cleaned up and ready for guests again. After three weeks, I still hadn't seen all of my friends, though it seemed like I was constantly having tea, coffee or a glass of wine with someone. Many people I know had changed jobs in the six months I was gone; this kind of mobility is so different to how it is in Europe. It was wonderful to be home in Lyall Bay. It even took me quite a while to want to dust off the campervan and leave my beach house for a little road trip. Just as before my departure, I realised anew how many good friendships I have made in the last three years in New Zealand. Nothing superficial here. I also realised how strong my professional network had become, which is important for job searching in Wellington. It was touching how my former clients and colleagues had recommended me to others and helped me along, not least a very generous former Māori client.

Suddenly, a wee declaration of love slipped out of my pen. To me, this country was simply the perfect mix: organized and yet flexible, trustworthy and yet spontaneous. Social well-being and security is not the government's responsibility, but mainly your own. It is a civilised place, featuring a gorgeous and pristine natural environment. There are workplaces in sight of the ocean. I can be who I am; titles are not important here. Jandals are socially acceptable footwear. People are unbelievably nice and smiley. They find my direct approach to things 'refreshing'. Crime rates are among the lowest in the world. New Zealand doesn't need to debate concepts like work-life balance – the lifestyle already embraces it. The country is free of dog poo in public places, as they is, of course, dog poo in New Zealand. Children can run freely, play in the woods and fields and on the beach instead of in sand boxes. There are fewer barriers and more opportunities, fewer problems and more 'shbireit'. Men aren't intrusive but are determined. They are in tune with their instincts and – in spite of their inventiveness with Number 8 wire and beyond – they can be as adorable and clumsy as the wingless kiwi bird. New Zealand men are manly, with fine manners and a sweet attitude. Nothing will make you feel safer than to be with a New Zealand man who knows his way around the wild outdoors of his country. New Zealand makes me happy and allows me to be the person I want to be. Thank you, New Zealand.

By the way, I brought a replacement with me for the crazy German clock that finally broke down after a guest's attempt to repair it. I am still waiting for the invoice for the repair of the faulty motion detector. And I took the door lock that didn't work to a locksmith, who saved me NZD400 for a new one because he didn't mind fiddling with it for hours until it worked again, and only asked for NZD20 as payment for his trouble.

When the rain finally stopped, the sun shone from a deep blue sky and made the emerald ocean glimmer all the way to the horizon. On such peaceful evenings, the only sounds are the waves from the shore down below and an occasional whistle from Kaitiaki in the garden.

## A month later – the day the Earth quaked

Two minutes after midnight on 15 November 2016. I was going to be signing a contract for a new project in the coming week. As was often the case due to the 12-hour time difference, I had spent most of the evening talking with family and friends in Europe. Now I was propped up in bed watching a movie. Suddenly the walls shook. I smiled and thought that my guests were sure having a good time in the next room. The shaking continued and then the closets started moving. I was beginning to be envious of the phenomenal orgasms they seemed to be having. The whole house rattled, and when the CD shelf (nowadays with anything in it other than CDs) looked like it was about to tip over, I jumped out of bed to hold on to it, thinking to myself, 'This is not normal!' It was the strongest earthquake I had ever felt. I could feel that something extraordinary had happened. I instantly knew the news would go around the world and that it would change the city forever, just as sure as when I knew my kiting trip was over after I broke my knee in Brazil. And it felt the same as when the AZF fertiliser factory in Toulouse exploded in the building right next to where I was teaching a German class in September of 2001, only 10 days after 9/11.[112]

I tried to capture a first impression about the situation on Facebook and then ran out of my room, straight into my guests who had the same idea. We excitedly told each other what we had felt, while trying to find out more on the internet. All the while the ground shook again and again. My sturdy timber house held up just fine. Nothing fell over; only a few pictures on the wall were crooked. One of the first things you learn in New Zealand is not to hang pictures above your bed or sofa. It shook again, hard. You can feel it more in a wooden house, though they are usually flexible enough to withstand wind and earthquakes. Strong tremors can easily destroy rigid buildings of stone, brick or concrete, as the devastating ones that hit Christchurch in 2010 and in Italy in 2016 have shown.

I skyped with my parents. to let them know 'You're calling late!' 'There has been a strong quake, though no one knows yet how bad the damage is. No doubt it will soon be in the news in Europe,' I told them. 'We are fine. The house is fine.' Then my Facebook chat buzzed.

I chatted with Manu, and Elena soon joined in. We had all been startled by the earthquake and were trying to find what had happened. Text messages came chiming in from everyone asking about each other's situation.

The aftershocks continued steadily. The epicentre appeared to be in Kaikoura, on the Pacific side of the northern end of South Island. A two-metre-high wave had also been seen in Kaikoura, so the coastal residents of the entire region, and also the Chatham Islands, were ordered to higher ground. People from central Wellington were evacuated up to Mount Victoria. At 3 am my mobile rang. Lower Hutt, at the other end of Wellington harbour, was also being evacuated. My friend had to leave her house and wanted to know how things were on my side. With the help of an internet tsunami zone map I found out that my house was on a hill outside of the tsunami zone.[113]

I contacted friends who lived near the coast to let them know that they were welcome to stay with me. Manu in Christchurch was evacuated from her home and spent the night with friends. Other friends in central Wellington reported cracks in every wall of their brand new, seventh-floor flat. And while I was keeping a close watch for unusual wave activity on the ocean – thanks to the bright full moon – and kept everybody informed, first messages from Europe arrived. The headlines over there: 'Tsunami in New Zealand – another earthquake in Christchurch. At least two dead.'

At around 5 am, most Wellingtonians tried to catch some sleep. The aftershocks continued. At 7 am, most working people were informed they should stay home. My guests' voices pulled me out of bed. During the night, I had already heard that Wellington's port had been extensively damaged. In Picton, the ferry terminal on the South Island, a ferry had tried to dock at the exact moment the earthquake hit – the land and the sea moved. Imagine you are trying to dock and the island in front of you is suddenly jumping in your direction. My guests had been informed that no ferries were running between the North and South Islands. Since the initial 7.8 quake (the third largest in New Zealand's history), there had been six more severe ones of between 5.1 and 6.3 on the Richter scale, with 'only' strong ones continuously in between.[114]

My tenants on the ground floor of my house came by for a cup of tea to tell me that everything was fine in their flat. Since we were all off work, there was time for a long chat. Time we hadn't had since I had come back from Europe. They had also been watching the ocean at night and saw how the water pulled back further than normal. Everyone in Wellington spent the day trying to piece together what had happened. There appeared to be no disturbance at the airport. Watching the planes take off and land was a bit of normality I could at least observe from my house. The population was warned not to go sightseeing at the coast. The tsunami warning remained in effect until the evening. More and more damage to buildings in Wellington central was reported. It seemed to be an abandoned ghost town, so few were out and about.

Altogether, Wellington suffered relatively little damage in this earthquake of 2016, as compared to Christchurch in 2010 and 2011. Construction in Wellington had always been cognisant of the fault line the city straddles, the so called Wellington Fault. The Miramar peninsula had once been an island. An earthquake in 1460 created the isthmus which now links Miramar with Kilbirnie.

This event hit Kaikoura on the South Island hardest, as well as Wellington, where 570 quakes were recorded in the following 24-hour period; 1,300 in 48 hours. My friends all said the initial 7.8 quake was the strongest they had ever felt. Kaikoura was cut off from the rest of the country by large landslides. A herd of cows was stranded on what was now a grassy island when the earth fell away around them. They became instant celebrities as pictures of their plight went around the world.[115] Cracks appeared in roads and fields. A piece of land had risen up exactly under a house. The owners said in an interview that they had known it was going to happen one day. 'Only not while we are still living in it.' New fault lines were discovered and at least four had moved.[116]

On the second day after the large quake, most people went back to work, provided their building had been declared safe to do so. As I watched numerous helicopters fly off towards the South Island, a storm hit Wellington. Wind speeds of over 140 km/hr and fierce rain pummelled the area. The sun really didn't show up that day. Streams

and rivers rose and flooded streets. Schools were closed for the day. The bus service was suspended. The main arteries leading north out of Wellington flooded too, effectively cutting Wellington off from the rest of the country for a while by both land and sea. The storm had nothing to do with the earthquake, of course. It is a fairly normal occurrence in windy Wellington, though highly unusual that two such events would happen in the 'middle of Middle-earth' in the same week.

I had hoped to have the day to myself. It was not meant to be. Late in the afternoon I received a booking request. Three friends felt very insecure in their flat as the building waved to and fro from the aftershocks like a wagging tail. They wanted to look for something else and move out as soon as possible. I took them in for a night. Only two of them stayed one more night, as I had other guests coming in for the second room.

On the next day, I was sitting on the sofa, looking out over the bay. I was telephoning with a friend who lived at the other end of Wellington when two more severe quakes shook the house. They were 5.9 and 5.7. Interestingly, my friend on the phone didn't feel a thing. His place was on the Australian Plate; my house was on the Pacific Plate. The latter was currently slipping beneath the Australian Plate – Wellington is on a subduction zone. Whoops! There was another one, 'only' 4.9 this time.

That night the friends of the person who had left that morning knocked on my door to ask if he could come back and sleep on the couch because of a fire alarm in his place. The other holiday guests didn't mind, so the three refugees were reunited and my house was full.

Thankfully, that same day friends in Kaikoura finally reported they were safe. They had been completely cut off for two days. We had happily spent the previous New Year's Eve at their place. They had just been without internet and cellphone reception for two days. 'Those were the longest two minutes and 20 seconds of my life!' Their dog had gone wild a few minutes before the first earthquake had hit, barking and growling. 'Even before we could quieten him down, the house jerked to one side and then the other, followed by stronger and stronger movements. It felt like the house wanted to spit us out! The noise was unbelievable: crashing mirrors, kitchen utensils spread

everywhere, furniture falling over, books flying around as the shelves popped open. Even the water in the toilet bowl spilled out. It went on and on!'

Kids in New Zealand learn early to heed the saying 'If it's long and strong, best be gone'. So they packed some things in the car and took off up the hill. The escape soon ended at an electric gate that they couldn't open because the power had gone. They hiked on foot until they met up with four other families and spent the night there together. The next morning they hiked down, expecting nothing left of the house. Amazingly, there it stood, looking fairly good from the outside. Inside it looked like someone had thrown a wild party while the parents were out. A sticky mix of wine, vinegar, milk, eggs, pickles and spices was all over the floor. A sign that read 'F#"k it, let's go to Kaikoura' hung crookedly on the wall. This sign was a homage to the simple life in a New Zealand bach (a small holiday-type cottage).

With no power and water, it was hardly possible to clean up. When they could finally get some water out of their tank, they cooked some of the most perishable of the food that was left. Lobster and pāua with champagne for breakfast, anyone? Of course, they deserved it!

It didn't take long to find out that the roads were solidly blocked, even with a 4x4. The many helicopters flying around made it clear that something serious had happened. They spent the following nights in the car up on the hill. During the day they met up with their neighbours, and everyone managed as best they could. In the end, a friend who owned a helicopter rescued them and brought them back to Christchurch.[117] In New Zealand it's not unusual for someone to know someone who knows someone who has a boat, or a kayak or... a helicopter.

As my friends from Kaikoura sat on the hill looking out over the ocean for signs of an impending tsunami, they noticed a number of cliffs and

riffs that hadn't been there before. They were surfers, so they knew their piece of coast very well. Later they found out that the sea floor had shifted upward significantly. Cape Campbell, the north-eastern point of the South Island, had shifted over two metres further north-north-east and risen vertically nearly one metre. Thus the South Island is now two metres closer to the North Island than before the earthquake.

My friend Manu in Christchurch always said she wished she lived closer to me, but this way…? Jokes aside, Kaikoura – at the epicentre – had also risen about 70 cm and shifted nearly a metre north-east. Hanmer Springs had shifted about 50 cm to the east. All of this happened within a few seconds.[118] Hadn't I already mentioned that New Zealanders are pretty mobile?

With typically kiwi humour, pictures were circulating of lobsters who sat on land asking 'Did someone say something about global warming?' Another picture showed some Māori people jumping into floodwaters and enjoying an unexpected swim. Prime Minister John Key missed a call from Donald Trump.[119] 'Who called? Oh, the president-elect of the United States! Sorry, I had other things to attend to. No doubt he will call back.' The same thing almost happened with still presiding Barack Obama because PM Key didn't recognise the mobile phone number.[120] Over the next few days, a tornado[121] swept through Wellington's northwest coast, followed by an unusual springtime hailstorm and finally a bomb scare in the city centre. It was probably the most eventful week Wellington had ever had.

In spite of the continuing aftershocks, it didn't take people long to get back to everyday life. New Zealanders live close to nature. They accept its vagaries and understand that Mother Nature can be angry at times. Recent immigrants from England and Germany had deeper, very personal reactions to the event. It seemed everything had changed; nothing was as before. New Zealanders shook it off with a surfing session.

Asian cultures also tend to take natural calamities in their stride. Of course things have changed! Life goes on and everything is in flow. You deal with it as best you can. To put it philosophically, and hinting at a different perception of time: the way the present, which was now the past, flowed into the future, is different for everyone.

# *F # \* K IT*

## LET'S <u>STILL</u> GO TO KAIKOURA

The following day things went back to normal, and a new sign was designed for our friends that read: 'F#"k it, let's still go to Kaikoura.' I feel more grounded since the earthquake; more like I am really a part of everything life here entails. The periodic rumbling doesn't faze me anymore. It will be a part of our daily life for quite a while, and even more so in Kaikoura. The aftershocks went on for months after the Christchurch earthquakes in 2010 and 2011.

# A week after the earthquake – back to work

New Zealanders are champions at getting back to normal. My new contract was signed sometime between work from home and some phone calls. My first day was the Monday following the week of calamity. It was to be my first project with a New Zealand bank. Since then, I can definitely confirm that the working atmosphere in a New Zealand bank is generally more relaxed than in a German one. In the second week, we worked together with potential external partners on a project. Some of them were Dutch. Saying, 'We know exactly how it works!' and 'This is the way to do it!' was how they tried to score points. I flinched and looked around to see how my New Zealand colleagues reacted. They flinched too. In the course of the project, some activities appeared that had not been mentioned before by Indian project participants. To make the story short: I emailed, trying to understand the context to avoid future misunderstandings. I received a slightly unapologetic reply, listing the overtime already invested. The whole point of the plan had been to avoid overtime.

## *Facework/face negotiation theory*

Kaitiaki felt it necessary to contribute some final cross-cultural observations: 'There are often situations when Indian or Asian business people tend to downplay risks in both the planning and execution phases. If a manager or project leader inquires how things are progressing, the response is that everything is fine. Difficulties are not mentioned.'

Dr Stella Ting-Toomey's research on communication has shown that negotiating face or facework – as she termed it – is a feature of every culture – some to lesser, others to higher degrees. In Asian cultures, facework is a very prominent component of communication and it can explain quite a few puzzling situations. As many Asians or people of Asian descent live in New Zealand, I didn't want to neglect this aspect of intercultural theory. In-depth information can be found in the suggested reading list for this section.

Kaitiaki continued. 'The people of collectivist and hierarchical cultures in Asia have a number of ways to mitigate conflicting situations to gain or give face, save face and hopefully not lose it. In collectivist cultures,

such as Asian cultures or the Māori culture, facework strongly focuses on the *us* or *you*, *in* or *out* groups: the face of the family, tribe, colleagues, workplace and so on, up to the 'face' of the nation. In contrast, in individualistic cultures such as we find in Germany or among the Pākehā, the focus is on a person's own feelings or on the 'face' of someone else – as individuals.

'Values build the foundation for facework; values are the reason face matters. As we have seen, different cultures place varying emphasis on a wide range of values. Divergent perspectives can cause conflicts on several unconscious levels. Do you remember the disparate understanding of inventiveness between Germans and New Zealanders? Misunderstanding or misinterpretation of values is fertile ground for conflict in areas such as autonomy, inclusion, status, trustworthiness, competence and morality. In order to save face or not lose face, the parties concerned take up strategies meant to solve a conflict as smoothly as possible. Theoretically, you can either avoid conflict, or control it. In addition, the following aspects play a role: integration, third party involvement, emotional expression, passive-aggressive behaviour, courteousness, and willingness to compromise. The goal can be to preempt loss of face or to repair damage already done. For people of cultures that place great importance on face-relevant communication, it is nearly impossible to regain lost face. For example, in a situation where a business partner from an individualistic culture has lost face in negotiations with a business partner from a collectivistic culture, it can happen that the latter will refuse to continue negotiations with the entire company.[122]

'Countless observations in international projects show that it may be beneficial to train teams and offer workshops on the topic of negotiating face to create awareness for these distinctive cultural features.'

With a flourish, Kaitiaki retired to his nest and let some aftershocks rock him to sleep.

# Six months after the trip – recovery incomplete

Yesterday I left my helmet behind on the seat of my motorbike. In my thoughts, I was already a few steps ahead with my client. I only noticed my lapse when I returned to the motorbike in the evening and saw it still sitting on the seat. Unsecured, in the middle of the capital city. I wondered if a helmet sitting like that was offensive to anybody. Only recently had I been reminded that leaning on the edge of a table is taboo in Māori culture.

## *Tikanga Māori – a blunder prevention kit*

The multicultural and welcoming lifestyle in New Zealand may cause newcomers to forget that it is very easy to commit a faux pas in dealings with the rich Māori culture. Whether in private or in business dealings, there are numerous rules that are unfamiliar to Westerners.

*Tikanga* is the term for a collection of customs and traditions stemming from the Māori word *tika*, meaning correct, as opposed to *teka*, meaning wrong. Many *tikanga* reflect the idea that the head and food is sacred and may not be defiled. A Māori saying goes: '*Nau te rourou, naku te rourou, ka ora te manuhiri*. With your food basket and my food basket, the visitors will be fed.'

Kaitiaki has requested that some *tikanga* be included here.
- Never sit or lean on a table, especially if it is used for serving or eating food. Bags and purses should also not be placed on a table. Māori culture considers every table a place for food. Food should never be allowed to get dirty.
- Never sit on pillows or cushions as these are reserved for a person's head.
- Do not touch anybody's head – it is sacrosanct.
- Food should not be passed over anyone's head.
- Hats should not be placed on tables.
- Do not climb over people in a row of seats. Ask politely if they will pull back their feet or stand to let you pass. Otherwise find another way. It is especially offensive for women to climb over the legs of a man.
- If you need to enter a room where a person of higher rank is speaking (in Māori culture often an elderly person), wait at the door until there

is a pause. Do not cut in front of the speaker. If there is no alternative entrance or absolutely no way to get to your seat without cutting in front, at least stoop to show respect.[123]

A year ago I set out on a journey to a wedding invitation and followed the call of my heart to visit Germany and a few other places. Towards the end of my long trip, I could hardly wait to get back home to New Zealand. I had originally thought of living here for six months of the year and in Europe for the other six. I had informed project agencies of this plan and now they were asking if I was available for work in Europe. No, I was not. 'Still recovering from the last one,' I thought to myself. By the end of my trip, coming home to New Zealand had felt like an escape, the same as when I had moved away from Europe over three years ago.

Looking at it from a New Zealander's perspective, I experienced Europe as being packed full of people who let the media whip them into a frenzy of fear from who knows what. My English colleague, who had left Berlin to work in London, has decided with his wife to return to Wellington. Only a year earlier they had wanted to leave New Zealand behind. Ping-pong Pom indeed. Welcome back.

Autumn came. I enjoy going to the gym, the sauna and getting comfy at home. Cheers to my German mole gene and *Gemütlichkeit*! It is the time of year the dolphins come to play with the surfers in my bay and the neighbouring waters. It is the time for the aurora australis to glow in the night sky above my house.[124]

My friend Manu in Christchurch recently became a mummy. She has been debating what it would be like to return to Germany for a while, since she misses it quite a bit. The posts of returned emigrants to Germany in different online forums are very interesting to read. They are already frustrated with feeling that the mega-feel-good-package of maternity leave and financial support from the government is hemming them in. They dream of freedom in New Zealand, while Manu is looking forward to the security the social net will afford her. We will see what she has to say about things after a few months of being back.

My stash of the personal care products I brought with me from Germany has been used up. My family sends me a package now and again, or a friend will bring something along on a visit, although I have started to find products in New Zealand that I like. There are fewer things from Germany that I really miss. When I visited Manu in Christchurch for Christmas, she looked a little ashamed when she said that she now eats New Zealand-style bread. I recently bought a loaf that looked good from a New Zealand bakery myself. It was a bit fluffier than what I really like and the crust could have been crunchier. Altogether not bad for a country that generally prefers soft and fluffy slices of bread. So we are coming together, New Zealand and I.

My present job is the best I have ever had. In Agile project management, the focus is on people over processes. I have a great multicultural team to spar with. Indian newcomers like to stand out from the crowd, which is not very compatible with the 'tall poppy syndrome' and New Zealand egalitarianism. They try to climb stairs that are not there, especially in an Agile environment with flat hierarchical structures. They would like to impress me, the Scrum Master, because they wrongly perceive my rather lateral position to be a disciplinary one. A Scrum Master's job is to smooth out obstacles, so that the team can work cooperatively. In the Indian world, there are no obstacles, especially when reporting to managers. The problems are addressed only if they actually occur. I don't like it if people want to impress me. I would rather argue points constructively. Problems should be out in the open to discuss freely. I relish debate and like to be challenged. This is, of course, a tightrope walk with people from cultures who are worried about losing face. One of the standard types of meetings in Agile project management is the Retrospective, where feedback is given. This is challenging for New Zealanders. Open, direct praise can make them uncomfortable in a society where people don't want to stand out. Talking about what has potential for improvement might not come naturally when 'shbireitmeit' is the usual reaction to everything.

I would like to heartily thank all of my colleagues and New Zealanders who still like me, in spite of my Germanness.

At Christmas, I started looking for contractors who could double-glaze the windows in my house. There is an endless selection of options, beginning with a 'second' window that you can click onto the existing one through to double-glazed windows imported from Germany, though not necessarily including a qualified installer. Making comparisons is nigh impossible. Some German importers would have liked to install high-grade plastic windows, which might be the most efficient solution from a German perspective. I prefer to try to retain the charm of wooden frames. Winters in New Zealand stay above freezing in most North Island regions. Whoever wants Germany in New Zealand is welcome to go back. 'They have no idea here, no quality, just terrible.' I, however, like the imperfection and natural vibe of houses here.

When I was looking to upgrade my heating system, I met Uwe. He understands the dichotomy. Typical New Zealand houses? Yes! German know-how? Yes! The big question is always, 'How can we bring both together?'

Summer hasn't come this year. 'In New Zealand it can be summer and winter in one day.' Winter in the summer season could make a good amendment to that axiom.

Instead of a holiday tenant, I had a flatmate for a time. A New Zealander. I'd been a little more of the 'grumpy' German than I wanted to be, I think. A good time to let more of New Zealand back into my life.


My best friend Verena, whom I have known since I was three years old, had been treated for breast cancer. She was one of the reasons I had taken that trip back to Europe. After I returned to New Zealand, her cancer came back with a vengeance. Her doctors said there were new tumours in her body and they don't have much hope for her recovery. I wanted to visit her so many more times.

Whether they return or stay away, our cultural fish will always find themselves somewhere between the river or the home lake. In the end, only a decision to build your own little world at your favourite place can make you happy. Even if New Zealand looks like a paradise and is often touted promoted as such, New Zealand is not

paradise. But if you decide to make it *your* paradise, then you are welcome here.

'Ladies and Gentlemen, in a few minutes we shall be landing. Please put your seat backs in the upright position, fasten your seatbelt and set your watch to twenty years ago. Relax, enjoy the headwind wind in your face – especially in Wellington – and prepare for the fancies of Mother Nature on peaceful and bumpy days, and look forward to loving a unique land.'

## Kupu opaniraa – closing remarks

Getting to know the world means getting to know yourself. On my temporary trip back into my past in Germany and again forwards into the future in New Zealand, I kept my eyes open. I have returned and departed many times; this time I looked at my encounters with people and my thoughts and feelings with a cross-cultural eye. Many important ideas regarding Europe and New Zealand have not been covered in this book.

Had I stayed there longer, I could probably have filled three books with my observations. I did try to address topics that you might not easily find in other books, topics that are part of ordinary, commonplace life, things that might frustrate you – perhaps even unconsciously – as you travel in Germany and New Zealand or the rest of the world.

Even if you have found your perfect spot like me, you will always live between cultures. Your roots will remain attached to you. Intercultural competence means that you have made your peace with two or more cultures and that you can navigate through them with ease. It is entirely possible that you know or have experienced things I have described differently. That's good. We are all individuals, each carrying our own cultural backpack with us, filled by our parents, families, the regions we have lived, the companies we have worked for and countless other 'cultures' we have been involved with.

I hope that some of the issues I have addressed in this book lead to fruitful discussion and reflection. It's important to ask how others view your experience and how it compares to their own. This applies not only to immigrants, returnees and travellers, but to daily life in our multicultural world.

A cross-cultural eye can help us make sense of what we experience in our own culture as well as foreign ones. Intercultural theories suggest explanations and a framework to help us analyse decisions and actions. They are thought-provoking and they are as versatile and as adaptable as each individual. Think of it this way: a Bavarian is a German, yet the stereotypical Lederhosen Bavarian is not representative of an entire nation.

It was important for me to demonstrate what happens if you get to know life from a completely new vantage point. You could be on a backpacking trip or be a bona-fide immigrant and you will never return home as the same person. This alone is reason enough to look at your experience with cross-cultural eyes. There is no place in this world where everything is perfect and shiny.
I hope everybody finds their place in the world and that they have family and friends who can understand.

## Whakawhetai – acknowledgments

This book could never have been written without my *whānau*. Heartfelt thanks to my family and friends who motivated me, supported me, opened their ears and made time for me.

Special thanks to:

- my mother, who passed on some of her language talents to me as I listened from in her tummy when she studied languages at university.
- my father for his creativity and unique drawings of Kaitiaki.
- to both parents for reading and re-reading this book a number of times, pretending it was always a fresh experience.
- my editor, Claudia Troßmann, who also writes travel guides filled with wonderful ideas and flashes of inspiration and directs the book world from the German Odenwald region.
- my editor in New Zealand of the English version of the book, Marja Stack, who made sure the kiwi spirit is maintained in the language and questioned sense and non-sense. She stands out with great professionalism and knowledge. The English translation wouldn't be the same without her.
- Nicole Raukamp, a black sheep, as her web address suggests: www.pecora-nera.eu. She immigrated to Sardinia, the 'other sheep island', and contributed with her unique sense of language and sharp, smart comments.
- first reader and commentator, Manuela Mühlbauer, in Christchurch who has always supported and helped me. My German friends in New Zealand are my haven in a sometimes foreign world. They have listened, comforted me and made me laugh with their German humour and great Denglish skills. Car bender or carpenter, anyone? These two have made all the difference to my immigrant experience.
- Susan Hoppe, my intercultural train-the-trainer. She jump-started my intercultural education. An American, she survived three decades of life in Germany. Like me, she has retreated to the Pacific Ocean, where she lives in Hawaii and regularly visits her Third Culture Kids and grandchildren in Germany.
- the many international and German friends I have known for

half of my life: Cornelia, Césare, Renata, Gemma, Verena and all of the colleagues, acquaintances and fellow travellers of this vibrant world who endure my Germanness, make appropriate fun of me and hold the mirror to my face. Our shared experiences that have found their way into this book – collectively, they are the reason I wrote it.

– and finally, Oliver, whose feedback has been simply invaluable.

## Kiwi Wiki – mini glossary

**ACC**

an acronym for the Accident Compensation Corporation – a government-run accident and invalidity insurance which also covers treatments for tourists.

**Afghans**

a popular kind of biscuit produced in New Zealand, made from chocolate, cornflakes and walnuts.

**Agile project management**

a project management method for IT and a number of other industries, which is gaining global interest. The Agile method is replacing traditional methods of software development. A step-by-step approach (e.g. iterative) as opposed to a big bang concept, is based on certain principles (Manifesto) aiming to change organisational culture and facilitate agile and open communications.

**Airbnb**

an internet portal for alternative accommodation around the world. It originated with the idea of connecting travellers with a 'night on the couch' so they could meet locals at their homes rather than staying in hotels and hostels. It has grown into a substantial platform for all manner of vacation rentals or bed & breakfast accommodation.

**ANZAC**

the acronym for 'Australian and New Zealand Army Corps'. They were soon called ANZACs; the appellation became legally protected in 1916. It was founded in 1915, joining some military forces of both countries in order to support the British war efforts in the Great War (WWI). Their defeat at Gallipoli against the Turkish army cost 8,500 Australian soldiers and 2,779 New Zealand soldiers their lives. The myth that ANZAC biscuits were sent to provision the troops prevails in both New Zealand and Australia. The men had other biscuits in their kits, known as 'rock hard tooth breakers' or 'Ship's ANZAC biscuits'.

**ANZAC biscuits**

another popular New Zealand biscuit, made with rolled oats and optionally with added coconut shreds. It is delicious in both its soft and hard versions. The latter has a caramel flavour. As is the case with pavlova and lamingtons, Australia and New Zealand maintain an enduring dispute as to which country invented them.

**Aotearoa**

the Māori name for New Zealand.

**Bach**

pronounced *batch*. It means a holiday or beach cottage in New Zealand.

**Backpacker**

person who travels as economically as possible with a large backpack as their only piece of luggage. Backpackers usually can't afford hotels, so they stay at cheap accommodation. The hostel-style accommodation is also called a *backpacker*. They believe they can connect more closely with the local culture in this way than package or luxury tourists.

**Blend**

a cuvée, or blended wine of several grape varieties or from different growing locations.

**Brexit**

an informal expression referring to the United Kingdom's planned withdrawal from the European Union. It is a mashup of the words *Britain* and *exit*.

**'Bring a plate'**

is a custom at many events, particularly potluck dinners, meaning that everyone brings a dish to be shared with other attendees.

**Bungy jump**

a modern, extreme sport in which a person dives headfirst off a tall building, high bridge, tower or crane.

The thrilling freefall is checked before hitting the ground by a strong cord (the bungy) connected to the dive platform and fixed to the body of the person jumping. The bungy's length is customised to the jumper's body weight. Its elasticity allows the jumper to rebound several times and swing before it eventually hangs still.

**Bushman's toilet paper, bushman's friend**

a colloquial name for the rangiora bush. The Māori people traditionally used its leaves for wiping.

**Casa particular**

the Cuban designation for accommodation similar to Airbnb or a bed & breakfast.

**Cheerio**

a pink-coloured sausage, also called a 'cocktail sausage' or 'little boy', which is traditionally eaten with Wattie's tomato sauce.

**Chocolate fish**

fish-shaped, strawberry-flavoured, chocolate-coated marshmallows.

**Crumpets**

a kind of griddle pancake typically featuring holes that result from the yeast in the batter.

## Cultural dimensions according to Fons Trompenaars

Alfons 'Fons' Trompenaars is a Dutch-French researcher of communication. He was a student of Geert Hofstede. Trompenaars distinguishes between seven cultural dimensions. The first five compare human relationships between cultures:

- Universalism vs Particularism: What is more important – rules or relationships?
- Neutrality vs Emotionality: How openly do we show our emotions?
- Individualism vs Collectivism: Do we function as individuals or as members of a group?
- Specific vs Diffuse: How involved are we in public life?
- Achievement vs Lineage: Do we work to achieve status or is it bestowed at birth?

Two more of Trompenaars dimensions are:

- Seriality vs Parallelity in time orientation. Do we do things one after another, or several at once?
- Internal control vs External control (dealing with the environment and nature). Do we try to control nature and the environment, or does it control us? Can we cooperate with it?

## Cultural dimensions according to Geert Hofstede

an intercultural theory. Between 1967 and 1978, Geert Hofstede conducted an extensive questionnaire study with around 116,000 employees in 50 countries in positions ranging from assembly line workers through to management. His goal was to create a tool that could scientifically and unambiguously define and compare cultures, which he called cultural dimensions. The six dimensions are as follows:

- Individualism vs Collectivism.
- High vs Low Power Distance.
- Weaker or Stronger Uncertainty Avoidance.
- Masculinity vs Femininity.
- Long-term Orientation.
- Indulgence.

Hofstede's dimensions are popularly used to measure competence, though methodically not at all comprehensively. Dimensions are aspects of cultural behaviours that can be compared to other cultures' behaviours on a kind of sliding scale.

## Cultural standards

descriptions and classifications of cultural mentalities that were first compiled by Alexander Thomas, a German professor emeritus of psychology.

**Deli**
the New Zealand word for a small café, not to be confused with a *dairy*, which is a convenience store or small grocery.

**Dick**
a colloquial term for penis, and also the New Zealand pronunciation of the word *deck*.

**DOC**
the acronym for the widely respected Department of Conservation, commissioned with protecting New Zealand's natural environment.

**Dubbeglass**
a drinking vessel for wine, popular in Germany's Palatinate region. Its name comes from the round depressions (Dubbe) all around the glass. Its volume is usually a half litre (500 ml).

**Egalitarianism**
an order of society in which all members have equal rights and equal access to resources. Leadership has limited power over the people. Social status, individual wealth and property are subordinate values.

**Facework/face negotiation theory**
an intercultural concept as analysed by Stella Ting-Toomey in which every culture has specific communication strategies for keeping face, gaining and losing face, etc. The importance of facework can be very profound, as in many collectivist (we) Asian cultures. In more individualistic (me) cultures such as Germany or the Pākehā in New Zealand, facework is less pronounced. Strongly hierarchical cultures place more emphasis on face than egalitarian societies. Ting-Toomey also describes how to recognise and use facework strategies in international communication and business.

**Feijoa**
a fruit, originally from South America, also called the Brazilian guava.

**Flight of the Conchords**
a New Zealand comedy duo, which is also known internationally.

**Fritter**
also called patty.

**Fush 'n' Chups**
the colloquial New Zealand pronunciation for *fish and chips*.

**German cultural standards**
a term coined by researcher Alexander Thomas. It describes German mentality and behaviours as seen by outsiders. Some standards for Germany include:
– formalism and rule-orientation.
– regard for hierarchies.

– separation of private and public/ work spheres.
– interpersonal distancing.
– a monochronic awareness of time.
– direct communication style.
– internalised control.

## Green-lipped mussels
a mussel found in the waters around New Zealand, with a signature green rim, or lip.

## Guy Fawkes (Bonfire Night)
a Catholic rebel officer who was involved in the failed Gunpowder Plot: the assassination attempt on King James I of England by bombing Parliament on 5 November 1605 in London. This event is remembered annually on Bonfire Night in England as well as in New Zealand. People carry torches and light fireworks and bonfires.

## Hapū
a subtribe in Māori culture which has significant importance as a political unit. A hapū is composed of several hundred members and whānau (extended families).

## Hāngi
a traditional Māori method of preparing food using heated rocks in an earth oven. Meat and vegetables are wrapped in ferns, laid on the heated stones in the hole, covered with wet ferns and earth and left to bake for several hours.

## Hokey pokey
a popular flavouring for sweets in New Zealand. Small chunks of honeycomb toffee is mixed into vanilla ice cream or chocolate. Hokey pokey is made of sugar, syrup and baking soda, which creates the honeycomb texture.

## Hoki
species of fish.

## Honey mead
honey fermented with water and sometimes other natural additives.

## Hongi
A traditional Māori greeting where they press their noses together, and sometimes their foreheads, although it is something really only reserved for cultural situations or between Māori people.

## Hui
the Māori word for meeting.

## Interpersonal distancing
a German cultural standard that describes German restraint and detached attitude towards unfamiliar people.

**Iwi**
the largest political grouping in pre-European Māori society, and means tribe.

**Jaf(f)a**
Jafa is a New Zealand colloquial acronym for 'Just another f**ing Aucklander', while Jaffa is a chocolate covered lolly with a sweet, hard orange coating.

**Jandals**
the New Zealand word for flip-flops or thongs.

**Kingfish**
a species of fish.

**Kite surfing**
a water sport where a person balances on a board similar to a short surfboard or wakeboard, and is pulled over water by an airborne kite riding the wind.

**Kiwi**
a nearly egg-shaped hairy fruit with green or yellow flesh; also a species of flightless bird, endemic to New Zealand, and a colloquial term for a New Zealander or something from New Zealand.

**Kiwiana**
a catch-all phrase for things that reflect New Zealand's culture, history, language and so forth, ranging from souvenirs to large sculptures of local specialties.

**Kiwi ingenuity**
the New Zealand ability and inventiveness to make do with limited resources when making or repairing things. The pioneering spirit and tinkering talents of the archetypal New Zealand bush man is often humorously satirised, especially in regard to his use of Number 8 wire to fix anything and everything.

**KiwiSaver**
a subsidised retirement savings plan in New Zealand.

**Koha**
the New Zealand word for donation or contribution. It originates from the Māori language and is in daily use.

**'Ladies a Plate'**
an old saying that refers to the female role of providing sustenance at official events.

**Lamington**
a cake claimed to have been invented in Australia, but has been proven to originate in New Zealand, where it was first called Wellington. Its respective names were in honour of

Lord Lamington, who visited Wellington in 1895.

**Lollies**
NZ English for sweets/candies.

**Long White Cloud**
the English-language translation of Aotearoa, the Māori name for New Zealand.

**Laughing Samoans**
a comedy duo from Samoa known and loved for its island humour.

**Māori**
the indigenous people of New Zealand.

**Marmite**
a food spread for bread and toast made from concentrated yeast extract.

**Mole gene**
Author's word creation for when Germans make the most of bad weather and coocoon in their houses, especially in winter (German *Gemütlichheit*)

**Moki**
a species of fish.

**Morning tea**
a mid-morning break gathering to which mostly everyone brings something to share. Morning tea is a very common feature of New Zealand's working environment.

**Mua**
a Māori language preposition meaning *in front of* and *past*.

**National Screening Unit**
a public institution which determines and coordinates health screenings and informs the general public about health issues.

**Neighbourliness**
describes a positive New Zealand attitude and helpfulness towards neighbours in the community.

**Number 8 wire**
the gauge of a commonly used wire in New Zealand. It symbolically represents the often only available resource in the past for fixing things. Number 8 wire is closely related to Kiwi ingenuity and reflects New Zealand's national self-confidence.

**Overseas**
used in reference to any place in the world that is not in New Zealand, or in the ocean immediately surrounding its shores.

**Pā**
the Māori word for village, the centre of social life, a group of traditional huts

which also serves as a defensive structure.

**Pākehā**
a New Zealander of European origin, a non-Māori, not indigenous. In the Māori language it means *foreigner*.

**Paradox of globalisation**
a theory of this author. In an increasingly globalised world, an increasing number of people live in countries they were not born in, whether intentionally or as immigrants and refugees. While living in a new culture, they slowly lose connections to their former home and consequently lose sight of new developments in their original culture. In their new home, they tend to look for people like themselves. An exaggerated nostalgia for the 'old country' can lead to social tension, even extremism. The paradox addresses the fact that the more globalised we become, the more opportunities become available – the price being a higher potential for conflict.

**Patty**
also called a fritter.

**Pāua**
the Māori word for the sea mollusc called abalone in English. The meat of this sea creature is considered a delicacy. It is black on the outside and white on the inside. The Māori people not only eat the pāua and use its beautiful shell to make jewellery, but incorporate it in cultural displays. Iridescent pāua mother-of-pearl is also called 'opal of the sea'. A caught pāua must have a minimal size or be thrown back into the ocean. The recreational limit is ten pāua per person per day. Only snorkel gear, no diving tanks, etc., may be used for fishing pāua.

**Pavlova**
a dessert made with meringue, fruit and whipped cream.

**'Piece of cake'**
a New Zealand idiom meaning very easy, no problem at all.

**Pineapple Lumps**
Pineapple lumps are small rectangles of a soft, pineapple-flavoured middle covered with chocolate.

**Ping-pong Poms**
a humorous reference to British people (Poms) who move back and forth between England and New Zealand or Australia like ping-pong balls.

**Pint**
a volume measurement for a glass of

beer or cider. It converts to 20 fluid ounces/568 ml in Great Britain or to 16 fluid ounces/473 ml in the USA.

**Pipi**
a species of tiny mollusc.

**Pōhutukawa**
a species of tree (*Metrosideros excelsa*), also called the Christmas tree in New Zealand because it blooms red blossoms in New Zealand's summer, the height of which is December and the Christmas season.

**Possum**
a major pest in New Zealand because it has no natural enemies on the islands. In Australia, however, the possum is a protected species as there are numerous animals that feed on them.

**Potluck (dinner)**
a popular gathering of family, friends or colleagues to which everyone brings a dish to share.

**Rangiora bush**
also called bushman's toilet paper or bushman's friend. Its leaves were traditionally used in the wild for wiping by the Māori people.

**Reintegration process**
a model by Hirsch which describes the three phases a person can go through when returning home after a period abroad. This process is often underestimated by returnees in contrast to the integration process of expatriation or immigration to a foreign country.

**Sandfly, sandflies**
New Zealand's tiny, biting monsters.

**Sauna (complex)**
Sauna complex and thermal baths – there are over 2,000 public saunas in Germany and around around 200 deluxe thermal baths which include an extensive sauna complex all around the country. Saunas can range from a basic arrangement in sport centres to luxurious themed complexes offering a variety of sauna types and numerous pools and relaxation zones. Thermal baths with sauna complexes are a very popular leisure activity in Germany.

**Shbireitmeit, Shbireit**
a transliteration by the author of the New Zealand saying 'She'll be right mate', which means everything is fine, no problem, all okay.

**Small talk**
casual chatting about the weather, leisure activities and other neutral topics before initiating negotiations or conversations on business issues.

English-speaking cultures use it to warm up or get to know someone.

## Space – personal space

an intercultural concept first described by researcher Edward Hall. He found that people of different cultures have a varying perception of personal space around themselves. Intrusion of this space or 'bubble' causes discomfort. Some cultures have a far larger bubble than others who are most comfortable standing close to each other. For example, New Zealanders tend to need a larger personal space than Germans, who are in turn uncomfortable with the close proximity Italians prefer. Hall believed that these issues with personal space and varying perceptions of time are the major causes of misunderstanding. He called these part of a 'silent language' that we unconsciously display in our daily communications.

## Steak and cheese pie

a savoury pastry stuffed with beef, gravy and cheese.

## SUP

is the acronym for the sport of standup paddleboarding which originated in Polynesia. A person balances on a wide surfboard and uses a long paddle for propulsion over the water.

## Superannuation

a retirement fund in New Zealand.

## Tall poppy syndrome

a descriptive term for the New Zealanders' desire to not stand out. The tall poppy is the flower that loses its head first because it reaches above the others. It is symbolic of egalitarianism, an important cultural value for New Zealand.

## Tamarillos

also called tree tomato. Although they originally come from South America. The name tamarillo was given to them in New Zealand.

## Tarakihi

a species of fish.

## Te Urewera Act 2014

The Māori people believe that fauna and flora are equal to humans. In 2014, New Zealand was the first country to grant the Te Urewara National Park the same status as a citizen, with the Te Urewara Act. The Whanganui River also has citizenship rights.

## Thermal bath

Please refer to *sauna* (complex).

## Third Culture Kids

a concept describing the unique qualities of people who grow up

between cultures, for example when their parents come from different cultural backgrounds, or when the TCKs grow up in another culture than their parents, or a combination of several multicultural aspects.

## Three-phase model
Please refer to *Reintegration Process* above.

## Tikanga
the collective term for Māori customs and traditions. It stems from the word *tika*, meaning right or correct, as opposed to *teka*, meaning wrong.

## Tip Top ice cream
Tip Top is a brand of ice cream in New Zealand.

## Tramping
local term for extreme hiking in New Zealand, not to be confused with *hitchhiking* in English or *trampen* in German, both of which mean thumbing a ride.

## Treaty of Waitangi
the original contract signed in 1840 in New Zealand by the first settlers under the British crown and the indigenous peoples. It has remained a bone of contention until today.

## Tuatuas
a species of mollusc.

## Value and development square
a communications model developed by Friedemann Schulz von Thun. The premise is that every value (every virtue, every leading principle, every human attribute) has a constructive effect only in connection with a positive contrasting value, a 'sister-virtue'. Without this balance, a value is easily devalued to an exaggeration of itself.

## Warehou
a species of fish.

## Wattie's
Wattie's or Heinz Wattie's Limited is a food manufacturing company in New Zealand.

## Whānau
the extended family in Māori society and ranks lower than the hapū and iwi as a political unit. It is pronounced *Faanau*.

## Whitebait
a species of tiny fish.

## Whittacker's chocolate
a brand of chocolate in New Zealand.

## Work visa
the legitimisation to work in New Zealand as a foreigner.

## Further literature

**Bönisch-Brednich**, Brigitte (2003). *Auswandern, Destination Neuseeland*. Berlin.

**Cryer**, Max (2006). *The Godzone Dictionary of Favourite New Zealand Words and Phrases*. Exisle Publishing.

**Duff**, Alan (1995). *Once Were Warriors*. Vintage International.

**Fletcher**, Adam (2016). *Wie man Deutscher wird. In 50 einfachen Schritten*. München.

**Fletcher**, Adam (2016). *Wie man Deutscher wird. In 50 neuen Schritten*. München.

**Gelfert**, Hans-Dieter (2005). *Was ist deutsch? Wie die Deutschen wurden, was sie sind*. München.

**Gelfert**, Hans-Dieter (2005). *Typisch Englisch. Wie die Briten wurden, was sie sind*. München.

**Heyse**, Dörthe, & **Heyse**, Volker (2017). *Das Neuseeland-Lesebuch: Alles, was Sie über Neuseeland wissen müssen*. Berlin.

**Hofstede**, Geert, & **Hofstede**, Gert (2017). *Lokales Denken, globales Handeln. Interkulturelle Zusammenarbeit und globales Management*. München: Beck.

**Hofstede**, Geert, **Hofstede**, Gert Jan, & **Minkov**, Michael (2010). *Cultures and Organizations. Software of the mind*. USA.

**Horrell**, Steve (2nd ed. 2010). *Emigrating to New Zealand: Comprehensive, up-to-date, practical information about everyday life in the other 'down-under'*. How To Books.

**Ihimaera**, Witi (2003). *The Whale Rider*. Harcourt Achieve.

**Klier**, Freya (2012). *Gelobtes Neuseeland. Fluchten bis ans Ende der Welt*. Berlin: Aufbau.

**Levine**, Robert (2006). *A Geography of Time: The Temporal Misadventures of a Social Psychologist, or How Every Culture Keeps Time Just a Little Bit Differently*. London.

**Kinsella**, Patrick (2016). *Toilets: A Spotter's Guide*. Melbourne.

**Mayr**, Stefan, & **Thomas**, Alexander (2009). *Beruflich in Frankreich*. Göttingen.

**Neudecker**, Eva, **Siegl**, Andrea, & **Thomas**, Alexander (2007). *Beruflich in Italien*. Göttingen.

**Noll**, Silke (2018). *Leben und Arbeiten in Neuseeland. Ein interkultureller Ratgeber für den beruflichen Alltag von Expatriates*. Wiesbaden: Springer.

**Pollock**, David C. (2017). *Third Culture Kids. The Experience of Growing Up Among Worlds*. Nicholas Brealey Publishing.

**Richter**, Anke (2011). *Was scheren mich die Schafe. Unter Neuseeländern. Eine Verwandlung*. Köln: KIWI.

**Schellenberger**, Uwe (2011). *Transmigration als Lebensstil. Selbstbilder und Erfahrungswelten von Pendlern zwischen Deutschland und Neuseeland*. Münster.

**Schroll-Machl**, Sylvia (2007). *Die Deutschen – Wir Deutsche. Fremdwahrnehmung und Selbstsicht im Berufsleben*. Göttingen.

**Schroll-Machl**, Sylvia (2016). *Beruflich in Babylon: das interkulturelle Einmaleins weltweit*. Göttingen.

**Smith**, Paul, & **Taylor**, Ken (2009). *German Secrets*. Norderstedt.

**Southward**, Phil (2015). *The soaring Kiwi and the Sauerkraut*.

**Storti**, Craig (1994). *Cross-Cultural Dialogues*. Boston.

**Thomas**, Alexander (2016). *Interkulturelle Psychologie. Verstehen und Handeln in internationalen Kontexten*. Göttingen: Hogrefe.

## Favourite Links

**Noll**, Silke: Wahlheimat Neuseeland.
Author's website and cross-cultural blog.
https://wahlheimat-neuseeland.de

**Te Ara** – The Encyclopedia of New Zealand.
https://teara.govt.nz

## Footnotes

### He kupu whakataki – Introduction

[1] Bönisch-Brednich, Brigitte. (2002). *Keeping a Low Profile: An Oral History of German Immigration to New Zealand*. (pp. 207–208). Wellington: Victoria University Press.

### How did I come to New Zealand – or, how did a world traveller become an immigrant.

[2] Slavik, A. (2016, August 13). In deutsche Unternehmen zieht das große Duzen ein. *Süddeutsche Zeitung*. Retrieved from https://www.sueddeutsche.de/karriere/arbeitsplatz-in-deutsche-unternehmen-zieht-das-grosse-duzen-ein-1.3120427

[3] Thomas, Alexander (1996). *Psychologie interkulturellen Handelns*. (A. Thomas, Ed.). Göttingen: Hogrefe.
Thomas, Alexander (1991). *Kulturstandards in der internationalen Begegnung*. (Alexander Thomas, Ed.). Saarbrücken: Breitenbach.

[4] Morrison, Terri, & Conoway, Wayne A. (2006). New Zealand. In *Kiss, Bow or Shake Hands*. (p. 338). Avon.

[5] Hoppe, Susan. (2013, June 11). Business Behave: Visitenkarten als Vehikel für Geschäftsleute. Management-Blog. *Wirtschaftswoche*. Retrieved from https://blog.wiwo.de/management/2013/06/11/business-behave-visitenkarten-als-vehikel-fur-geschaftsleute-gastbeitrag-von-trainerin-susan-hoppe/

[6] Hofstede, Geert, Hofstede, Gert J., Minkov, Michael (2017). *Lokales Denken, globales Handeln: Interkulturelle Zusammenarbeit und globales Management* (6th ed.). München. dtv Verlagsgesellschaft.
Hofstede, Geert (2003). *Culture's Consequence* (2nd ed.). SAGE Publications.
Hofstede, Geert, Pedersen, Paul B., & Hofstede, Gert (2002). *Exploring Culture*. Intercultural Press.

[7] Cole Catley, Christine (1996). *The Xenophobe's Guide to The Kiwis*. (p. 14). West Sussex.

[8] New Zealand. Retrieved from Hofstede Insights: https://www.hofstede-insights.com/country/new-zealand/

[9] Germany. Retrieved from Hofstede Insights: https://www.hofstede-insights.com/country/germany/

[10] Thomas, Alexander (1996). *Psychologie interkulturellen Handelns*. (A. Thomas, Ed.). Göttingen: Hogrefe.
Thomas, Alexander (1991). *Kulturstandards in der internationalen Begegnung*. (Alexander Thomas, Ed.). Saarbrücken: Breitenbach.

[11] Kevin D. Lo, Carla Houkamau. Exploring the Cultural Origins of Differences in Time Orientation between European New Zealanders and Māori. *NZJHRM*. 2012 Spring. 12(3),105–123. Retrieved from https://repository.usfca.edu/olc/10/

[12] Morrison, Terri, & Conoway, Wayne A. (2006). New Zealand. In *Kiss, Bow or Shake Hands*. (p. 335). Avon.

[13] Trompenaars, Fons, & Hampden-Turner, Charles (1993). *Riding the Waves of Culture: Understanding Cultural Diversity in Business*. Random House Business Books.

[14] Cole Catley, Christine (1996). *The Xenophobe's Guide to The Kiwis*. (p. 13). West Sussex.

[15] Derby, Mark (2015, February 24). Inventions, patents and trademarks. *Te Ara - the Encyclopedia of New Zealand*. Retrieved from https://teara.govt.nz/en/inventions-patents-and-trademarks

[16] Goetheinstitut Neuseeland. (2014, April). *Lifeswap Episode 3 – The Winter Deniers* [Video file]. Retrieved from http://www.lifeswap.info/2014/04/episode-three.html Lifeswap. (2016, September 16). *Lifeswap Episode 3 – The Winter Deniers* [Video file]. Retrieved from https://www.youtube.com/watch?v=bLGY_btzU70

[17] GeoNet Home. Retrieved from https://www.geonet.org.nz/

[18] Condor Flugdienst GmbH. (2011, April 5). *Condor Safety Video Bordeinweisung* [Video file]. Retrieved from https://www.youtube.com/watch?v=daed7gAch6I

[19] Harker, Caroline (2013, September 19). *Humour - Funny-business time – the 21st century*. Te Ara - the Encyclopedia of New Zealand. Retrieved from https://www.teara.govt.nz/mi/humour/page-4

[20] Flight of the Conchords. (n.d.). In *Wikipedia*. Retrieved August 27, 2019, from https://en.wikipedia.org/wiki/Flight_of_the_Conchords

[21] Laughing Samoans. (n.d.). In *Wikipedia*. Retrieved August 27, 2019, from https://en.wikipedia.org/wiki/Laughing_Samoans

## Departure from New Zealand

[22] Harper, Tim, & Thom, Murray (2019). *The Great New Zealand Cookbook: The Food We Love from 80 of Our Finest Cooks, Chefs and Bakers*. Bonnier Pub Australia. Thom, Murray (2015). *Das große Neuseeland Kochbuch: 190 Rezepte gegen das Fernweh*. Knesebeck.

[23] Theunissen, M. (2017, August 27). Kingie smokes the competition. *NZ Herald*. Retrieved from https://www.nzherald.co.nz/nz/news/article.cfm?c_id=1&objectid=11388080

International Underwater Spearfishing Association. Retrieved from http://www.iusarecords.com/ViewRecord.aspx?id=749

[24] Cole Catley, Christine (1996). *The Xenophobe's Guide to The Kiwis*. (pp. 30–31). West Sussex.

[25] Marine. Department of Conservation. Retrieved from https://www.doc.govt.nz/nature/habitats/marine/

[26] Ministry for Primary Industries (2018, April 30). *Recreational fishing*. Retrieved from https://www.mpi.govt.nz/travel-and-recreation/fishing/

## En route to Europe – Cuba

[27] NZ Transport Agency. (2015, February 27). *About driving*. Retrieved from https://www.nzta.govt.nz/resources/roadcode/about-driving/giving-way-at-roundabouts/

[28] Maier, Anja (2016, August 22). Schöner Scheißen. *Die ZEiT*. Retrieved from https://www.zeit.de/kultur/2016-08/neuseeland-hundertwasser-kawakawa-10nach8/komplettansicht

[29] Air New Zealand. (n.d.). *Home* [YouTube Channel]. Retrieved from https://www.youtube.com/user/airnewzealand

Sky News. (2012, November 2). *Air New Zealand Hobbit Safety Video A Hit* [Video file]. Retrieved from https://www.youtube.com/watch?v=XCbPFHu3OOc&t=5s

PLANEtalking. (2013, February 27). *Air New Zealand A320 Safety Video with Bear Grylls* [Video file]. Retrieved from https://www.youtube.com/watch?v=xJheoLUtX_Q

TheSafetyVideos. (2011, October 23). *Air New Zealand Hilarious Flight Safety Video*. [Video file]. Retrieved from https://www.youtube.com/watch?v=_r9rlrRt-sk

[30] Thomas, Alexander (1996). *Psychologie interkulturellen Handelns*. (A. Thomas, Ed.). Göttingen: Hogrefe.

Thomas, Alexander (1991). *Kulturstandards in der internationalen Begegnung*. (Alexander Thomas, Ed.). Saarbrücken: Breitenbach.

Hofstede, Geert, Hofstede, Gert J., Minkov, Michael (2017). *Lokales Denken, globales Handeln: Interkulturelle Zusammenarbeit und globales Management* (6th ed.). München: dtv Verlagsgesellschaft.

Hofstede, Geert (2003). *Culture's Consequence* (2nd ed.). SAGE Publications.

Hofstede, Geert, Pedersen, Paul B., & Hofstede, Gert (2002). *Exploring Culture*. Intercultural Press.

[31] Schulz von Thun Institut. *Das Werte- und Entwicklungsquadrat*. Retrieved from https://www.schulz-von-thun.de/die-modelle/das-werte-und-entwicklungsquadrat

## Europe – German winelands – the Palatinate

[32] Accident Compensation Corporation (ACC). Retrieved from https://www.acc.co.nz

[33] National Screening Unit (NSU). Retrieved from https://www.nsu.govt.nz

[34] Thomas, Alexander (1996). *Psychologie interkulturellen Handelns*. (A. Thomas, Ed.). Göttingen: Hogrefe.

Thomas, Alexander (1991). *Kulturstandards in der internationalen Begegnung*. (Alexander Thomas, Ed.). Saarbrücken: Breitenbach., p. 268

[35] Hirsch, Klaus (1996). Reintegration von Auslandsmitarbeitern. In Bergemann, Nils, & Sourisseaux, Andreas L. J. (2003) *Interkulturelles Management* (pp. 417–430). Berlin Heidelberg: Springer.

[36] Trompenaars, Fons, & Hampden-Turner, Charles (1993). *Riding the Waves of Culture: Understanding Cultural Diversity in Business*. Random House Business Books.

[37] Hall, Edward T. (1973). *The Silent Language*. Anchor Books.

[38] Lewis, Richard D. *The Lewis Model*. Retrieved from https://www.crossculture.com /about-us/the-model/

[39] Lewis, Richard D. (2014, June 1). How Different Cultures Understand Time. *Businessinsider*. Retrieved from https://www.businessinsider.com/how-different-cultures-understand-time-2014-5?IR=T

[40] Lo, Kevin D., Houkamau, Carla. *Exploring the Cultural Origins of Differences in Time Orientation between European New Zealanders and Māori*. (p. 116) NZJHRM. 2012 Spring. 12(3),105-123. Retrieved from https://repository.usfca.edu/olc/10/

[41] Lo, Kevin D., Houkamau, Carla. *Exploring the Cultural Origins of Differences in Time Orientation between European New Zealanders and Māori*. (pp. 115) NZJHRM. 2012 Spring. 12(3),105-123. Retrieved from https://repository.usfca.edu/olc/10/

[42] Hall, Edward T. (1973). *The Silent Language*. Anchor Books.

[43] Lewis, Richard D. *The Lewis Model*. Retrieved from https://www.crossculture.com /about-us/the-model/

## A visit to a sauna paradise

[44] All films of Kiwi-German lifeswap. Retrieved from https://www.goethe.de/ins/nz /de/kul/sup/lsw.html

Lifeswap. (n.d.). *Home* [YouTube Channel]. Retrieved from https://www.youtube.com /channel/UCqG-VKS5cezLwZPX8hR1sbw

[45] Fletcher, Adam (2016). *Wie man Deutscher wird. In 50 neuen Schritten*. München.

### Frankfurt – welcome to the city of penguins

[46] Kreft, Steffen, & Connor, William (2013, December) *Lifeswap Episode 2 - The Tea Towel stinks* [Video File]. Retrieved from http://www.lifeswap.info/2013/12/episode-two.html

[47] WebID. Retrieved from https://www.webid-solutions.de/de/

### London – the city where everything began

[48] Hofstede, Geert, Hofstede, Gert J., & Minkov, Michael (2017). *Lokales Denken, globales Handeln: Interkulturelle Zusammenarbeit und globales Management* (6th ed.). München: dtv Verlagsgesellschaft.

Hofstede, Geert (2003). *Culture's Consequence* (2nd ed.). SAGE Publications.

Hofstede, Geert, Pedersen, Paul B., & Hofstede, Gert (2002). *Exploring Culture*. Intercultural Press.

Germany. Retrieved from Hofstede Insights: https://www.hofstede-insights.com/country/germany/

[49] Germany. Retrieved from Hofstede Insights: https://www.hofstede-insights.com/country/germany/

New Zealand. Retrieved from Hofstede Insights: https://www.hofstede-insights.com/country/new-zealand/

[50] See following books:

Wiggins, Clara (2015). *The Expat Partner's Survival Guide*.

Gorman, Donna Scaramastra (2015). *Am I going to Starve to Death? A Survival Guide for the Foreign Service Spouse.*

or following websites:

Expat's Manual. *Trailing Spouse*. Expat Info Desk. Retrieved from https://www.expatinfodesk.com/expat-guide/moving-with-your-partner/being-a-trailing-spouse/

Elliot, Andrea (2011, September 9). *Global Immigration and the Trailing Spouse: Barrier to Mobility or Stealth Competitive Advantage?* Retrieved from https://definingmoves.com/2011/global-immigration-and-the-'trailing'-spouse-barrier-to-mobility-or-stealth-com petitive-advantage/

or onlineresearch e.g.: "trailing spouse in New Zealand"

[51] Inland Revenue (2018). *Bright-line property rule has changed*. Retrieved from https://www.classic.ird.govt.nz/campaigns/2018/brightline.html

[52] Land Information new Zealand. (2018) *Overseas Investment Amendment Act 2018*. Retrieved from https://www.linz.govt.nz/overseas-investment/about-

overseas-investment-office/legislation-ministers-delegated-powers/overseas-
investment-amendment-act-2018

## Barcelona – pura vida

[53] Bundeszentrale für politische Bildung. (2008, July 20). *Dossier Frauenbewegung*. Retrieved from https://www.bpb.de/gesellschaft/gender/frauenbewegung/

Strobl, I. (2019, February 25). *Frauenbewegung: Alice Schwarzer*. Retrieved from https://www.planet-wissen.de/geschichte/deutsche_geschichte/frauenbewegung_der_kampf_fuer_gleichberechtigung/pwiealiceschwarzer100.html

Bergeron, R. (2015, August 17). *'The Seventies': Feminism makes waves*. Retrieved from https://edition.cnn.com/2015/07/22/living/the-seventies-feminism-womens-lib/index.html

Feminism in New Zealand (n.d.). In *Wikipedia*. Retrieved August 27, 2019, from https://en.wikipedia.org/wiki/Feminism_in_New_Zealand

[54] Thomas, A., Schroll-Machl, S., & Kinast, E.-U. (2003). *Handbuch interkulturelle Kommunikation und Kooperation* (Vol. 1, p. 26). Göttingen: Vandenhoeck & Ruprecht.

[55] Cole Catley, Christine (1996). *The Xenophobe's Guide to The Kiwis*. (p. 60). West Sussex.

[56] Cole Catley, Christine (1996). *The Xenophobe's Guide to The Kiwis*. (pp. 14–15). West Sussex.

[57] Wellington Women's Boarding House. Retrieved from http://wwbh.org.nz/

[58] Heritage Te Manatu Taonga. (2018, September 21). *Women and men*. Te Ara - the Encyclopedia of New Zealand. Retrieved from https://teara.govt.nz/en/women-and-men

[59] Erll, Astrid, & Gymnich, Marion (2010). *Interkulturelle Kompetenz*. (pp 42–43) Stuttgart.

[60] Goetheinstitut Neuseeland. (2014, Dezember). *Kiwi-German life swap, Episode 5, Christmas Special* [Video file]. Retrieved from http://www.lifeswap.info/2014/12/lifeswap-5-yule-love-it-christmas.html

[61] InterNations. Retrieved from https://www.internations.org/

[62] Antipodr. Retrieved from https://www.antipodr.com/

## Berlin – an exploding new world

[63] King, Carolyn M., & Barrett, Priscilla (2006). *The handbook of New Zealand Mammals*. Oxford.
Cowan, P. E., & Tyndale-Biscoe, C. H. (1997). Australian and New Zealand mammal species considered to be pests or problems. *Reproduction, Fertility and Development 9*(1) 27–36. https://doi.org/10.1071/R96058

## The day-to-day – museums, media, childhood, helicopter parenting and the world of work

[64] YouShop. Retrieved from https://www.nzpost.co.nz/tools/youshop

[65] Employment New Zealand. (n.d.). *Trial and probationary periods*. Retrieved from https://www.employment.govt.nz/starting-employment/trial-and-probationary-periods

[66] Bönisch-Brednich, Brigitte. (2002). *Keeping a Low Profile: An Oral History of German Immigration to New Zealand*. (pp. 210–212). Wellington: Victoria University Press.

[67] Cole Catley, Christine (1996). *The Xenophobe's Guide to The Kiwis*. (p. 60). West Sussex.

[68] New Zealand. Retrieved from Hofstede Insights: https://www.hofstede-insights.com/country/new-zealand/
Germany. Retrieved from Hofstede Insights: https://www.hofstede-insights.com/country/germany/

[69] Morrison, Terri, & Conoway, Wayne A. (2006). New Zealand. In *Kiss, Bow or Shake Hands*. (p. 333). Avon.

[70] Boenisch-Brednich, Brigitte (2008). Watching the Kiwis: New Zealanders Rules of Social Interaction - an Introduction. *The Journal of New Zealand Studies*, (6/7). https://doi.org/10.26686/jnzs.v0i6/7.131

[71] United Kingdom. Retrieved from Hofstede Insights https://www.hofstede-insights.com/country/the-uk/

[72] Cole Catley, Christine (1996). *The Xenophobe's Guide to The Kiwis*. (pp. 24–25). West Sussex.

[73] Walters, Laura (2016, January 21). A look back at New Zealand school uniforms. *Stuff*. Retrieved from https://www.stuff.co.nz/national/education/75972895/A-look-back-at-New-Zealand-school-uniforms

[74] HomeExchange. Retrieved from https://www.homeexchange.com/

## My old home – Hamburg and Sylt

[75] Department of Conservation (n.d.). Whales. Retrieved from https://www.doc.govt.nz/nature/native-animals/marine-mammals/whales/
Department of Conservation (n.d.). Killer whale/orca. Retrieved from https://www.doc.govt.nz/nature/native-animals/marine-mammals/dolphins/killer-whale-orca/

[76] Cook, Frances (2016, December 16). Orcas and dolphins visit Wellington's Lyall Bay. *NZ Herald*. Retrieved from https://www.nzherald.co.nz/nz/news/article.cfm?c_id=1&objectid=11768384

[77] König Appartement Sylt GmbH (2016). *70er Jahre Special*. König Appartment Sylt, 2016(1), 12–17.

[78] Kollenbroich, B. (2016, August 18). "Economist"-Ranking: Die lebenswertesten Städte der Welt. *SPIEGEL Online*. Retrieved from http://www.spiegel.de/wirtschaft/soziales/staedte-ranking-hamburg-unter-zehn-lebenswertesten-staedten-der-welt-a-1108290.html

[79] Elbphilharmonie. (n.d.). In *Wikipedia*. Retrieved August 27, 2019, from https://en.wikipedia.org/wiki/Elbphilharmonie

[80] Zaninelli, S. M. (1994). *Was passiert, wenn „Coconut" und „Peach" miteinander kommunizieren, oder: Das berühmteste Missverständnis der Welt zum Thema: Interpersonale Distanz USA – Deutschland*. In Institut für Auslandsbeziehungen, (Ed.). *Materialien Zum Internationalen Kulturaustausch*, (33), 5–8. Stuttgart.
Zaninelli, Susanne M. (Revised January 2005). *Was passiert, wenn „Coconut" und „Peach" miteinander kommunizieren, oder: Das berühmteste Missverständnis der Welt zum Thema: Interpersonale Distanz USA – Deutschland*. [PDF file]. Retrieved from http://www.culture-contact.com/resources/coconut_und_peach.pdf

[81] Miniatur Wunderland. (n.d.). In *Wikipedia*. Retrieved August 27, 2019, from https://en.wikipedia.org/wiki/Miniatur_Wunderland

## A former stage in life in the Rhineland – Düsseldorf and Cologne

[82] Morrison, Terri, & Conoway, Wayne A. (2006). New Zealand. In *Kiss, Bow or Shake Hands*. (p. 333). Avon.

[83] Cole Catley, Christine (1996). *The Xenophobe's Guide to The Kiwis*. (p. 16). West Sussex.

[84] Thomas, Alexander (1991). *Kulturstandards in der internationalen Begegnung*. (Alexander Thomas, Ed.). Saarbrücken: Breitenbach.
Thomas, Alexander (1996). *Psychologie interkulturellen Handelns*. (A. Thomas, Ed.). Göttingen: Hogrefe.

[85] Hall, Edward T. (1973). *The Silent Language*. Anchor Books.
[86] Bäcker, Eva Maria (2013). *Bienvenue en Afrique – Interkulturelle Kompetenz für Gabun*. (p. 116). Nordhausen.

## My old love – Tuscany
[87] Ediltermica di Bernardi Enrico. Retrieved from https://bernardiediltermica.com
[88] Schwan, H. (2016, September 2). Flughafen Frankfurt: Falscher Alarm wegen Fehlers eines Mitarbeiters. *Frankfurter Allgemeine Zeitung*. Retrieved from https://www.faz.net/aktuell/rhein-main/flughafen-frankfurt-falscher-alarm-wegen-mitar-beiter-14418199.html
[89] Rhue, Morton (2007). *The Wave*. New York.

## Close to a former study home – Nice, France
[90] Pollock, David C., & Van Reken, Ruth E. (2009). *Third Culture Kids. Growing up among worlds*.
Selasi, Taiye (2014, October). *Taiye Selasi. Don't ask where I'm from, ask where I'm local* [Video file]. TEDGlobal 2014. Retrieved from https://www.ted.com/talks/taiye_selasi_don_t_ask_where_i_m_from_ask_where_i_m_a_local
Selasi, Taiye (2005, March 3). Bye-Bye Babar. *The LIP Magazine*. Retrieved from http://thelip.robertsharp.co.uk/?p=76
Iyer, Pico (2013, June) *Pico Iyer. Where is home?* [Video file]. TEDGlobal 2013. Retrieved from https://www.ted.com/talks/pico_iyer_where_is_home

## Hello Germany – or, what is it like to return home after a long time abroad?
[91] Hirsch, Klaus (1996). Reintegration von Auslandsmitarbeitern. In Bergemann, Nils, & Sourisseaux, Andreas L. J. (Ed.) *Interkulturelles Management* (2003, pp. 417–430). Berlin Heidelberg: Springer.

## En route to New Zealand – Nicaragua
[92] Hall, Edward T. (1973). *The Silent Language*. Anchor Books.
[93] Morrison, Terri, & Conoway, Wayne A. (2006). New Zealand. In *Kiss, Bow or Shake Hands*. (p. 183). Avon.
[94] Morrison, Terri, & Conoway, Wayne A. (2006). New Zealand. In *Kiss, Bow or Shake Hands*. (pp 183–184). Avon.
[95] Thomas, Alexander (1991). *Kulturstandards in der internationalen Begegnung*.

(Alexander Thomas, Ed.). Saarbrücken: Breitenbach.

Thomas, Alexander (1996). *Psychologie interkulturellen Handelns*. (A. Thomas, Ed.). Göttingen: Hogrefe.

[96] Schulz von Thun Institut für Kommunikation (n.d.). *Das Werte- und Entwicklungsquadrat*. Retrieved from https://www.schulz-von-thun.de/die-modelle/das-werte-und-entwicklungsquadrat

[97] GeoNet. *Geological hazard information for New Zealand*. Retrieved from https://www.geonet.org.nz/volcano/whiteisland

[98] Department of Conservation. (n.d.). Great Walks. Retrieved from https://www.doc.govt.nz/great-walks

[99] Outdoor Education New Zealand. Retrieved from https://www.outdoorednz.co.nz

[100] Rousseau, Bryant (2016, July 13). In New Zealand, Lands and Rivers Can Be People (Legally Speaking). *New York Times*. Retrieved from https://www.nytimes.com/2016/07/14/world/what-in-the-world/in-new-zealand-lands-and-rivers-can-be-people-legally-speaking.html

[101] Cole Catley, Christine (1996). *The Xenophobe's Guide to The Kiwis*. (p. 9). West Sussex.

[102] Department of Conservation. (n.d.). White sharks. Retrieved from https://www.doc.govt.nz/nature/native-animals/marine-fish-and-reptiles/sharks-mango/white-shark/

[103] Cole Catley, Christine (1996). *The Xenophobe's Guide to The Kiwis*. (p. 45). West Sussex.

[104] Lonely Planet. (n.d.). In *Wikipedia*. Retrieved August 27, 2019, from https://en.wikipedia.org/wiki/Lonely_Planet

[105] Die Zeit. (2012, September). Wie die Welt verhandelt. Spanien und USA. *Die Zeit*. Retrieved from https://www.zeit.de/2012/38/interkulturelle-kompetenzen-karriere/seite-4

[106] Lo, Kevin D., Houkamau, Carla. Exploring the Cultural Origins of Differences in Time Orientation between European New Zealanders and Māori. (pp. 114) *New Zealand Journal of Human Resource Management* (NZJHRM). 2012 Spring. 12(3), 105–123. Retrieved from https://repository.usfca.edu/olc/10/

[107] Passport to Trade 2.0. (n.d.) *Business meeting etiquette*. Retrieved from http://businessculture.org/western-europe/business-culture-in-germany/meeting-etiquette-in-germany/

[108] Bäcker, Eva Maria. (2013). *Bienvenue en Afrique - interkulturelle Kompetenz für Gabun* (p. 97). Nordhausen: Bautz.

## Arrival in New Zealand

[109] See one variation of amusing ad: GSentertainment. (2013, October 19). *Deck Maintenance Banned Commercial Very Funny Try Not To Laugh* [Video file]. Retrieved from https://www.youtube.com/watch?v=QhUXR1VPwi8

## Three weeks later – home in New Zealand

[110] Cole Catley, Christine (1996). *The Xenophobe's Guide to The Kiwis*. (p. 37). West Sussex.

[111] Neighbourly. Retrieved from https://www.neighbourly.co.nz

## A month later – the day the Earth quaked

[112] Schuh, Hans (2001, October 4). Das Rätsel von Toulouse. *Die Zeit*. Retrieved from https://www.zeit.de/2001/41/Das_Raetsel_von_Toulouse

[113] Wellington Region Tsunami Evacuation Zones: LyallBay to EvansBay [PDF file]. Wellington: *Wellington Region Emergency Management*. Retrieved from http://www.gwrc.govt.nz/assets/Emergencies--Hazards/Tsunami-Maps/11lyall-evans.pdf

[114] GeoNet (n.d.) Recent Quakes. Geological hazard information for New Zealand. Retrieved from https://www.geonet.org.nz/quakes/felt/severe
Wellington Quake Live. Retrieved from http://wellington.quakelive.co.nz/Top100Wellington30Days/

[115] Nicoll, Dave, Manch, Thomas, McConnell, Glenn, & Clayton, Rachel. (2016, November 16) Pictures of rescued quake cows realeased. *Stuff*. Retrieved from https://www.stuff.co.nz/business/farming/86512978/Pictures-of-rescued-quake-cows-released

[116] Noble, F. (2016, November 17). New Zealand earthquake: Land moves 10 METRES and new fault lines found after quake. *Mail online*. Retrieved August 27, 2019, from https://www.dailymail.co.uk/news/article-3943818/New-Zealand-earthquake-Land-moves-10-METRES-new-fault-lines-quake-power-400-atom-bombs.html

[117] NZ Herald. (2017, August 24). Finally home, quake evacuees tell of two days trapped on coast. *NZ Herald*. Retrieved from https://www.nzherald.co.nz/nz/news/article.cfm?c_id=1&objectid=11749902

[118] GeoNet (n.d.) Geological hazard information for New Zealand. Retrieved from https://info.geonet.org.nz/pages/viewrecentblogposts.action?key=quake
GeoNet (n.d.) Geological hazard information for New Zealand. (2016, November 18).

*GPS allowed rapid detection of land movements due to M7.8 earthquake*. Retrieved from https://www.geonet.org.nz/news/5rfEJCYGfmWmMw0SyuyYUU

[119] Sachdeva, Sam (2016, November 15). Prime Minister John Key missed a call from US President-elect Donald Trump after quake. *Stuff*. Retrieved from https://www.stuff.co.nz/national/politics/86460713/prime-minister-john-key-misses-call-from-us-presidentelect-donald-trump-after-earthquakes

[120] Davison, Isaac (2014, September 23). Key close to missing Obama call. *NZ Herald*. Retrieved from https://www.nzherald.co.nz/nz/news/article.cfm?c_id=1&objectid=11329574

[121] NZ Herald. (2016, November 16). Tornado hits Kapiti Coast. *NZ Herald*. Retrieved from https://www.nzherald.co.nz/nz/news/article.cfm?c_id=1&objectid=11749456

## A week after the earthquake – back to work
[122] Ting-Toomey, Stella (1994). *The Challenge of Facework: Cross-Cultural and Interpersonal Issues*. New York.

## Six months after the trip – recovery incomplete
[123] Victoria University Wellington. (n.d.) *Tikanga tips for learning and teaching*. Retrieved from https://www.victoria.ac.nz/maori-at-victoria/ako/teaching-resources/tikanga-tips

[124] Stuff. (2017, April 24) *Southern lights delight New Zealand for the second night in a row*. Retrieved from https://www.stuff.co.nz/national/91832560/southern-lights-delight-new-zealand-for-the-second-night-in-a-row

# Index

HOUSE
HOMESTAY
WELLINGTON
LYALL BAY
KIWIANA
TASMAN SEA
ART DECO
EVANS BAY
BO3SEAS.CO.NZ

Enjoy your Wellington visit in a homestay with locals in a stunning area with no hotels. You are literally staying home away from home. You will stay in a double bedroom in sunny 3bedroom timber, Art Deco house from 1939, "sitting in the sky".

It opens to dramatic views of Lyall Bay, Evans Bay and the Tasman Sea. Aviation devotees will have the perfect vantage point to observe planes landing and departing from one of the world's most difficult airport runways.

Having breakfast while watching penguins does happen!

Interested? Mail to silke@bo3seas.co.nz